The Strategy Factor in Successful Language Learning

SECOND LANGUAGE ACQUISITION
Series Editor: Professor David Singleton, *Trinity College, Dublin, Ireland*

This series brings together titles dealing with a variety of aspects of language acquisition and processing in situations where a language or languages other than the native language is involved. Second language is thus interpreted in its broadest possible sense. The volumes included in the series all offer in their different ways, on the one hand, exposition and discussion of empirical findings and, on the other, some degree of theoretical reflection. In this latter connection, no particular theoretical stance is privileged in the series; nor is any relevant perspective – sociolinguistic, psycholinguistic, neurolinguistic, etc. – deemed out of place. The intended readership of the series includes final-year undergraduates working on second language acquisition projects, postgraduate students involved in second language acquisition research, and researchers and teachers in general whose interests include a second language acquisition component.

Full details of all the books in this series and of all our other publications can be found on http://www.multilingual-matters.com, or by writing to Multilingual Matters, St Nicholas House, 31–34 High Street, Bristol BS1 2AW, UK.

The Strategy Factor in Successful Language Learning

Carol Griffiths

MULTILINGUAL MATTERS
Bristol • Buffalo • Toronto

Library of Congress Cataloging in Publication Data
A catalog record for this book is available from the Library of Congress.
Griffiths, Carol
The Strategy Factor in Successful Language Learning/Carol Griffiths.
Second Language Acquisition: 67
Includes bibliographical references and index.
1. Language and languages—Study and teaching. I. Title.
P51.G733 2013
418.0071–dc23 2013001852

British Library Cataloguing in Publication Data
A catalogue entry for this book is available from the British Library.

ISBN-13: 978-1-84769-941-1 (hbk)
ISBN-13: 978-1-84769-940-4 (pbk)

Multilingual Matters
UK: St Nicholas House, 31–34 High Street, Bristol BS1 2AW, UK.
USA: UTP, 2250 Military Road, Tonawanda, NY 14150, USA.
Canada: UTP, 5201 Dufferin Street, North York, Ontario M3H 5T8, Canada.

The policy of Multilingual Matters/Channel View Publications is to use papers that are natural, renewable and recyclable products, made from wood grown in sustainable forests. In the manufacturing process of our books, and to further support our policy, preference is given to printers that have FSC and PEFC Chain of Custody certification. The FSC and/or PEFC logos will appear on those books where full certification has been granted to the printer concerned.

Typeset by Techset Composition Ltd.
Printed and bound in Great Britain by Short Run Press Ltd.

Contents

Acknowledgements

I would like to express my gratitude to the many colleagues, students, friends and significant others in my life as well as the institutions where I have worked and my publishers, Multilingual Matters who have supported me during the time and energy consuming process of getting a book together.

Xie xie
Kam sa ham ni da
Çok Teşekkürler
Many thanks
Carol

Introduction

I.1 A Personal Perspective

I learnt about the importance of strategies at a relatively early age. Up until the time I was about 12 years old, my school life had been very happy. I had been blessed with patient teachers who encouraged me with praise and good advice. Therefore, I had done well at school and had enjoyed my time there.

Shortly after my 12th birthday, however, my father changed his job. My new school was very different from my old one. Instead of the kindly teachers I was used to, Miss Campbell was a strict disciplinarian who seemed to take great delight in finding fault with anything I did. She never called me by my name: I was always 'the new girl' to her. Discipline could be extremely punitive, from writing out many pages of repetitive lines to long periods of detention, although only the boys got the strap, for which, at least, I was grateful.

Although I found the whole atmosphere of the school repressive, this was not my major difficulty. The main problem was the curriculum. My previous school had emphasized creativity and self-expression, whereas my new school had a much more formal approach. I found myself being expected to answer questions on nouns, pronouns, verbs, adjectives, adverbs, articles, prepositions, subjects, objects, complements, predicates. I had never even heard these terms, and had absolutely no understanding of what they meant. If Miss Campbell had been talking Martian I could hardly have been more bewildered. My grammatical ignorance proved to be fertile ground for Miss

Campbell's ridicule, since she knew almost certainly that if she asked me a question I would get it wrong.

The time came for a big test which, it was announced, would be held the following Monday. Forlornly, I went to Miss Campbell to ask for help. With a sweeping gesture of impatience, she told me to ask one of the other pupils. The other kids, however, had better things to do than to spend their lunch-time tutoring a newcomer.

I took my textbook home on Friday night and, without too much expectation of success, set to work to try to make sense of its contents. I read the definitions of the unfamiliar concepts, wrote them out to help myself remember them, read the examples, did the exercises and checked my answers from the back of the book. By means of these strategies I found myself gradually achieving some understanding of the alien subject matter.

By Sunday night, I found I could do the exercises and get most of them right. And on Monday I got full marks in the test. Miss Campbell seemed surprised and even a little disappointed: she now had to find someone else to serve as the object of her scorn. Although she never paid me the compliment of calling me by my name, I suppose I earned from her a kind of grudging respect for having achieved beyond her expectations. And although we never actually liked each other, at least she more or less left me alone after that.

This was a most uncomfortable experience, and a most unhappy time. However, it taught me a valuable lesson which I have never forgotten: in this life we are ultimately responsible for our own success or failure. Although other people, such as good teachers, can be very helpful, and can make the task easier and more enjoyable, in the end it is we who do the learning. If we develop sound strategies which are helpful to us, which suit our individual characteristics and which are appropriate for the situation and the task at hand, there is almost nothing we cannot achieve with sufficient effort and determination.

I.2 Overview

The language learning strategy concept was first brought to wide attention with the publication of Joan Rubin's seminal article 'What the "Good Language Learner" can teach us' (1975). At the time, few people probably expected that it would sow the seeds of controversies which would still be unresolved several decades later. The debates which have raged over the intervening years have often been quite heated, but have frequently failed to produce the desired illumination.

I.2.1 Objectives

In the hope of resolving some of the controversies, the objectives of this book are therefore to:

- clarify basic concepts, especially of terminology, definition, effectiveness, theoretical underpinnings and classification;
- address fundamental questions regarding the relationships among successful language learning and strategy frequency and quantity, strategy type, strategy use according to learner, situational or target variables and strategy development;
- consider strategy effectiveness from an individual point of view, particularly in relation to a range of learner variables;
- discuss pedagogical issues, especially relating to teacher perceptions and training, classroom and learner factors, methodology and content, as well as considering situational and target variables;
- identify areas still requiring research clarification.

I.2.2 Aims

The book aims to achieve these objectives by means of:

- an extensive review, analysis and re-interpretation of the existing literature;
- providing quantitative research evidence for the fundamental questions noted above by means of empirical studies;
- providing qualitative research evidence regarding individual strategy use by means of interviews;
- providing pedagogical research and drawing implications for classroom practice and teacher education;
- recommending areas still requiring further research.

I.2.3 Audience

The strategy concept is of interest to a potentially wide range of readers, but this book is especially intended for an audience of:

- students working on a variety of diploma or degree programmes in the language learning area for whom the discussion and references would be extremely useful when completing assignments or theses;
- teacher educators, practising teachers or teacher trainees for whom the pedagogical implications of the numerous findings described in the book are especially relevant;

- researchers, for whom the numerous under-researched areas pointed out may help to indicate directions for future useful studies.

I.2.4 Organization

The topics of the book are organised into four main chapters:

- Chapter 1 deals with the essential concepts of terminology, effectiveness, underlying theory and classification, and attempts a definitive definition based on essential elements extracted from the literature.
- Chapter 2 looks at the answers to some basic questions regarding strategy use and its relationship with other variables and to successful learning outcomes. It reports on a number of studies which address some of the vexed issues involved.
- Chapter 3 approaches the strategy issue from the individual student's point of view. Although quantitative findings such as those presented in Chapter 2 are valuable, and may well be used to inform teaching practice, individuals never quite conform to statistical expectations, and it is essential to allow for individual variation when considering effective language learning and strategy use.
- Chapter 4 looks at the pedagogical research. Studies of teacher perceptions and of strategy-based instruction are reviewed, along with findings regarding methodology and content. Learner, situational and target variables are considered, as well as issues for teacher training.

I.3 How This Book Is Different

- The learning strategy field has at times been criticized for being atheoretical (e.g. Dornyei, 2005; Dornyei & Skehan, 2003; Macaro, 2006). This book addresses underlying theoretical issues in the first chapter by looking at terminology, definition, theoretical underpinnings and classification systems.
- Rather than merely discussing the concepts, this book presents evidence from empirical studies for each of the fundamental questions posed in Chapter 2.
- In addition to the quantitative view taken in Chapter 2, the book takes a qualitative look at strategy use by individuals in Chapter 3 and considers the implications of the interview data.
- Finally, in Chapter 4, rather than looking at strategies divorced from the 'real world' of the classroom, this book looks at the issues from the teaching/learning point of view.

In addition, the book contains:

- multiple suggestions for further research;
- a glossary which explains essential terms;
- an extensive bibliography;
- appendices containing the instruments used in the studies which might be useful for replication studies;
- an index for ease of reference.

It is my own firm belief that effective strategies are an essential tool for learners who want to succeed at learning language. I therefore hope that this book may contribute to this success.

1 A Conceptual Perspective

1.1 Basic Concepts

There is an old proverb which states: 'Give a man a fish and he eats for a day. Teach him how to fish and he eats for a lifetime.' Applied to the language teaching and learning field, this proverb might be interpreted to mean that if students are provided with answers, the immediate problem is solved. However, if they are taught the strategies to work out the answers for themselves, they may be empowered to manage their own learning. It is on this fundamental premise that this book is based.

Over the years, a great deal of effort has gone into developing theories, methods and approaches for *teaching* language (such as the Grammar Translation Method, audiolingualism and the communicative approach). However, issues relating to the learner have been treated with 'relative neglect' (Dansereau, 1978: 78) and much less attention has been paid to the language development process from the *learning* point of view (Tarone & Yule, 1989). Although valuable work has been and continues to be done on the questions of how language is acquired/learnt/developed (e.g. Doughty & Long, 2003; Eckman *et al.*, 1984; Ellis, 1986, 1994, 2008; Krashen, 1981; Spada & Lightbown, 2002; Winitz, 1981), when it is considered that the learner forms one half of the teaching/ learning partnership, it might be considered surprising that, in general, the significance of the learner's role has continued to be 'underestimated' (Larsen-Freeman, 2001: 12).

In the 1970s, the possibility that success in language learning might be related to *how* students go about the task was explored by writers such as Naiman *et al.* (1978), Rubin (1975) and Stern (1975). Writers such as O'Malley (1987), Oxford (1990, 2011b), Wenden (1991), Cohen (1998, 2011), Chamot (2001, 2008), Macaro (2006) and Griffiths (2008a) have continued to suggest that learners might be able to learn language more effectively by the use of language learning strategies, which have the potential to be 'an extremely powerful learning tool' (O'Malley *et al.*, 1985: 43). O'Malley *et al.* (1985: 22) noted, however, that there was 'no consensus' regarding basic concepts such as terminology, definition, classification and underpinning theory. Although this was written more than 20 years ago, much of the 'conceptual ambiguity' (Dornyei & Skehan, 2003: 610) remains to this day.

1.2 Terminology

Some of this ambiguity arises at the very basic level of terminology. This applies especially to the learning tool phenomenon itself, to the language being learnt, and to those who are trying to learn a new language.

1.2.1 Strategies

Although promising in terms of its potential to facilitate successful learning, there is 'considerable confusion' (O'Malley *et al.*, 1985: 22) in the language learning strategy field; indeed, there is a great deal of controversy over the very term *strategy* itself, before we even begin to think about definition, classification and theory. Consensus is not assisted by some writers' use of conflicting terminology such as *learning behaviours* (Politzer, 1983; Politzer & McGroarty, 1985; Wesche, 1977), *tactics* (Seliger, 1984) and *techniques* (Stern, 1992). These rival terms are often used more or less (but not always exactly) synonymously with the term *strategy* as used elsewhere in the literature.

Strategy, of course, is originally a military term, as some (e.g. Larsen-Freeman & Long, 1991; Oxford, 1990, 2011b) point out, and there are those who find the somewhat bellicose overtones of the term unfortunate. A military strategy tends to be an overall plan of attack or 'plans for winning a war' (Oxford, 2011a: 168); the term *tactics* tends to be applied to smaller manoeuvres within the overall strategy. Perhaps, however, we do not need to concern ourselves too much with the way the term was used in battle when we are applying it to language learning, although it is an interesting comparison!

According to Larsen-Freeman and Long (1991: 199), the term *strategy* was used by Rubin (1975) 'in perhaps the earliest study in this area and it enjoys the widest currency today' (for instance, among many others, Chamot, 1987; Cohen, 1991, 2011; Cohen & Macaro, 2007; Lam & Wong, 2000; O'Neil, 1978; Oxford, 1990, 2011b; Pearson, 1988; Purpura, 1999; Weinstein, 1978; Wenden, 1985). It is acknowledged, however, that *strategy* is not the only term which has been, or which might be, used to cover the thoughts and behaviours involved.

Although the term *tactics* is employed by some writers to denote a specific activity within an overall *strategy* (e.g. Oxford, 2011b), the point at which a given behaviour ceases to be a tactic and becomes a strategy or vice versa is not entirely easy to pinpoint. Is an action such as *asking a teacher for help with words I don't understand*, for instance, a tactic or a strategy? If it is considered a tactic within, say, a broader strategy such as *reviewing vocabulary regularly*, what then would *writing down the teacher's explanation* become – a sub-tactic? And what about *learning what I have written down*? It all becomes very messy. And does it matter? Do we really need to introduce yet more terms into an already confused picture?

Terminology: Strategy

Of all the competing terms which might be chosen, the term *strategy* would seem to have the longest history and to have been used most frequently and consistently over the years. For this reason, *strategy* is the term which will be used for the purposes of the present book.

1.2.2 Target language

No less controversial than the term *strategy* itself is the term for the language the strategies are being used to learn. Many writers opt for the term *second language* (SL or L2) (for instance, among many others, Ausubel, 1964; Chaudron, 1995; Cook, 1991; Donato, 2000; Harley *et al.*, 1990; Hylenstam & Pienemann, 1985; Krashen, 1982; Phillipson *et al.*, 1991; Schumann, 1978; Sharwood Smith, 1994; Spolsky, 1989; Wolfson & Judd, 1983), even though it may be used 'somewhat confusingly' (Ellis, 1994: 12). The term is confusing because it does not allow for the many students who may already be multilingual and who may be in the process of learning a third, fourth or subsequent language, and therefore it does not reflect the resource that learners may already possess. There is also frequent confusion between the terms *second language* (studied in the environment where the language is spoken, for instance international students studying English in New Zealand or the USA), *foreign language* (FL) (studied in an environment other than where it is spoken, for instance French as it is taught in England or Turkey) and *heritage language* (the language derived from a particular cultural heritage spoken in a dominant language environment, for instance Hebrew as spoken in the USA). Other terms such as *non-native language* (NNL) and *non-primary language* (NPL), where *native* and *primary* are usually defined as the one spoken in the home, are not always as straightforward as might initially be supposed, since many homes and backgrounds around the world operate in more than one language. Still other terms which have been suggested, such as *additional language* or *additive language*, tend to make the language sound either marginalised or like a brand of food or petrol! In the face of these debates, the term used in this book will be *target language* (TL) – the one the students are aiming to learn.

Terminology: Target Language (TL)

The language the students are trying to learn will be termed the *target language* for the purposes of this book, since this term encapsulates the idea of the learning goal and is applicable irrespective of how many languages the learner already speaks, where the learning is taking place or what the heritage/native/primary language may be.

1.2.3 Speakers of other languages

Yet another controversial term is that used for those who are trying to learn a target language. The term *SOL* (speakers of other languages), as favoured by publications such as *TESOL Quarterly, TESOL Matters* and *TESOLANZ Journal*, although somewhat long and clumsy, has arisen partly to avoid the second/foreign language learner confusion. Descriptors such as *non-native, non-primary* and *non-English-speaking-background* (NESB) have been used, but the intrinsically negative perspective of these terms make them less than universally acceptable.

Unfortunately, the universally acceptable term for those who already speak other languages and are trying to learn a new one has yet to be coined. For the purposes of the present work, however, the term *speakers of other languages* (SOL) will be used.

Terminology: Speakers of Other Languages (SOL)

The term *speakers of other languages* (SOL) will be used for this book since it is well established in the field (for instance with publications such as *TESOL Quarterly*), avoids the confusion between second and foreign languages, allows for the possibility that the student may speak any number of other languages and avoids the negative connotations of terms like *non-native, non-primary* and *non-English-speaking background*.

1.3 Definition

Language learning strategies have been notoriously difficult to define (e.g. Oxford, 1990; Oxford & Cohen, 1992). One of the earliest researchers in this field, Rubin (1975: 43) provided a very broad definition of learning strategies as 'the techniques or devices which a learner may use to acquire knowledge'. By means of observing students in classrooms, observing herself, talking to good language learners and eliciting observations from teachers, Rubin isolated seven strategies characteristic of good language learners, namely:

- *guessing/inferring* (by using clues);
- *communicating* (for instance, by means of circumlocution, gestures, etc.);
- *managing inhibitions* (for instance, of appearing foolish);
- *attending to form* (for instance, by looking for patterns);
- *practising* (for instance, pronunciation);
- *monitoring one's own and the speech of others;*
- *attending to meaning* (for instance, by attending to context).

At around the same time as Rubin published her 'good learner' study, Stern (1975) produced a list of 10 language learning strategies used by good language learners. He believed that good language learners are characterised by positive learning strategies, among which he included:

- *experimenting;*
- *planning;*
- *developing the new language into an ordered system;*
- *revising progressively;*
- *searching for meaning;*
- *practising;*
- *using the language in real communication;*
- *self-monitoring;*
- *developing the target language into a separate reference system;*
- *learning to think in the target language.*

Although Stern's work was an important addition to the developing body of research on the relationship between language learning strategies and the successful language learner, these strategies were listed as a rather confused mixture with 'characteristics', such as 'active', 'tolerant' and 'outgoing' (Stern, 1975: 316).

In another pioneering piece of research at around the same time, Naiman and colleagues (1978) also tried to find out what people known to be good at languages had in common. Identified as 'essential for successful language learning' (Naiman *et al.*, 1978: 225) were strategies for:

- *coming to grips with the language as a system;*
- *using the language in real communication;*
- *monitoring the interlanguage;*
- *coming to terms with the affective demands of language learning;*
- *coping with ambiguity.*

As we can see, there is little agreement among these three important early studies, causing O'Malley *et al.* (1985: 22) to lament that 'there is no consensus on what constitutes a learning strategy in second language learning'. Subsequently, Wenden and Rubin (1987: 7) talk of 'the elusive nature of the term' and Ellis (1994: 529) describes the concept as 'fuzzy', while Cohen (1998: 3) talks of 'conflicting views'.

Difficulties such as those noted above, as well as 'a lack of theoretical rigour' (Macaro, 2006: 320), have led Macaro to despair of achieving an all-encompassing definition. He opts instead (Macaro, 2006: 327–330) for listing defining characteristics according to:

- location of strategies;
- size, abstractness and relationship to other strategies;
- explicitness of goal orientation;
- transferability

Dornyei and Skehan (2003: 610) go even further and discuss abandoning the strategy concept altogether in the face of a 'theoretical muddle' which has never been 'cleared away'. They recommend the adoption of the 'more versatile' concept of self-regulation, which 'refers to the degree to which individuals are active participants in their own learning' (Dornyei & Skehan, 2003: 611).

However, the slippery strategy concept hangs on tenaciously, and refuses to be so easily dismissed. This is evidenced by an ongoing stream of publications on the subject (e.g. Chamot, 2008; Cohen, 2011; Cohen & Macaro, 2007; Griffiths, 2008a; Oxford, 2011b, etc.).

If we look carefully at the literature of the last several decades, I would like to suggest:

- that it is possible to identify the essential characteristics of language learning strategies and to incorporate them into a workable definition;

- that there are six key features (listed and explained below) which define language learning strategies and distinguish them from other learner characteristics or learning behaviours (such as learning style, skills and communication strategies).

1.3.1 Activity

Rubin (1975) stressed the active nature of strategies – they are what learners *do*. Larsen-Freeman (2001: 12) is another who argues that the learner is not 'merely a passive recipient' and that language learning is not merely a 'unilateral process . . . dependent on some benevolent, skilful, more proficient interlocutor'.

It needs to be understood, however, that although there is a considerable degree of consensus that strategies are active, not all writers agree on the nature of the activity. Macaro (2006), for instance, insists that strategies are a mental activity. Oxford (for example, 1990), however, would include physical activities, such as writing in a notebook or physically acting out new words, as examples of strategic behaviour. Since these two experts disagree on this question, researchers need to be aware that they will need to make their own decision about where they stand on the issue, to select strategy items according to their own contexts, participants, research purpose and understanding of the concept, and to be prepared to justify their choices.

Macaro and Oxford's mental/physical divergence notwithstanding, there seems to be fairly general agreement in the literature about the activity dimension of strategies. For this reason, verbs (especially gerunds) are often used to specify strategic activities, for instance:

- *revising regularly;*
- *controlling schedules so that English study is done;*
- *studying English grammar;*
- *consciously learning new vocabulary.*

and so on (taken from the *English Language Learning Strategy Inventory (ELLSI)*: Griffiths, 2003b, see Appendix).

Oxford (1990) in the well-known *Strategy Inventory for Language Learning (SILL)* chooses to express the strategic activity in terms of first-person verbs, such as:

- *I use rhymes to remember new English words.*
- *I try to find patterns in English.*
- *I think about my progress in learning English.*
- *I look for words in my own language that are similar to new words in English.*

As we can see from these two inventories, the active nature of strategies tends to be reflected in the very nature of the grammar which is used to itemise them.

It is this activity component which distinguishes *strategies* from *style*, a closely related concept with which the strategy concept is frequently confused. The confusion began early in the literature. Working at much the same time as Rubin in the mid-1970s, Stern (1975) produced a list of 10 language learning strategies which he believed to be characteristic of good language learners. At the top of the list he put 'personal learning style' (Stern, 1975: 311), thereby confusing the concepts of learning style and learning strategy and contributing to the difficulties with definition which remain to this day.

The key distinction drawn by Wenden (1991: 36) between styles and strategies is that styles are 'the learner's characteristic, and consistent way of perceiving, interacting with and responding to the learning environment'. Styles are relatively enduring, whereas strategies are *'amenable to change'* (Wenden, 1991: 18, author's italics). According to Reid (1998a: ix), learning styles are 'internally based characteristics', whereas learning strategies are activities which students use to improve their learning. Because of this distinction, whereas strategies are usually expressed by means of verbs (*practising, using, planning*, and so on), learning styles are commonly identified either in adjectival terms, such as:

- *aural*
- *visual*
- *kinaesthetic* (Fleming & Mills, 1992)

or as nouns, such as:

- *converger*
- *accommodator*
- *assimilator*
- *diverger* (Kolb, 1976)

Learning styles, or 'general approaches to learning' (Cohen, 1998: 15) are therefore related to, but distinct from, language learning strategies, although strategy choice may be influenced by learning style (Cohen, 2012; Griffiths, 2012; Wenden, 1991). We might expect, for instance, that a student who prefers an aural style would tend to choose strategic activities which involve the sense of hearing, a converger might select strategies which synthesise information, and so on.

1.3.2 Consciousness

Bialystok (1978) and Oxford (1990), among others, argue for the inclusion of the dimension of consciousness in a definition of language learning strategies. The issue of consciousness is, of course, another highly controversial area. Even in a medical environment, using sophisticated equipment, deciding whether a person is conscious or unconscious is far from as straightforward as it might seem. In relation to language learning, Schmidt (1990) points out that 'conscious' or 'unconscious' have a variety of meanings, including whether the learner is aware or not, or whether something has been noticed or not, and he suggests that it is important to be clear what is meant by the terms when using them. These ambiguities led McLaughlin (1990: 617) to recommend that the terms should be abandoned, since they have 'acquired too much surplus meaning'.

Although Wenden (1991) believes that strategies may be used automatically, this is not exactly the same as saying that they are used unconsciously. In the same way, much of our driving behaviour, although automatic (since experienced drivers do not need to deliberately decide on each action), is neither subconscious nor unconscious (hopefully!). Perhaps 'deliberate' versus 'automatic' would be a more useful distinction when talking about language learning strategies than 'conscious' versus 'unconscious'.

However, despite the reservations expressed by Schmidt (1990) and McLaughlin's (1990) recommendations for abandonment, the 'conscious' versus 'unconscious' distinction is well established. Cohen (1998: 4) argues that 'the element of consciousness is what distinguishes *strategies* from those processes that are not strategic' (author's italics), and he suggests that learners who use learning strategies must be at least partially conscious of them even if they are not attending to them fully. As evidence of this argument, Cohen points out that, if interrupted in the course of strategy application, learners can usually verbalise what they were doing. Macaro (2006) is another who uses the adjective 'conscious' when discussing strategic activity.

So what to recommend about the 'consciousness' dimension? Clearly, it is a controversial area, with many dissenting voices (e.g. DeKayser, 2009). There has, however, been so much debate over the issue over the years that it perhaps needs to be included in the definition. It should be remembered, however, that a 'conscious' activity can be either 'automatic' or 'deliberate'. Although Oxford (2011b: 12) describes strategies as 'deliberate', I would like to suggest that strategies can operate somewhere on a continuum between deliberate and automatic. Novice learners, for instance, or those trying out new strategies, are likely to need to make deliberate decisions, whereas experienced learners' strategy selections are likely to be more automatic, to the point where they may not even be aware of having made choices.

1.3.3 Choice

In her model of second language learning, Bialystok (1978: 71) described language learning strategies as 'optional means for exploiting available information to improve competence in a second language'. It would seem self-evident that strategies are chosen by learners, since it would, in any practical sense, be impossible to force them to employ strategies against their will. Furthermore, given the emphasis on active learner involvement which underpins the strategy concept, students who passively accept learning activities from others can hardly be considered strategic.

Strategy selection will depend on a variety of factors, especially:

- *Individual* – strategy choice is likely to vary according to a wide range of personal variables such as motivation, personality, style, age, gender, affect, beliefs, nationality, ethnicity, culture, anxiety, attribution, self-efficacy, self-esteem, proficiency level and so on.
- *Contextual* – learning situation is another variable which has a strong influence on strategy selection. For instance, a student studying in a distance-education environment which is physically isolated from teachers, peers and library resources might be expected to need different strategies from a student in a well-equipped urban school or university with library resources readily available (e.g. White, 2003). Other contextual factors which might affect strategy choices might include whether students are full-time or studying in night classes after work (such as Alberto in the classic study by Schumann, 1975) or whether they are local or whether they must cope in a non-native language (e.g. Freed, 1998). Teaching/learning method might be considered another environmental factor which students would need to consider when making effective choices regarding the strategies they wish to use: for instance, students learning in a traditional grammar-translation environment may well need different strategies if they are to be successful from those learning in a communicative environment (e.g. Griffiths, 2008d).
- *Purpose* – the purpose for which students are studying also affects strategy choice. If, for instance, students are in the fortunate position of being able to study for their own interest or personal satisfaction, they will be able to choose those strategies which best suit their own individual or situational needs. However, students studying for an exam or a specific qualification will need to focus on whatever it is that the exam or the

qualification requires, and 'successful' students (that is, those who pass the exam) will select strategies which achieve this goal.

1.3.4 Goal orientation

According to a number of writers and researchers (e.g. Chamot, 2001; Cohen, 2003; Oxford, 2001, 2011b) strategic behaviour implies goal-oriented, purposeful activity on the part of the learner, aiming at a particular learning target. Goals, of course, vary considerably according to the individual and the situation. But for a particular activity to be considered strategic, it must be purposefully related to a goal, and not just some kind of random behaviour which is undertaken in a haphazard fashion for no particular purpose.

The specification of a goal or purpose is also listed by Macaro (2006) among his identifying features of strategies. As he points out: 'Human action is normally considered to be directed by purpose and dependent on the pursuance of goals. ... Therefore, a key feature of a strategy should be the explicitness of its goal orientation' (Macaro, 2006: 328).

The purposeful/goal-oriented dimension is what distinguishes strategies from *skills*, another concept with which strategies are commonly confused. Skills relate to the way language is used (Richards *et al.*, 1992), and they are usually conceptualised in terms of reading, writing, listening and speaking. These may be further broken down into sub-skills such as: skimming and scanning (for reading); paragraphing and cohesion (for writing); inferring and listening for gist (for listening); fluency and turn-taking (for speaking). All of these relate to the way students use the language they have learnt in order to send or receive messages. If we accept that language use is the key distinguishing feature of skills, we might say that, whereas learning strategies are engaged in the learning process (for instance, grammar or vocabulary), skills are employed to use what has been learnt.

In addition, however, to their essential function to facilitate language use, skills may be employed as a strategy to promote a learning goal. For instance, students may decide to read in order to learn idioms, to write in order to practise grammar, to listen in order to improve pronunciation, or to use their speaking skills in order to develop vocabulary.

Although Oxford (2011b) distinguishes between strategies and skills along the lines that strategies are deliberate and skills are automatic, we have already seen in Section 1.3.2 that strategies can be automatic, especially for experienced learners; it is a little hard to see how the use of, say, writing skills to write a letter can be anything other than deliberate even for students who have had plenty of practice. If, however, we draw the learning strategy/skill distinction according to goal orientation (that is, learning strategies are aimed at learning; skills are aimed at using what has been or is in the process of being learnt), we can see that, when used as an activity to develop idioms, grammar, pronunciation, vocabulary or whatever, skills are being employed as a tool to achieve a learning goal – in other words, used this way they are strategies.

In practice, of course, the distinction between learning/using is not so clear cut. For instance, if a student comes to me, as his teacher, and asks me a question about a weekend activity, how am I to know if he really wants to use his language to gain information, or if he actually wants to practise his grammar, or if he just wants someone to talk to? Maybe he wants all of these, and maybe he achieves one or the other, all or none – human relations and intentions are rarely so cut-and-dried in real life! For the purposes of definition, however, it is important to keep the distinction clear:

- Skills are related to how language is used.
- Learning strategies are activities chosen by learners to achieve a learning goal.

However, aspects of language which are usually thought of as skills or sub-skills may be used for a strategic purpose, although this involves a change in the basic nature of the skill, as a means to an end rather than as an end in itself. This produces a circular (rather than linear) pattern of learning which may contribute to the Tornado Effect discussed in 2.10, 4.9.

Another complicating factor which it is important to keep in mind is that the nature of the goal itself may affect the strategies chosen and how effective the chosen strategies may be in achieving the goal in question. This issue will be further discussed in Section 1.4.

1.3.5 Regulation

Language learning strategies are used by learners for regulating or controlling their learning (Wenden, 1991). The degree to which individuals are active participants in their own learning has been called 'self-regulation' (Dornyei, 2005; Dornyei & Skehan, 2003), which has become a hot topic in language learning in recent years.

As Oxford and Lee (2008) point out, self-regulation also involves *metacognition* and *autonomy*. These are more related concepts which sometimes cause confusion.

Long recognised as a key ingredient of successful learning (e.g. O'Malley *et al.*, 1985; Short & Ryan, 1984), metacognition involves the ability to prepare for and reflect on learning, to plan, monitor and evaluate and, where necessary, to make changes (Anderson, 2008). The ability to think metacognitively is an essential component of self-regulation, since it is impossible for students to be active participants in their own learning if they are unable to think beyond the immediate cognitive demands of a particular task.

In turn, the ability to self-regulate is a vital component of autonomy, defined by Cotterall (2008: 110) as 'learners' ability to assume responsibility for their learning'. Autonomy, then, requires students to regulate their own learning and, in order to do this, they must be able to think metacognitively.

Winne (1995) includes strategies as one of the means used by learners to self-regulate. Viewed in this way, rather than being replaced by the self-regulation concept as Dornyei and Skehan (2003) have suggested, strategies become a tool, pro-actively employed by learners in the process of regulating their own learning.

1.3.6 Learning focus

Yet another concept with which language learning strategies are often confused is that of *communication strategies*. Learning strategies and communication strategies are seen by some as two quite separate manifestations of language learner behaviour. Brown (1980: 87), for instance, draws a clear distinction between learning strategies and communication strategies on the grounds that 'communication is the output modality and learning is the input modality'. Brown (1980) suggests that, while a learner generally applies the same fundamental strategies (such as rule transference) used in learning a language to communicating in that language, there are other communication strategies, such as avoidance or message abandonment, which do not result in learning. Indeed, Ellis (1986) argues that it is even possible that successful use of communication strategies may actually prevent language learning, since skilful compensation for lack of linguistic knowledge may obviate the need for learning.

Tarone (1980), however, takes a different point of view, suggesting that by helping students to say what they want or need to say, communication strategies can help to develop language. Even if the communication is not perfect in grammatical or lexical terms, the process of using the language for communication will expose the learner to language input and could therefore be considered a learning strategy since it may result in learning. The problem with classifying strategies according to result, however, is that even strategies that are clearly intended for learning (such as *repeating vocabulary to myself until I know it*) do not necessarily result in learning.

The key point in this somewhat circuitous argument would seem rather to be intention, so that, in order to be considered a learning strategy rather than a communication strategy the 'basic motivation is not to communicate but to learn' (Tarone, 1980: 419). The problems with differentiating between communication strategies and learning strategies on the grounds of motivation or intention, however, as Tarone (1981) acknowledges, are that we have, in practice, no way of determining what motivates a learner, that learners may have a dual motivation to both learn and communicate, or that learners may learn language even when the basic motivation was to communicate. These difficulties are recognised also by Faerch and Kasper (1983: xvii) who concede: 'one particular act of verbal behaviour can have both learning and communication functions', while Dornyei (1995: 60) observes that the difference between communication and learning strategies 'is not so clear at a closer glance'.

However, I would like to suggest that it is possible to identify the point at which a communication strategy becomes a learning strategy. For instance, recently when I was travelling in Turkey, I wanted to have a photo of myself with a particular set of magnificent ruins in the background (not to mention the foreground!), so I appealed to a couple of locals for help. I communicated in gestures what it was that I wanted and handed them my camera.

'Ah,' they said, 'Çok güzel fotoğraf makinesi'.

So they took my photo and handed the camera back to me with smiles all round. And there it might have ended – photo taken, communication achieved.

But what had they said?

Now I know *çok güzel* – it means 'very good'. As for the rest, cognates were sufficient for me to recognise *fotoğraf* – indeed, it sounds very similar to the English word when spoken. And *makinesi* is sufficiently close to the English 'machine' for me to be able to put the two together as 'photograph machine', therefore 'camera'.

So I repeated it to myself several times to help me to remember it, and checked the spelling in the dog-eared little pocket dictionary that I always carry in my bag, and wrote it down in my notebook of useful words and phrases when I could find a pencil with which to do so. And recently I used *fotoğraf makinesi* in conversation, which impressed everyone with how much my Turkish has improved! So, in fact, a number of strategies were involved in this rather minimal piece of learning, including:

- *using cognates;*
- *repeating new language to oneself to activate memory;*
- *using a dictionary;*
- *recording new language in a notebook;*
- *using new language in order to practise it.*

The key point is that I did not have to carry the communicative experience through to a learning experience: I could have left it at the point where communication had been achieved. The point at which the communication strategies changed into learning strategies really was quite clear: it was the point where I consciously chose to learn from the encounter rather than settling for merely having communicated and got what I wanted.

We can say, therefore, that:

- Communication strategies are used to facilitate interaction.
- The goal of learning strategies is the regulation of language development.

1.3.7 Synthesis

Griffiths (2008a) identified these six essential characteristics of language learning strategies (they are active, conscious, chosen, purposeful, regulatory and learning-focused) which were synthesised into a suggested definition (Griffiths, 2008a: 87), according to which:

Definition of language learning strategies

Language learning strategies are activities consciously chosen by learners for the purpose of regulating their own language learning.

1.4 Effectiveness

The issue of definition should be kept separate from the question of strategy effectiveness. A definition (see above) aims to identify and describe a phenomenon and should not imply any kind of value judgement, for instance, whether it is good or bad or more or less effective (Grenfell & Macaro, 2007). If the activity is consciously chosen by learners for the purpose of regulating their own language learning it is a strategy.

When considering how effective a strategy may be we need also to consider:

- 'Why?' (aim/objective/target/goal)
- 'Where?' (situation/context/environment)
- 'How?' (selection/co-ordination/orchestration)
- 'For whom?' (individual/personal)

1.4.1 The nature of the learning aim/objective/goal/target

As the heading for this section implies, the underlying concept of what it is that a learner is trying to achieve goes by a number of names: sometimes it is referred to in terms of aims and objectives; sometimes it is the learning goal; sometimes the learning target. And these aims or objectives, goals or targets may vary from the general to something quite specific (Hutchinson & Waters, 1990). As discussed previously, goal orientation or purpose is a defining characteristic of a strategy, but the definition should be independent of how effective a chosen strategy may or may not be in terms of achieving the goal.

As an example, at one of the universities where I used to work, it was common for the students when preparing for a writing exam to memorise huge tracts of text. To do them justice, they had very good memories, but for some reason that I still do not completely understand, the argument that this was not an effective strategy when it came to having to write on an unfamiliar topic, and that there were other much more effective strategies that they might have employed which would have taken no more time and produced better results, failed to impress them or to greatly change their behaviour in most cases.

So can we say that memorising these texts was not a strategy? Or was the behaviour not strategic?

I would like to argue 'No'.

What they were doing was an example of an activity which they chose consciously for the purpose of regulating their learning: therefore, it was, by definition, a strategy. The fact that it was not effective is another matter. It might, after all, have been effective for a different purpose – a perfectly good strategy for learning lines for a play, for instance (which, sometimes, they did). Or it might be effective in a different situation.

1.4.2   Learning situation/context/environment

Although long overlooked or ignored as a factor which influences learning, learning situation (also often referred to as context or environment) has in more recent years been recognised as having a major effect on learning outcomes (e.g. Norton & Toohey, 2001). This issue has been discussed previously and will be dealt with again later in the book, but suffice it here to say that learning context must obviously be a factor when considering strategy effectiveness. For instance:

- It would seem to be of little use to debate the effectiveness of a strategy such as *using computers to develop grammatical accuracy* in a poor rural school where the possibility of obtaining and maintaining such expensive hi-tech equipment and software is minimal.
- Whether students are studying the target language in their own countries surrounded by those who speak their own language or whether they

are in a country where the target language is spoken as the native language will clearly affect the degree to which strategies such as *watching TV in the target language to learn idioms* or *reading target language newspapers to expand vocabulary* are easy or even possible.

* Family and/or cultural environments are also likely to have a strong influence on the strategies which given individuals are able to choose and which may or may not be effective for them given the contexts in which their lives are conducted. A strategy such as *reading for pleasure in the target language,* for instance, is unlikely to be an option for a girl in a situation where the women of the family are not expected to be educated.

To return to the example of memorising texts noted previously, in some environments, the ability to memorise is highly valued. Some religions, for instance, place strong emphasis on the importance of remembering and reciting, and those who can do this well are considered to be successful, and rewarded and given status accordingly. In these kinds of situations, then, an effective strategy might be quite different from the kind of activity a learner might choose to achieve success in a more 'creative' or 'communicative' environment. In other words, the very definition of 'success' is context dependent.

Given the all-pervading effect that learning environment inevitably has on learners, it is surprising that there is so little on the subject in the literature. Distance learning situations have existed for many years, especially for students who for one reason or another are unable to attend face-to-face lessons in a conventional classroom, and this kind of learning context has expanded considerably since the advent of the internet (White, 2003). White (1993) discovered that the successful learners in a distance learning situation were those most adept at using metacognitive strategies.

Another context which has received attention is that of students learning in native-speaking (study abroad) environments. In recent years, the demand for English tuition has been keenly felt in English-speaking countries. According to Skyrme (2005), students often expect that the mere fact of studying in a target language environment will somehow make the learning easier. Some studies have indeed shown that significant gains in linguistic proficiency have been made during study-abroad programmes (e.g. Tanaka & Ellis, 2003). However, the rather naïve belief in some kind of linguistic osmosis has not always proved to be well founded (e.g. Isabelli-Garcia, 2003; Pellegrino, 1998; Regan, 1998; Skyrme, 2005; Wilkinson, 1998). In reality, students often find it difficult to cope in learning and living situations which may be very different from those they are used to, and where they are linguistically, culturally and socially challenged in ways which may threaten their very sense of identity (Kline, 1998) and severely reduce motivation.

Clearly, then, studying in a target language environment is not in itself sufficient to guarantee successful learning, and a form of culture shock may well be the result. Students urgently need strategies to help them cope with their new learning environment, and there are different types of strategies, all of which may play a part in the armoury of the self-regulating learner: strategies for maintaining motivation, communication and social strategies, strategies for managing the learning/living situation, and so on. Students who leave their own familiar environments to study in a target language situation may well need all of these in addition to language learning strategies.

1.4.3 How strategies are employed

A third factor which affects how effective strategy choices may be is how they are used. Frequently mentioned in this regard is the individual learner's ability to co-ordinate strategy use. Language learning is a very complex activity, and effective learners do not use strategies in isolation (Anderson, 2008). Rather, successful learners use strategies in clusters, and are able to choose from a repertoire of strategies those which best suit their own goals, situations and individual characteristics.

The *orchestration* metaphor is often employed to convey the idea that strategies need to be harmonised with each other if they are to produce the desired learning outcome. Anderson (2008: 103) describes a student engaged in a think-aloud protocol who verbalises his strategies while listening to a radio announcement:

> [He] uses his background knowledge of radio call-in contests, he identifies vocabulary that he does not know, he guesses at that unknown vocabulary, he expresses doubts about his comprehension. In short, [he] can identify what he knows as well as what he does not know by orchestrating various strategies.

The importance of being able to select and orchestrate appropriate strategies is underlined by two well-known studies of unsuccessful learners. Both Porte (1988) and Vann and Abraham (1990) discovered that their unsuccessful learners in fact used many strategies: the problem was not so much with the quantity or with the frequency. However, these students were not always able to select strategies appropriate for themselves, their situation or the task at hand, and they were not able to use them effectively in combination.

1.4.4 Individual/personal variables

The range of individual variables which might affect strategy choice is almost limitless. In recent years, interest in the influence of individual factors on language learning has been strong (e.g. Dornyei, 2005; Skehan, 1989; Takeuchi *et al.*, 2007), resulting in what Ellis (1994: 472) has called a 'veritable plethora' of such factors in the literature.

Some of the most commonly researched of these individual variables include:

1.4.4.1 Motivation

The importance of motivation in language learning has been dealt with by many. Brown (1994: 152), for instance, claims that motivation is 'a key to learning', while Williams and Burden (1997: 111) suggest that 'it seems only sensible to assume that learning is most likely to occur when we *want* to learn' (authors' italics). Cohen and Dornyei (2002: 172), put forward the intuitively logical argument that 'motivation is often seen as the key learner variable because without it, nothing much happens'.

Ushioda (2008: 19) defines motivation as 'what moves a person to make certain choices, to engage in action, and to persist in action'. From a human point of view, it is difficult to disagree with the basic premise that motivation is important if students are to learn language successfully.

Over the years, motivation has been viewed from a variety of perspectives. In one of the earliest distinctions, Gardner and Lambert (1959, 1972) identified two different motivational orientations:

- integrative (arising from a desire to identify with those who speak the language, perhaps in a social context, in a workplace or as an immigrant);
- instrumental (arising from a desire to benefit practically from acquiring the language, for instance by gaining access to desired educational institutions, by getting a better job, higher salary etc.).

Using a general measure of motivation (including both integrative and instrumental orientations) with students of French in Canada, Gardner (1985) found that motivation (especially integrative motivation) was significantly positively related to achievement. In a later study, Gardner and MacIntyre (1991) found that students did significantly better on a vocabulary task when offered a reward (instrumental motivation). Other studies (such as Chihara & Oller, 1978), however, have failed to show a significant relationship between motivation and achievement.

Taking a somewhat different perspective, Deci and Ryan (1980) and Ryan and Deci (2000) typified motivation as:

- intrinsic (originating from within the learner – it is something the learner wants for his/her own satisfaction);
- extrinsic (arising from outside the learner, for instance from a parent, a teacher/school system or an employer).

In a study based on the distinction between intrinsic and extrinsic motivation, Noels *et al.* (2000) surveyed Anglophone learners of French in Canada. They discovered that intrinsic motivation was more strongly correlated with the criterion measures than extrinsic motivation.

Although the two dichotomous models of motivation (integrative versus instrumental and intrinsic versus extrinsic) have proven to be enduring, they may be overly simplistic. For one thing, as Ushioda (2008) points out, the different concepts may not necessarily be mutually exclusive, but may be 'working in concert with one another' (Ushioda, 2008: 22). Also, as Cohen (2011: 42) colourfully puts it:

> The problem with this approach is that it is pitched at too macro a level to capture those moment-to-moment decisions based on actual language experiences. It is these in-the-trenches experiences that may make or break a learner's desire to stick with a language or call it quits.

Drawing on sociocultural theory (e.g. Lantolf, 2000; Vygotsky, 1978), Norton and Toohey (2001) draw attention to the social context of motivation by describing the experiences of two Polish immigrants (Eva and Julie) who both managed to negotiate well-respected identities for themselves within their respective social situations. The point here is that it is impossible to assess motivation except in relation to the context with which it interacts. If Eva and Julie had not managed to gain acceptance by their communities, their level of motivation might well have suffered accordingly.

Rather than viewing motivation as a static phenomenon which can be described according to integrative/instrumental, intrinsic/extrinsic criteria, Dornyei (2001) presents motivation as dynamic and constantly changing. According to this view, language learners are complex individuals whose motivation derives from their vision of themselves, from social pressures, and the effects of prior learning experiences (Dornyei & Ushioda, 2010).

As far as the relationship between language learning strategies and motivation goes, Oxford (2011b: 74) points out, 'strategies can be fruitfully used to support a number of motivational orientations'. Studies which investigate the relationships between/among strategies, motivation and successful learning are not common, however. One such study is reported in Chapter 2.

1.4.4.2 Nationality

Not always an easy concept to define, nationality is frequently confused with the often closely related concepts of culture and ethnicity. Defined as 'the software of the mind' (Hofstede, 1997: 4), culture is usually considered to include the customs, attitudes, family organisation, social systems and other day-to-day practices of a people which identify them as a distinctive group. Culture may also include language (Scollon & Scollon, 2000). Ethnicity relates to race, while nationality is essentially a political concept (what goes on the passport) which may or may not be identified with a typical culture (ways of behaving), ethnicity (racial origin) or language.

It is, of course, not always easy to classify people in terms of culture, ethnicity, language or nationality in absolute terms. In New Zealand, for instance, there is a large community of ethnic Chinese. Many of these people's families have been in New Zealand since the gold rushes of the late 1800s, were born in New Zealand and have New Zealand nationality. Although most of this community would speak English as their native language, there are varying degrees to which individuals adhere to the heritage language and cultural practices (such as food preferences) and family celebrations (such as weddings). The same applies to ethnic Indians in Fiji, ethnic Koreans in Japan or Russia, ethnic Africans in America, ethnic Japanese in Brazil, and so on, a picture which becomes even more complex if we consider intermarriage, bilingualism and those who have dual or multiple nationalities.

It is a common observation that students from different backgrounds do not always learn language in the same ways (e.g. Connor, 1996; Finkbeiner, 2008; Griffiths & Parr, 2000; Kaplan, 1966; Lado, 1957; Lavine, 2001; Oxford, 1996a; Pennycook, 1997; Pierson, 1996; White, 1989). Some students, for instance, come from very 'talkative' backgrounds where they are brought up from an early age to express ideas freely; others come from backgrounds where they are taught to think carefully before speaking and where imposing one's ideas on others is considered extremely impolite (Corbett, 1999). Some students are brought up in an environment where people communicate naturally without worrying too much about correctness; others are brought up to feel keenly the loss of face which comes from being seen to make mistakes (Ching, 1992; Clarke, 1996). Some students are encouraged to be active in their approach to their learning; others are traditionally passive (Usuki, 2000). These kinds of general national characteristics may well affect the different ways students of varying nationalities behave and interact in a teaching/learning situation and the kinds of learning strategies they typically employ.

Although in the 1950s and 1960s Contrastive Analysis, which hypothesises that students will find characteristics of a target language which are similar to the native language easier to learn than those which are different (Lado, 1957) and Contrastive Rhetoric, which considers cultural in addition to linguistic aspects (Kaplan, 1966) seemed to hold the promise of helping to guide students of varying linguistic/cultural backgrounds to learn a target language more effectively, in more recent years it has often been considered not 'politically correct to generalize' about such issues (Pierson, 1996: 51). Perhaps because of this, studies of language learning strategy use according to nationality are not easy to find. However, there are some studies which have produced findings on nationality-related differences in language learning strategies.

Politzer and McGroarty (1985) administered a strategy survey to 19 Hispanic and 18 Asian graduate students in the USA. They found that the Asian students made significantly greater progress in their language acquisition over the period of the study although they exhibited fewer of the strategies expected of 'good' language learners than did Hispanic students.

In order to investigate the role of language learning strategies in successful learning, O'Malley (1987) and his colleagues randomly assigned 75 students to one of three instructional groups, two of which received instruction in various listening, speaking and vocabulary strategies while the third group served as the control. They discovered a significant difference in favour of the treatment groups for speaking, but not for listening, while the control group for vocabulary actually scored slightly higher than the treatment groups, an unexpected finding which O'Malley attributes to the persistence of familiar strategies among Asian students who were unwilling to adopt the strategies presented in training, especially when a test was imminent.

At a university in South Africa, the language learning strategy use of 305 Afrikaans-speaking students of English was surveyed using the *SILL*. The authors (Dreyer & Oxford, 1996) report that 45% of the variance in TOEFL scores was found to be attributable to strategy employment.

Following a review of 36 studies in a variety of different backgrounds, Bedell and Oxford (1996: 60) conclude: 'Cultural influences on the selection of language learning strategies is clear. Learners often – though not always – behave in certain culturally approved and socially encouraged ways as they learn'.

In a study involving a questionnaire and group interviews in Taiwan, Yang (1998) made some interesting discoveries about her students' language learning strategy use, and in a later study (1999), she found that, although her students were aware of various language learning strategies, few of them actually reported using them. As a result of her research, Yang produced recommendations aimed at helping teachers adapt programmes to students' needs more effectively.

Acknowledging that Japanese learners are typically believed to be passive, Usuki (2000) undertook a study in a Japanese university. After discussing the psychological barriers to the adoption of effective language learning strategies by Japanese students, Usuki recommends more cooperation between students and teachers.

A study which explores the relationships among nationality, strategies and successful language learning is reported in Chapter 2.

1.4.4.3 Age

Issues associated with the age of students who are speakers of other languages learning a new language have been long and sometimes hotly debated (e.g. Ausubel, 1964; Bialystock, 1999; Birdsong, 1999a; Griffiths, 2008b; Hylenstam & Abrahamsson, 2003; Singleton, 1989; Singleton & Lesniewska, 2012). We would all like to envisage ourselves striding into our mature years full of vim, vigour and vitality, with intellectual batteries not only undimmed but supercharged. With untold megabytes of experience to add RAM to our ROM, we could take on the world. We could study, we could read, we could write, we could learn languages...!?

Popular wisdom generally has it that children are better at learning languages than adults (e.g. Bellingham, 2000; Littlewood, 1984). In one of the earliest studies into age-related differences in language development by speakers of other languages, Oyama (1976) discovered that the younger people were when they started learning English the more native-like was their pronunciation. Other studies have shown that, although adults may learn more quickly initially, younger learners are often more successful in the long run (Snow & Hoefnagel-Hohle, 1978). Harley (1986) also discovered that, although older students demonstrated greater overall control of the verb system than younger students after 1000 hours of instruction, those students who started younger were ultimately more successful.

Other studies, however, indicate there that there may be 'optimism for older learners' (Ehrman & Oxford, 1990: 317). Although they discovered that performance ratings corresponded roughly inversely to age, they found that the oldest student was not the weakest, nor was the youngest the best. Furthermore, some results suggest that the benefits of early instruction for language development may not be long term (Burstall et al., 1974). Although Fathman (1975) found that younger students did better than older students on learning phonology, older students did better on morphology. Neufeld (1978) produced results which seemed to indicate that adults could acquire native-like pronunciation, and a study of Canadian immersion programmes by Swain (1981) concluded that an earlier start had much less effect than might have been expected.

A well-known case study which supports the idea that older learners can learn language successfully is that of Julie (Ioup *et al.*, 1994). At the age of 21, Julie moved from England to Cairo with her Egyptian husband who was called away for military service soon after their arrival. Left with non-English-speaking relatives in a situation of total immersion until her husband's return, Julie kept a notebook in which she recorded vocabulary, idioms, and what she observed regarding the structure of the language. According to Ioup *et al.* (1994), after six months, Julie was communicating well, and after two and a half years she could pass as a native speaker.

However, by no means all adults are as successful as Julie. Schumann (1975), for instance, describes a 10-month study of a 33-year-old Costa Rican living in the USA. Although Alberto appeared to have good motivation and positive attitudes towards America, he socialised mainly with speakers of Spanish, and chose to work at night, limiting his opportunities to interact in and study English. As a result, his linguistic development was slow.

Like Alberto, Wes, a Japanese artist living in Hawaii, was also 33 years old. According to Schmidt (1983), when Wes first arrived in Hawaii, his ability to communicate in English was minimal, although he was extroverted with a strong drive to communicate. As a result, during a 3-year observation period, Wes's ability to communicate orally in English increased impressively, but his grammatical control of English improved very little.

A variety of possible theories has been put forward to explain apparent age-related differences in language learning, including the Critical Period Hypothesis (e.g. Birdsong, 1999b; Lenneberg, 1967). Brown (1980: 46) defines the critical period as 'a biologically determined period of life when language can be acquired most easily and beyond which time language is increasingly difficult to acquire'. According to Long (1990), another possible biological explanation might be the process of myelination which progressively wraps the nerves of the brain in myelin sheaths as the brain matures. Myelination means that learning pathways are delineated in the brain, thereby preserving previous learning, but it reduces flexibility. Like concrete pathways in a garden, the myelin sheaths facilitate movement to and from a point, but also make it more difficult to deviate from set patterns. None of the biological explanations for age-related differences is without controversy, however (e.g. Singleton & Munoz, 2011), and Dulay *et al.* (1982) believe that we must look elsewhere for an explanation for observed age-related differences in second language development. For this reason the term 'sensitive' period rather than 'critical' period has been proposed in order to indicate that there is no 'abrupt or absolute criterion after which L2 acquisition is impossible but rather a gradual process within which the ultimate level of L2 attainment becomes variable' (Ioup *et al.*, 1994: 74). Munoz and Singleton (2011: 1) also argue for a 'loosening of the association' between biological age and the ability to learn language.

Socio-affective factors are considered by some to be the most powerful influences on the differences in language learning ability according to age. Describing his own 'distinctly unsatisfactory' (Burling, 1981: 280) attempts to learn Swedish when he spent a year as a guest professor in Sweden, Burling is in no doubt that 'generalized social changes' (Burling, 1981: 290) are the main cause of age-related differences in language development, which mean that 'an adult is likely to give up and conclude that he has lost the capacity to learn a language' (Burling, 1981: 284). Schumann (1976) proposed the concept of social distance to refer to the similarity or dissimilarity of cultures which come into contact with each other, resulting in greater or lesser degrees of culture shock, and Brown (1980) suggests that social distance is a factor in the difficulty the learner will have in learning a target language. According to Ellis (1986: 109), socio-affective factors are often less inhibiting for younger learners since they tend to be 'less culture bound than adults . . . and so acquire L2 more quickly'.

Cognitive variables may be another factor contributing to age-related differences in language development. Krashen (1985) explains the older learners' faster initial progress in terms of their ability to obtain more comprehensible input by means of their greater experience, knowledge and ability to negotiate communication. According to Ellis (1986), older learners are able to learn language by consciously thinking about the rules; cognitive factors could help to explain Snow and Hoefnagel-Hohle's (1978) findings that older students are initially faster than younger students since they are capable of rationalising the systems of the target language and of comparing them with existing knowledge. More mature students might also be expected to have a larger and well-established strategy repertoire from which they can select and orchestrate appropriate learning activities to regulate their own learning. In addition, older students might be expected to be able to exercise better metacognitive control over their learning, for instance by means of time management, and by planning, monitoring and evaluating their own progress.

According to their age, it is possible that learning context may affect students differently. Learning situation can vary considerably from a formal classroom, to naturalistic environments where students learn by being immersed in the target language, to distance learning. Classrooms can also vary greatly, and classes may be conducted during the day or at night. Methods may vary from structure-based grammar-translation, to behaviourist audiolingualism, to interactive communicative approaches, and may include some of the lesser known methods such as Total Physical Response (TPR), the Silent Way or Suggestopaedia. These various situations may suit older or younger students depending on variables such as previous learning experience, learning style, metacognitive ability, motivation, autonomy, personal circumstances and, of course, the strategies they choose to employ.

Studies which explore the relationships among age, strategies and successful language learning are not easy to find. One such study is reported in Chapter 2.

1.4.4.4 Sex/gender

This is another learner variable sometimes thought to affect success in language learning. The concept of sex is usually used to mean a biological attribute, whereas the concept of gender refers more to a culturally determined characteristic.

When drawing distinctions along sex/gender lines, care needs to be taken to avoid 'oversimplification and unproductive generalizations' (Sunderland, 2000: 149). However, women are often believed to be better language learners than men (Ellis, 1994; Larsen-Freeman & Long, 1991).

On a biological level, research appears to indicate that women have more nerve cells in the left half of the brain where language is centred. In addition, women often use both sides of the brain (Legato, 2005).

However, it is also possible that girls' linguistic development may be as much a social phenomenon as it is a biological one. As Nyikos (2008: 75) notes: 'much of the perceived female superiority in language capability may be due to the added effort which adults tend to lavish on baby girls compared with baby boys'.

Oxford et al. (1988) argued that women have an advantage over men with regard to language development because they are more likely to be interactive. In addition, they are more likely to strive for higher grades and to use language learning strategies more frequently because of a stronger desire for social approval. Research has consistently found that females are prepared to invest more time and effort in studying language because of the greater perceived benefits for their future (Gu, 2002), and girls' culture appears to be more study oriented and supportive of academic achievement (Van Houtte, 2004). In contrast, men are often interested only in the ultimate goal (Nyikos, 1990). Men also tend to work alone more, thereby missing out on the benefits of interactive strategies (Young & Oxford, 1997), and they tend more often to use rote memorisation, repetition and translation, all of which are more likely to be used more frequently by less successful language learners (Nyikos, 1987).

There are, in fact, a number of studies which investigate the relationship between language learning and sex (e.g. Bacon, 1992; Boyle, 1987; Burstall, 1975; Eisenstein, 1982; Farhady, 1982; Nyikos, 1990, 2008; Sunderland, 1998, 2000). However, studies which explore language learning strategy use according to sex are not common. Nevertheless, there are a few.

Most studies in this area seem to have reported a greater use of language learning strategies by women. Tran (1988), however, discovered that Vietnamese women use fewer language learning strategies than men.

After studying the language learning strategies used by more than 1200 undergraduate university students, Oxford and Nyikos (1989: 296) concluded that sex differences had a 'profound influence'. These differences indicated that females used strategies more frequently than males.

Reporting on an exploratory study undertaken as part of a larger study at the Foreign Service Institute, Ehrman and Oxford (1989) concluded that women reported definitely more use of strategies than men. The same authors in a later article (1995) again reported that females tended to use conscious language learning strategies more often than males.

At the University of Puerto Rico, Green and Oxford (1995) investigated the language learning strategy use of 374 students using the *SILL*. They also concluded that females used strategies significantly more often than males, and that different environments can influence the use of specific strategies by the two sexes, since men used television and movies to learn English far more than women because English language programming, especially sport, appealed more to men than to women.

Some studies have looked at language learning strategies and sex in relation to a third variable. One such study explored the relationships among sex, strategies and visual style (Nyikos, 1990). Women were found to be significantly more successful when utilising colour association than men, while the men were more successful when combining visual linking and colour association. According to Nyikos (1990: 285), results showed that men and women who used 'learning strategies that are in tune with their socialized learning style' were equally successful.

A study which explores the relationships among sex, strategies and successful language learning is reported in Chapter 2.

1.4.4.5 Learning style

Learning style is another possible contributor to variations in individual language learning strategy use. Although care should be taken to keep the concept of learning style separate from the concept of language learning strategy, it is well recognised that learning style can have a major influence on the way students learn and on the types of language learning strategies which they choose (e.g. Carrell *et al.*, 1989; Cohen, 2011; Cohen & Dornyei, 2002; Griffiths, 2012; Nel, 2008; Reid, 1987, 1995, 1998b; Willing, 1987).

Reid (1995: viii) provided a definition of learning styles which has proved to be enduring. According to this definition, learning styles are 'an individual's natural, habitual and preferred way(s) of absorbing, processing, and retaining new information and skills'.

The learning style concept has been recognised in the field of education since at least the mid-1970s. One of the earliest instruments was the *Learning Style Inventory* by Dunn *et al.* (1975), which divided learning style into five domains of preference: environmental, emotional, sociological, physiological and psychological. Around the same time, another influential inventory appeared: Kolb's (1976) *Learning Style Inventory*. According to Kolb's model, learning preferences can be described using two intersecting continua: active versus reflective, and abstract versus concrete, resulting in four types of learners: converger (active/abstract), accommodator (active/concrete), assimilator (reflective/abstract) and diverger (reflective/concrete). Three years later, Gregorc (1979) continued the quadrant model for conceptualising learning style when he produced *The Gregorc Style Delineator* with two axes (concrete versus abstract, and sequential versus random) which delineated four styles: concrete sequential, concrete random, abstract sequential and abstract random. In the early 1980s, Honey and Mumford (1982) published their *Learning Styles Questionnaire*, which retained Kolb's quadrant model but added some new categories: reflector, theorist, pragmatist and activist. Then, Curry (1983) conceived of style in terms of a metaphorical onion where the outer cognitive/personality layer influences the information processing layer which then contributes to instructional preferences.

One of the first well-known applications of the style concept to language learning was by Reid (1987) who developed the *Perceptual Learning Style Preference Questionnaire (PLSPQ)*, which was based on five modalities: visual (learning by seeing), auditory (learning by hearing), tactile (learning by touching), kinaesthetic (learning by moving) and individual versus group preference. In the same year, Willing (1987) conducted a large-scale survey of immigrants to Australia using a Kolb-style quadrant model with a twin-axis framework (passive–active and analytic–holistic) which produced four more learner types: convergers, conformists, concrete learners and communicative learners. Using a modified version of Reid's perceptual learning style model, Fleming and Mills (1992) produced the *VARK* (Visual, Aural, Read/write and Kinaesthetic). The *Style Analysis Survey* (Oxford, 1993) analysed learning style according to other preferences including intuitive/random, concrete/sequential, closure-oriented/open and global/analytic. In addition, Oxford also contributed to the *Learning Style Survey* (Cohen *et al.*, 2002) with yet more style dimensions, including sharpener/leveller, global/particular, synthesising/analytic, deductive/inductive, impulsive/reflective, metaphoric/ literal, field dependent/independent and memorisation. A year later, Ehrman and Leaver (2003) produced the *Learning Style Questionnaire*, which operates between the two poles of ectasis (exercising conscious control) versus synopsis (relying on subconscious processing) and employs style concepts including random/sequential, analogue/digital and concrete/abstract.

As one considers the multitude of style inventories and dimensions noted above (which is by no means exhaustive), it is difficult not to feel intimidated by the 'quagmire' (Dornyei, 2005: 120) they represent. And although there have been many attempts over the years to identify, label and categorise learning styles and to develop inventories, studies that empirically investigate the concept are surprisingly difficult to find.

Perhaps the aspect of style which has been most thoroughly researched has been field in/dependence (e.g. Chapelle, 1988; Witkin, 1962). Field-dependent learners are unable to separate details from the background, are more holistic or global in their approach, and more concerned with the overall picture than with particulars. Field-independent learners, on the other hand, are able to analyse tasks into sections and focus on discrete aspects. Field in/dependence is usually assessed by means of Witkin's *Embedded Figures Test* (1971), which requires students to discern patterns among more complicated shapes. This inevitably raises questions about its relevance to language learning and renders the role of field in/dependence as an aspect of learning style somewhat dubious.

Though much controversy remains regarding the learning style concept, Nel (2008: 57) reminds us that 'every learner does have a learning style'. Although, as Nel (2008) points out, learning style is generally considered to be a relatively stable learner characteristic, according to Oxford (2011b: 40) learning styles 'are not set in stone'. Reid (1987: 100) agrees that learning styles 'can be modified and extended', and Cohen and Dörnyei (2002) also suggest that the ability to remain somewhat flexible with regard to learning style preferences is a characteristic of successful learners.

The interview data reported in Chapter 3 will be examined for possible relationships among learning style, strategy use and successful language learning.

1.4.4.6 *Personality*

Learning style is often assumed to be an aspect of the broader concept of personality, which is generally considered to be a relatively stable characteristic of an individual. Personality has been defined as 'those aspects of an individual's behaviour, attitudes, beliefs, thought, actions and feelings which are seen as typical and distinctive of that person' (Richards *et al.*, 1992: 340).

A well-known instrument to measure personality is the *Myers–Briggs Type Indicator* (*MBTI*) (Myers, 1962), a widely used personality inventory based on Jung's (1921) theories of psychological types. The MBTI measures personality according to four dichotomous scales:

- *Extraversion–Introversion*: extraverts are focused primarily toward the outer world whereas introverts are focused primarily inwards – they are commonly abbreviated E and I respectively (note that the spelling 'extravert' was used by Isabel Myers in the original 1962 version).
- *Sensing–Intuition*: a person who relies primarily on sensing (S) uses one or more of the five senses to attend to observable facts or happenings whereas someone who relies on intuition (N) attends to meanings, relationships and/or possibilities beyond what is observable.
- *Thinking–Feeling*: thinkers (T) rely on logical consequences whereas feelers (F) tend to make decisions on the basis of value judgments.
- *Judging–Perceiving*: someone with a judging personality (J) tends to use rational processes to deal with the world whereas a perceiver (P) relies more on instinct when interacting with others or making decisions

The four *MBTI* scales combine into 16 possible four-letter personality types:

ISTJ	ISFJ	INFJ	INTJ
ISTP	ISFP	INFP	INTP
ESTP	ESFP	ENFP	ENTP
ESTJ	ESFJ	ENFJ	ENTJ

Key: I = introversion; E = extròversion; S = sensing; N = intuition; F = feeling; T = thinking; J = judging; P = perceiving.

Another common framework for conceptualising personality is known as the Big Five Model (McCrae & John, 1992). The Big Five factors are openness, conscientiousness, extraversion, agreeableness and neuroticism (OCEAN):

- Those with an open personality are intellectually curious and enjoy variety.
- Conscientious individuals are disciplined, organised and achievement oriented.
- Extroverts are sociable and talkative and enjoy interacting with others.

- Agreeable personalities are helpful, cooperative, friendly and sympathetic.
- Neurotics display anxiety, nervousness, insecurity and lack of confidence.

The salient common factor of the *MBTI* and the Big Five models is the extrovert/introvert dimension, first introduced into the literature by Jung (1921). Extroverts tend to be gregarious, interested in interacting with others and, therefore, likely to use social strategies in order to learn language. Introverts, on the other hand, tend to be less sociable, quite happy to spend time on their own, and may tend to favour cognitive strategies (such as reading for pleasure) or metacognitive strategies (such as time management).

Although extroverted personalities are commonly believed to be the best language learners, Ehrman (2008) discovered that, contrary to expectations, the really high-level learners in her study had introverted personalities and were significantly overrepresented among the top learners. Ehrman (2008: 70) concludes that according to the results of her research good language learners tend to be characterised by introverted personalities which, as she comments

> is a finding which runs contrary to much of the literature, and, even, to pedagogical intuition. ... However, it is clear from the fact that there are high level language learners in a wide variety of personality categories that motivated individuals can become good language learners whatever their personalities.

The interview data is examined for possible relationships among personality, strategy use and successful language learning in Chapter 3.

1.4.4.7 Autonomy

It is generally Henri Holec (1981) who is credited with first applying the term *autonomy* to language learning, defining it as 'the ability to take charge of one's own learning' (Holec, 1981: 3). Since then, the autonomy concept has been widely discussed (for example, among many others, see Aoki & Smith, 1999; Benson, 2007; Benson & Voller, 1997; Pemberton *et al.*, 1996; Sturtridge, 1997). According to Wenden (1991), strategies are an important element of learner autonomy, since it is by using strategies that learners are able to become autonomous. Recognition of the importance of the role of autonomy in language learning is evidenced by the proliferation of self-access centres in language schools or departments in the years since. In these centres, which often provide computers and a range of books, tapes, CDs, DVDs and other materials and equipment, students are encouraged and supported to pursue their own studies according to their own interests or needs, thereby demonstrating autonomous learning behaviours which they exercise independently of teacher supervision.

Learner autonomy is generally assumed to be advantageous (e.g. Dam, 1995) and 'a desirable objective' (Jones, 1995: 228). According to Crabbe (1993: 443) 'learning is more meaningful, more permanent, more focused on the processes and schemata of the individual when the individual is in charge'.

Jones (1995), however, is not so certain that autonomy is always beneficial, since he claims 'the concept of autonomy is laden with cultural values', which may not be relevant to less individualistic societies. Little (1999: 12), nevertheless, disagrees that autonomy is only a 'western cultural construct and, as such, an inappropriate pedagogical goal in non-Western societies' since, he argues, the capacity for autonomy is universal.

Autonomy is a complex phenomenon, which Benson (2001: 47) describes as 'a multidimensional capacity that will take different forms for different individuals, and even for the same individual in different contexts or at different times'. Cotterall (2008: 118) makes a similar point: 'A defining characteristic of autonomous learners is their ability to make decisions about their learning which take account of the context in which they are learning.' Autonomous behaviour is likely to involve metacognitive strategies (e.g. Anderson, 2008) to enable learners to control their own learning.

In recent years, the term *autonomy* has sometimes been replaced by the term *self-regulation* (Cohen, 2011), which Dornyei and Skehan (2003: 611) define as 'the degree to which individuals are active participants in their own learning'. In turn, *self-regulation* has been seen as resulting at least in part from *volition* (Corno, 2001), defined by Oxford (2011b: 74) as 'persistence after initial motivation is over'. According to Kuhl (1984), *volitional competence* is responsible for controlling intention, attention, action, arousal, motivation, emotion, encoding, self-reflection, thinking and planning. Volitional strategies are 'designed to help the learner keep learning despite many kinds of difficulties' (Oxford & Lee, 2008: 313), and they represent the antithesis of *learned helplessness* where individuals do not believe they can control their situations (Seligman, 1975).

The question of the relationships among autonomy, strategy use and successful language learning will be further discussed in Chapter 3.

1.4.4.8 Beliefs

Beliefs might be defined as 'the psychological state in which a person holds a premise to be true' (Oxford, 2011b: 277). A number of researchers have investigated learner beliefs in language learning over the years. When Wenden (1987a) interviewed learners, she found that in addition to describing their strategy use they were able to articulate beliefs about how best to learn language. And Abraham and Vann (1987) discovered that l‹ beliefs affect how they approach learning which, in turn, influences ʜᴜⱳ. successful they will be in their studies.

An important development in the field of learner beliefs was Horwitz's (1987) *Beliefs about Language Learning Inventory (BALLI)*, an instrument which has been used in much of the research into learners' beliefs since that date. The *BALLI* was developed as a result of a brainstorming session with 25 language teachers from which Horwitz constructed a list of beliefs to which participants were asked to respond on a five-point Likert-scale ranging from 'strongly disagree' to 'strongly agree'. Items in the *BALLI* include beliefs such as:

* Children learn language more easily than adults.
* Some people are naturally better at learning language than others.
* Women are better than men at learning language.
* Some languages are easier than others.
* Vocabulary is the most important part of learning a new language.
* Grammar is the most important part of learning a new language.
* Pronunciation is important when learning a new language.
* Students who are allowed to make mistakes will have difficulty speaking correctly later.

In turn, these items were divided into five belief areas:

* aptitude;
* language learning difficulties;
* the nature of language learning;
* strategies;
* motivation.

A year after publishing the *BALLI*, Horwitz (1988: 283) comments: 'Although student beliefs about language learning would seem to have obvious relevance to the understanding of student expectations of, commitment to, success in, and satisfaction with their language courses, they have remained relatively unexplored.' And, indeed, even in the years since, beliefs have been a relatively under-researched area of language learning. Nevertheless, there have been some belief-focused studies, of which a number are reviewed by Horwitz (1999) and Barcelos (2003).

Although an individual's beliefs are often assumed to be a relatively stable individual characteristic, White (2008: 125) reports that, according to a longitudinal study which she conducted (White, 1999, 2003) good language learners are not 'those who have particular sets of beliefs but [those] who succeed in sensing out the affordances of a particular learning context, and developing a productive interface between their beliefs and attributes and different possibilities and experiences within that context'. According to White (2008), good language learners believe in themselves as able to learn and they also believe that the language they are studying is worth learning. Furthermore, according to Ehrman and Oxford (1989, 1990), successful learners develop insights into beliefs about the language learning process and the use of effective learning strategies.

The interview data are examined for possible relationships among beliefs, strategy use and successful language learning in Chapter 3.

1.4.4.9 Aptitude

For some time the idea that natural aptitude might contribute to success in language learning has been rather unfashionable (Ranta, 2008). For some reason, we are often quite comfortable with the idea that some people are naturally better at sport, or music, or maybe even subjects like maths. But the possibility that some might be innately better at language, to be able to learn language more rapidly and easily than others, is somehow undemocratic (e.g. Dornyei & Skehan, 2003). Nevertheless, the question of language aptitude is actually an important one (Diller, 1981) in order that less able students may be adequately supported (Ranta, 2008; Wesche, 1981).

Perhaps the instrument which is most strongly connected with the aptitude concept is the *Modern Language Aptitude Test* (Carroll & Sapon, 1959). The *MLAT* is a commercial product which has been used to select promising language learners, to place them in the most beneficial environment, and to diagnose learning difficulties. Carroll (1965) suggested that aptitude consisted of four areas of ability:

- phonemic coding ability – the ability to identify and remember distinct sounds;
- grammatical sensitivity – the ability to recognise grammatical relationships;
- rote learning ability – the ability to remember linguistic information;
- inductive language learning ability – the ability to infer rules.

Other tests of aptitude include the *Pimsleur Language Aptitude Battery* (*PLAB*) aimed at high school students (Pimsleur, 1966), and the *Cognitive Ability for Novelty in Acquisition of Language – Foreign* (*CANAL-F*) based on the premise that successful language learners are able to cope with new ideas (Grigorenko *et al.*, 2000). However, according to Williams and Burden

(1997: 18) the predictive value of aptitude tests is not particularly high, and they run the risk of 'placing limitations on the way in which we view learners and consequently the way we treat them'.

The relationship of aptitude to working memory has been investigated (e.g. Baddeley & Hitch, 1974; Juffs & Harrington, 2011), as well as the possibility that rather than being a unitary phenomenon, aptitude involves utilising combinations of cognitive abilities or aptitude complexes (e.g. DeKeyser & Koeth, 2011; Robinson, 2012; Snow, 1987). But the possibility that low aptitude might be compensated for by means of effective strategies remains surprisingly under-researched.

The interview data is examined for possible relationships among aptitude, strategy use and successful language learning in Chapter 3.

1.4.4.10 Affect

The role of affect in language learning has long been recognised. Schumann (1975) investigated the affective factors which created problems for his subjects. Lozanov (1978) developed Suggestopaedia around the idea that feelings/emotions play a key role in language development. Krashen and Terrell (1983) discussed the Affective Filter Hypothesis in relation to language teaching methodology, explaining that the higher the affective filter, the more difficulty the learner will experience. And Arnold (1999) has devoted a book to various aspects of affect in language learning.

Affect can itself be broken down into a number of areas, each of which tends to have its own literature:

- *Anxiety* – According to Oxford (1999: 59), 'Language anxiety is fear or apprehension occurring when a learner is expected to perform in a second or foreign language'. Language anxiety is sometimes divided according to whether it is considered a state (that is, a response to a specific situation or event which will pass when the situation or event is no longer a threat) or a trait (that is, a person's characteristic reaction to experiences which is more likely to be enduring) (Gardner & MacIntyre, 1993). Although anxiety is often assumed to be negative in its effects on behaviour, it may not always be unproductive. Indeed, a certain level of anxiety may be motivating and spur learners to achieve beyond the level that they might have otherwise achieved (e.g. Scovel, 1978).

- *Attitude* – According to Baker (1988), attitudes are learnt and have feelings and emotions attached to them. Furthermore, they are related to motivation (Gardner, 1985; Gardner & Lambert, 1972) which, in turn, is related to successful language learning (e.g. Ushioda, 2008). Oxford (2011b: 71) suggests that 'attitudes are generally viewed as either positive or negative and can strongly affect L2 learning', and she goes on to recommend the use of strategies to modify attitudes where appropriate.

- *Attribution* – Attribution theory relates to an individual's perception of the causes for successes or failures (Arnold & Brown, 1999). Failure attributed to internal factors (such as aptitude, age, nationality or sex) tend to be much more limiting than failure attributed to external factors (such as the learning situation or teacher limitations) which do not devalue the self (Weiner, 1974, 1985).

- *Empathy* – Empathy refers to the ability to identify with another, the ability to understand (though not necessarily agree with) another's point of view. Hogan (1969) and Mehrabian and Epstein (1972) published empathy scales which have been used in a number of studies in the years since. However, although 'there is strong intuitive support' for believing that empathy would facilitate the language learning process 'the jury is still out on the question of the degree of correlation between empathy and success in language learning' (Arnold & Brown, 1999: 19). Guiora *et al.* (1972: 111), nevertheless, do report that, according to their study, empathy 'is positively related to the ability to authentically pronounce a second language'.

- *Inhibition* – One of the first to note the effect of inhibition on successful language learning was Rubin (1975: 47) who writes that the good language learner 'is willing to appear foolish if reasonable communication results ... [and] willing to make mistakes in order to learn to communicate'. As Arnold and Brown (1999: 10) explain, inhibitions relate to 'the need to protect a fragile ego'. Inhibitions are what individuals use to protect their *ego boundaries* (Ehrman, 1999; Federn, 1928; Hartmann, 1991). In a language classroom, perhaps the area where inhibitions are most obvious, as Rubin (1975) suggests, relates to error correction.

- *Self-concept* – 'A person's self-concept consists of the beliefs one has about oneself' (Mercer, 2011: 14), and it can in turn be broken down into a number of sub-fields, each of which has a literature of its own, although there are numerous points at which the sub-fields overlap, making them difficult to separate into totally mutually exclusive categories.
  - *Self-confidence* – self-confidence relates to the degree to which an in individual believes in him- or herself. According to Williams and Burden (1997: 72) 'teachers should see one of their primary functions as encouraging ... self-confidence'.
  - *Self-efficacy* – self-efficacy relates to the belief that one can achieve a particular goal (Bandura, 1997). As such, it is a more targeted concept than the more general concept of self-confidence.

- *Self-esteem* – self-esteem is another closely related concept which Coppersmith (1967: 5) defines as 'a personal judgement of worthiness that is expressed in the attitudes that the individual holds towards himself'. According to de Andres (1999: 87) there is a 'strong link' between self-esteem and academic performance.
- *Self-image* – self-image relates to the way one views oneself, and it is likely to be closely linked to motivation, which has been previously discussed as a strong predictor of language learning outcomes. If students see themselves as good language learners, they are likely to be motivated to invest time and effort in fulfilling their own vision of themselves.

The interview data is examined for possible relationships among affect, strategy use and successful language learning in Chapter 3.

1.4.4.11 Identity

All of the individual factors noted above (and perhaps others) contribute to learner identity, which has been recognised in recent years for the pivotal role that it plays in language learning (e.g. Cummins, 1996, 2001; Day, 2002; LoBianco *et al.*, 2009; Norton, 1997, 2000, 2010; Pavlenko & Blackledge, 2003; Peirce, 1995; Toohey, 2000). However, perhaps because the concept of learner identity ranges over such a wide variety of factors, contributing to a potentially infinite number of permutations of variables producing unique identities, debates on the issue are often 'inconclusive and indeterminate' (Norton, 1997: 409).

Nevertheless, although slippery, the identity concept remains important in the field of language learning. Learners are not, after all, idealised theoretical clones of each other. They are unique individuals who interact with one another and with their environment in distinctive ways and employ combinations of strategies which are all different. And herein lie both challenge and reward for a teacher.

The interview data is examined for possible relationships among identity, strategy use and successful language learning in Chapter 3.

1.4.4.12 Investment

The concept of *investment* was introduced into the language learning literature by Peirce (1995), drawing on the economic metaphors of Bourdieu (1977) in which he describes linguistic development as *cultural capital*. According to Peirce (1995), when learners invest in language learning, they expect to get an identity-enhancing return on their investment.

In addition to a possible financial input, investment can take the form of time, attention and effort. One indicator of the amount of effort a learner is willing to invest may well be the level of strategic activity which they report, since uncommitted students would seem likely to be less strategically involved than more committed learners who could be expected to be more pro-actively seeking ways to promote their learning.

The interview data is examined for possible relationships among investment, strategy use and successful language learning in Chapter 3.

1.4.5 Summary

To summarise, it is not possible to label any given strategy as either 'good' or 'bad' or 'effective' or 'ineffective' in itself. A given strategic activity can only be judged in this way according to its suitability for a given learner in a given context studying for a given purpose and in relation to other strategies being deployed. Individual, situational and target factors and their effects on strategy choice and orchestration will be further discussed in later chapters.

Strategy effectiveness

A strategy or cluster of strategies is effective if it works for a particular individual in a particular learning situation working towards a particular goal.

1.5 Theoretical Underpinnings

Although the learning strategy concept is 'intuitively appealing' and has been 'embraced with enthusiasm' (Dornyei, 2005: 166), Dornyei and Skehan (2003: 610) believe that strategy research has often been carried out in a 'theoretical muddle' which has resulted in a great deal of 'conceptual ambiguity'. In the face of such criticism, it is important to examine the theoretical underpinnings of the concept before proceeding further.

The general concept of using strategies to enhance learning is not new. Generations of us must have used the first-letter mnemonic strategy to remember information such as the colours of the rainbow (Roy G. Biv = red, orange, yellow, green, blue, indigo and violet) and the order of the elements in chemistry. Gage and Berliner (1992) discuss a number of general learning strategies, such as highlighting important ideas and summarising. These strategies are often so basic that it is easy for experienced students to take them for granted, but it must be remembered that the strategies themselves had to be learnt initially before they could be used to enhance other learning, and some students never manage to acquire this kind of procedural knowledge.

It is widely accepted that language learning strategies are a factor in successful language learning (e.g. Chamot, 2008; Cohen, 1998, 2011; Cohen & Macaro, 2007; Griffiths, 2008a; Macaro, 2006; Oxford, 1990, 2011b; Rubin, 1975; Wenden, 1987a). A possible reason for this is that they require the learner to be 'more active cognitively' than a learner who is less strategically engaged (Gage & Berliner, 1992: 302). The awareness of the importance of cognition in language learning led to the interest in the strategies used by 'good language learners' in the mid- to late 1970s (e.g. Naiman *et al.*, 1978; Rubin, 1975; Stern, 1975).

This view of a cognitive basis to learning strategies is developed at length by O'Malley and Chamot (1990), drawing on the work of cognitive psychologist John Anderson (for instance, 1980). According to a cognitive perspective, the learner is seen as 'an active participant in the learning process' (Williams & Burden, 1997: 13), capable of thinking through the language learning process until the required knowledge to understand the new language system is achieved. This conception, according to which the student must actively process information, 'places great responsibility on the learner' (Bialystok, 1991: 77). As Larsen-Freeman (2001: 12) argues, the learner is not 'merely a passive recipient' and learning is not merely a 'unilateral process . . . dependent on some benevolent, skilful, more proficient interlocutor'. In order to learn effectively, learners must become thinking participants who can influence their own learning and who share responsibility for that learning. This implies that learners are capable of consciously choosing strategies for the purpose of actively regulating their own learning according to their individual goals and situations.

The importance of cognition in language learning has been widely recognised (for example, among many others, J. Anderson, 1980; Ausubel, 1968; Chamot, 2005). From a cognitive point of view, learning language is not merely a matter of habit formation as the Behaviourists believed but, like any other kind of learning, involves taking in information which is then processed and acted upon (Bialystok, 1978, 1981, 1991; Dornyei, 2005; McLaughlin, 1978; McLaughlin *et al.*, 1983; O'Malley & Chamot, 1990; Rubin, 1975, 1981; Skehan, 1998; Williams & Burden, 1997). From a cognitive perspective, learners are viewed as active participants in the learning process, capable of generating rules (Chomsky, 1959, 1965, 1968), learning from errors (Corder, 1967), developing an interlanguage system (Selinker, 1972), establishing schemata (R. Anderson, 1977) and consciously managing their own learning (N. Anderson, 2008), in a way which ultimately brings order into a complex and chaotic system (Larsen-Freeman, 1997). Learning strategy theory, however, may also include some audiolingual/behaviourist elements in the form of repetition/

memory strategies. There may also be a sociocultural/communicative/interactive dimension (e.g. Lantolf, 2000; Littlewood, 1981; Long, 1996; Vygotsky, 1978; Widdowson, 1978) in the form of interactive strategies which involve taking in information from the socio-cultural environment which is then processed and acted upon (Leont'ev, 1978).

In other words, although essentially cognitive, we can see that strategy theory has a somewhat eclectic theoretical base, including elements of Schemata Theory, Complexity/Chaos Theory, Behaviourism, Sociocultural Theory, Activity Theory and, perhaps, others. This has produced a 'web of interlocking theories' (Oxford, 2011b: 60) which may help to explain why language learning strategy theory has been so resistant to theoretical clarification for so long.

Language learning strategies: Theoretical underpinnings

Although language learning strategies belong essentially to a cognitive theoretical paradigm according to which learners take in information which is then processed and acted upon, strategy theory also draws on a variety of other theories of learning, producing a complex theoretical scenario.

An important corollary which follows logically from placing language learning strategies within an essentially cognitive theoretical paradigm is that not only are learners able to bring cognition to bear on their learning processes, but that the strategies themselves are also able to be learnt and, furthermore, that teachers are able to facilitate strategy development. In other words, from a cognitive perspective, language learning strategies are learnable and teachable.

In actual fact, although this sounds straightforward enough in principle, the learnability/teachability dimension of language learning strategies has proven to be not quite so straightforward in practice. We will look more carefully at this issue in the chapter on pedagogical perspectives (Chapter 4).

1.6 Classification

If definition of and establishing a theoretical base for language learning strategies has been difficult, classification has certainly been no less so. Over the years there have been numerous attempts to itemise and label strategic activities and to list them in inventories or organise them into taxonomies.

In 1981 Rubin identified two kinds of learning strategies: those which contribute directly to learning, and those which contribute indirectly to learning. The direct learning strategies, which involve the learner interacting directly with the material to be learnt, she divided into six types:

- *clarification/verification*
- *monitoring*
- *memorisation*
- *guessing/inductive inferencing*
- *deductive reasoning*
- *practice*

The indirect learning strategies she divided into two types:

- *creating opportunities for practice*
- *production tricks*

Of the indirect strategies, the first would probably be called metacognitive by some (e.g. Anderson, 2008), while the inclusion of strategies related to communication under 'production tricks' (Rubin, 1981: 12) is controversial in a list of learning strategies since, as discussed previously, communication strategies do not necessarily lead to learning.

When O'Malley *et al.* (1985) came to conduct their research, 10 years after Rubin's (1975) original landmark article, they based their definition on Rigney's (1978) definition of learning strategies as procedures which facilitate acquisition, retention, retrieval and performance. In an attempt to produce a classification scheme with mutually exclusive categories, O'Malley and his colleagues developed a taxonomy of their own, identifying 26 strategies which they divided into three groups:

- *metacognitive* (knowing about learning);
- *cognitive* (specific to distinct learning activities);
- *social* (relating to interaction with others).

The metacognitive and cognitive categories correspond approximately to Rubin's indirect and direct strategies. However, the addition of the social mediation category was an important step in the direction of acknowledging the importance of interactional strategies in language learning.

Oxford (1990) took this process a step further. Like O'Malley *et al.* (1985), Oxford (1990) also began with Rigney's (1978) original definition which she expanded to define language learning strategies as 'specific actions taken by the learner to make learning easier, faster, more enjoyable, more self-directed, more effective, and more transferable to new situations' (Oxford, 1990: 8). From an extensive review of the literature, Oxford (1990) gathered a large number of strategic activities, producing a very comprehensive inventory, although it is still, of necessity, somewhat selective since 'dozens and perhaps hundreds of such strategies exist' (Oxford et al., 1989: 29). On the basis of factor analyses, Oxford (1990) divided the strategy items into six groups:

- *memory strategies* (which relate to how students remember language, such as *using flashcards* or *visualising*);
- *cognitive strategies* (which relate to how students acquire knowledge about language, such as *formulating rules* or *looking for cognates*);
- *compensation strategies* (which enable students to make up for limited knowledge, such as *guessing* or *gesturing*);
- *metacognitive strategies* (relating to how students manage the learning process, such as *planning* or *evaluating*);
- *affective strategies* (relating to students' feelings, such as *trying to relax* or *talking about feelings*);
- *social strategies* (which involve learning by interaction with others, such as *asking for help* or *talking to classmates*).

These six categories underlie the *SILL* (*Strategy Inventory for Language Learning*, Oxford, 1990), used by Oxford and others for a great deal of research in the learning strategy field.

However, agreement on the validity of classifying strategies according to these kinds of groupings is by no means universal, as Oxford herself (2011b) acknowledges. Stern (1992: 264), for instance, points to 'a certain arbitrariness in the classification of learning strategies'. LoCastro (1994) questions the grouping of memory strategies as separate from cognitive strategies in the *SILL*, since memory involves mental (cognitive) processing, and memory and cognitive strategies might therefore be considered as belonging to the same group. Another classification difficulty relates to the *SILL*'s compensation group of strategies which, according to Ellis (1994: 539), are included 'somewhat confusingly', since they might be considered communication strategies rather than learning strategies.

Since memory may be considered an aspect of cognition and the items in the *SILL*'s compensation group may be classified as communication rather than learning strategies, Cohen and Dornyei (2002) recommend reducing the *SILL*'s six groups to four (cognitive, metacognitive, affective and social). If we extend this argument still further, however, and accept that metacognitive strategies are those used to 'supervise or manage ... language learning' as Cohen and Dornyei (2002: 181) themselves define them, it might be suggested that social and affective strategies are themselves used metacognitively to manage social interaction and affective states. This line of argument would reduce the basic strategy categories to two: cognitive strategies which are used to interact directly with the material to be learnt and metacognitive strategies which are used to control this interaction. Viewed in this way, socio/affective strategies become a metacognitive subcategory and memory strategies become a subcategory of cognitive strategies as set out diagrammatically in Table 1.1.

If we accept this kind of binary view, which kind of strategy is more important? Cognitive or metacognitive? According to O'Malley *et al.* (1985), students who do not have metacognitive strategies are like ships without rudders: they cannot direct their own learning and risk drifting aimlessly and achieving very little. Anderson (2008) is another who firmly advocates the importance of metacognition since the ability to manage their own learning makes students less dependent 'on the vicissitudes of the learning situation' (Anderson, 2008: 108).

It is, perhaps, impossible to disagree that the ability to manage, control, organise and regulate their own learning is an essential feature of good language learners. However, we might also argue that students who orga-

Table 1.1 Taxonomy of language learning strategies

METACOGNITIVE
Activities which involve controlling/managing/regulating the learning process, e.g. *Checking test requirements.* *Planning sequence of homework.*

AFFECTIVE	SOCIAL
Activities aimed at controlling feelings or emotions, e.g. *Consciously trying to relax when I am nervous.* *Giving myself a reward when I have done well.*	Activities aimed at managing interaction with others, e.g. *Doing homework with classmates.* *Inviting a native-speaking friend out for coffee.*

COGNITIVE
Activities which directly process the material to be learnt, e.g. *Learning vocabulary for the test.* *Practising pronunciation.*

MEMORY
Activities which are aimed at remembering the target material, e.g. *Repeating vocabulary items to oneself until they are remembered.* *Writing out idiomatic expressions in order to remember them.*

nise themselves to take books out of the self-study room but then never read them, who plan a vocabulary-learning schedule but then never actually do it, who select grammar-learning strategies but then never actually apply them to their own learning – such students are unlikely to achieve a great deal in spite of a well-developed repertoire of metacognitive strategies. It really isn't until these learners engage cognitively by reading the books they have taken out, by remembering the vocabulary they have listed, by internalising and applying the grammar rules they have written down that learning actually takes place.

We can conclude, then, that metacognitive strategies and cognitive strategies really go hand-in-hand. It is no use planning unless there is follow-up action – it is like the plan of a house that never gets built. At the same time, acting without a sound plan is likely to be much less effective, and to result in much more wasted time, frustration and a less successful outcome than action which is well managed and supported by sound metacognitive strategies.

Another of the difficulties with classification is that, in practice, it is often not possible to exclusively classify a particular strategy into one group or another. This difficulty is acknowledged by Green and Oxford (1995), who concede that the *SILL's* sub-groups do not always correspond to *a posteriori* factor analyses. For instance, is a strategy such as *reading books I have got from the self-study room* cognitive or metacognitive? Is *listening to songs in order to relax myself* cognitive or affective?

Although a framework such as that suggested in Table 1.1 might go some way towards resolving some theoretical issues, when constructing a valid instrument for research purposes we are still left with the practical difficulties of deciding on appropriate item selection and assigning the selected items to appropriate categories.

In the case of the *ELLSI* (*English Language Learning Strategy Inventory*), Griffiths (2003b), after repeated attempts at factor analysis, gave up trying to assign strategy items to statistically justifiable categories and dealt with the items individually rather than in groups. However, data obtained from large numbers of unrelated strategies can be indigestible, unwieldy and difficult to interpret. Such data, therefore, risk ending up as just a meaningless jumble, without some means of classifying them into some sorts of meaningful clusters.

Perhaps the best advice (at least for the present until further research manages to achieve some enlightenment) might be that, if strategies need to be grouped for a particular research project, the grouping should be done on a case-by-case basis and justified according to the particular learners, situations and goals involved and the purpose for which the research is being carried out. Pre-existing classification systems should be considered with care in the light of the intended participants, the learning purpose and the context in which they are to be used. They should, perhaps, be customised and tailored to the needs and characteristics of the group with which they are to be employed, and results should be interpreted with care and with due consideration of the research participants, their goals and the learning environment factored into the analysis.

Classification of language learning strategies

In fact, issues regarding the classification of strategies remain an unresolved source of controversy and a focus of research effort right up to the present and efforts to classify strategies into neat and universally agreed categories have met with only limited success.

1.7 Issues in Research Methodology

One of the difficulties with researching language learning strategies has been that only a few (such as *writing vocabulary in a notebook* or *using a dictionary*) can be observed directly: most can only be inferred from language learner behaviour or elicited by means of learner reports. As Ellis (1986: 14) rather colourfully puts it: 'It is a bit like trying to work out the classification system of a library when the only evidence to go on consists of the few books you have been allowed to take out.' Given the difficulties of such a task, the challenge has been to devise a means first of all to record and subsequently to interpret the phenomena involved, a process which Ellis (1986: 188) likens to 'stumbling blindfold round a room to find a hidden object'. Grenfell and Harris (1999: 54) agree that 'it is not easy to get inside the "black box" of the human brain and find out what is going on there. We work with what we can get'.

Over the years, a common method used in strategy research has been the questionnaire, the use of which has been widely debated (e.g. Aldridge & Levine, 2001; Dornyei, 2003, 2007; Oxford, 1996b, 2011b; Reid, 1990; Turner, 1993). Gu *et al.* (1995) question the degree to which student self-report ratings on Likert scale instruments such as the *SILL* can be relied on to be an accurate reflection of actual use, since what is 'often' to one respondent may be rated quite differently by another. However, Gu *et al.* (1995) point out that such scales can be useful if administered and interpreted with care.

Many major studies of language learning strategy use have employed the *SILL*. Although issues related to the *SILL* have been discussed in the previous section, Oxford's taxonomy is possibly the most comprehensive currently available (Ellis, 1994). According to Oxford (1996b) many major strategy studies have used the *SILL* which has appeared in several different versions and in a number of different languages. The *SILL* is a self-scoring, paper-and-pencil survey which consists of statements such as *I review English lessons often* or *I ask questions in English*, to which students are asked to respond on a five-point Likert scale ranging from one (never or almost never) to five (always or almost always) according to perceived frequency of use.

According to Green and Oxford (1995), reliability is generally high for the *SILL*, and is quoted as ranging from 0.93 to 0.95 (Cronbach alpha) depending on whether the students take the survey in their own language or in the target language, a level which, according to Oxford and Burry-Stock (1995: 6), is 'very acceptable'. Oxford (1996b) also argues that the construct validity (how well the theoretical construct is measured), the criterion-related validity (demonstrated in the relationship between the *SILL* and performance), and the content validity (the degree to which the content is appropriate) are all very high. In addition, according to Oxford and Burry-Stock (1995: 6) the *SILL* has utility (defined as 'the usefulness of an instrument in real-world settings for making decisions relevant to people's lives') and low fakability. As Oxford and Burry-Stock (1995: 11) point out: 'If people are not honest in their answers, validity is destroyed.' Dishonest answers are ascribed to two main reasons: to please the researcher, or to make the respondent appear in a more favourable light. Oxford and Burry-Stock (1995) claim that repeated studies have failed to discover any social desirability response bias, a result which Oxford (1996b: 33) ascribes to the 'nonthreatening' nature of the *SILL*.

Oxford (2011b) acknowledges, however, that the *SILL* may not be appropriate for all students in all contexts. For instance, in the study by Griffiths (2003b), there were some strategy items (such as *using rhymes* or *flashcards*) which did not seem to be rated highly by any of the students – indeed students often had difficulty understanding what these strategies involved. Conversely, there were other strategies which students mentioned during discussions, or identified as key strategies during interviews, or were commonly observed using, which are not included in the *SILL* (as noted also by Lunt, 2000). Examples of these 'missing' strategies might be:

- *looking up a dictionary*
- *referring to the teacher*
- *using a self-study room*
- *keeping a notebook*
- *listening to radio*
- *reading newspapers.*

Another pragmatic difficulty with the *SILL* can be its length. Although the 50-item version is considerably shorter than other versions, it nonetheless takes students up to an hour to complete which, at times, can lead to some impatience among students who are keen to proceed with learning English rather than bothering too much with *how* to learn. Students (who often believe they know all they need to know about learning strategies anyway) will often tolerate a certain amount of strategies-focused material, but fail to see the relevance of extended exercises or discussions. Oxford (2011b) therefore encourages researchers to make adaptations to suit their particular learners in their specific situations.

One such instrument is the *ELLSI* (Griffiths, 2003b, 2008a) which was constructed using a 'bottom up' approach including only the strategies students actually said they used. These were gathered over a period of several weeks into an original questionnaire consisting of strategy items such as:

* *Reading books in English* (Item 4);
* *Consciously learning new vocabulary* (Item 16).

An attempt was made to divide the items of the *ELLSI* into sub-groups before administering it in class. However, the same difficulties with assigning strategies to mutually exclusive categories experienced with the *SILL* also applied to the *ELLSI* (see the discussion of issues with strategy classification in Section 1.6). A strategy such as Item 8: *Listening to songs in English*, for instance, might be considered to relate to the use of resources or to the management of feelings. A strategy such as Item 13: *Using a dictionary* might relate to the management of learning or to the use of resources.

Because of difficulties with deciding on appropriate sub-groupings for the strategy items, the *ELLSI* was initially not subdivided. Instead it was decided to use a factor analysis procedure on the first batch of questionnaires as a possible guide to establishing sub-groups for subsequent versions of the survey. When a Principal Component Analysis was carried out, however, 18 of the 32 *ELLSI* items were found to form a unified group which could not be statistically subdivided. The strategies in this group included such conceptually diverse items as *Reading books in English* (Item 4), *Talking to other students in English* (Item 12), *Pre-planning language learning encounters* (Item 21), *Listening to the radio in English* (Item 31) and *Writing a diary in English* (Item 32). In the face of these results, attempts to establish fixed groupings for the *ELLSI* were abandoned.

Another instrument developed to suit the needs of a particular group is the *Language Skills Development* (*LSD*) survey (Griffiths, 2004), modelled on established instruments by Oxford (1990), Cohen and Chi (2002) and Griffiths

(2003b). Since this survey focused on skills development, strategy items which relate to more general language learning behaviour (such as strategies for learning vocabulary or grammar or for organising the learning environment) were not included. Although these more general strategies may, of course, lead on to skills development (for instance, strategies which expand vocabulary may help students to write or speak more effectively, or to understand what they read or hear), they are somewhat removed from strategies which directly address the skill under development, and to have included them would have created a questionnaire of daunting length.

The *LSD* strategy survey was divided into four sections according to the traditional four skills (reading, writing, listening, speaking). Ten statements were made regarding each skill, for instance:

- *I make summaries of what I read;*
- *I plan my writing before I start;*
- *I listen for key words;*
- *I plan in advance what I want to say.*

When constructing the *LSD* questionnaire, every effort was made to consider the issues raised by de Vaus (1995) regarding questionnaire construction. The language was kept as unambiguous and simple as possible, and items were kept as short as possible. Double-barrelled items were avoided, although at times similar elements (such as radio, TV, movies) were combined in order to avoid making the questionnaire unduly lengthy. Negative questions, which can be difficult to understand and answer appropriately, were also avoided. The *LSD* questionnaire was trialled with three groups of trainee teachers whose suggestions were noted and changes made as appropriate.

Another commonly used technique for researching strategy use has been the interview. Valuable as figures may be for indicating trends and general truths, we must bear in mind that they can never represent more than paper profiles of flesh and blood learners in all their complexities. As Wong Fillmore (1982: 157) points out: 'Anyone who works with second language learners, whether in teaching or in research, discovers quickly how much individual variation there is.'

Learners, in fact, cannot be reduced to mere animated columns of data. As Horwitz (1999: 558) reminds us: 'language learners are individuals approaching language learning in their own unique way'. In reality, individual language learners are often full of statistically inconvenient contradictions which an analysis of the aggregated data can never portray. Over a sufficient number of cases, these contradictions tend to become levelled out, but this does not alter the fact that, on an individual level, learner characteristics of one kind or another can be a real force to be reckoned with, and it is here that qualitative research methods can be useful (e.g. Emery, 1986).

Interviews have been used by many researchers to probe the complexities of the individual learner which help to 'capture the richness of learners' constructions' (Oxford, 2001: 94) and produce insights 'that are at once broadly applicable and rich in observed detail' (Green & Oxford, 1995: 293). Interviewing real learners can help to contextualise depersonalised statistics and add 'qualitative refinement' to quantitative analysis of data (Chaudron, 1986: 714). In support of the advantages of using the interview as a research method, Wenden (1987a: 103) presents the common-sense point of view that 'the best way to get at what strategies learners actually use as they go about their learning tasks is to ask them'.

As explained by Nunan (1992), interviews vary from structured, through semi-structured to unstructured. According to Gillham (2000: 65), the semi-structured interview is 'the richest single source of data'. In a semi-structured interview, 'Although there is a set of pre-prepared guiding questions and prompts, the format is open-ended and the interviewee is encouraged to elaborate on the issues raised in an exploratory manner [which does not] limit the depth and breadth of the respondent's story' (Dornyei, 2007: 136).

The interview technique has been used successfully by many strategy researchers. These include Naiman *et al.* (1978: 37) who comment that 'the interview proved to be a useful research technique', O'Malley *et al.* (1985: 35) who report that 'generally we had considerable success in identifying learning strategies through interviews', and Griffiths (2003b) who used interviews to add depth to questionnaire data.

1.8 Conclusion

At a conceptual level, language learning strategies have almost limitless potential as a tool for facilitating language learning, and because of the promise which they present, they have been widely researched and extensively written about. In spite of this potential, however, the strategy concept has proved difficult to nail down and it has proved difficult to entirely eliminate fuzzy terminology, conflicting definitions, theoretical inconsistencies and incompatible classification systems.

This chapter has attempted to clarify these basic concepts. In particular, the chapter has suggested that:

(1) At the level of terminology, *strategy* has been and probably remains the term which has been most consistently used to cover the behaviours

involved, and for this reason it is probably the term which best deserves to be accepted as the established one for behaviour aimed at *target language* development by *speakers of other languages.*

(2) From an extensive review of the literature spanning more than 30 years, a definition is suggested of language learning strategies as **activities consciously chosen by learners for the purpose of regulating their own language learning**.

(3) This definition excludes several related but distinct concepts with which learning strategies are often confused (styles, communication strategies and skills).

(4) Strategy effectiveness must be considered in relation to learning target, situation, learner characteristics and co-ordination with other strategies.

(5) If we consider the main theories which have underpinned contemporary language learning, it becomes clear that by far the majority of language learning strategies are essentially cognitive in their nature. That is, they assume that learners can think through and consciously manage their own learning.

(6) Although essentially cognitive, we can nevertheless see that strategy theory has an eclectic theoretical base, including elements of Schemata Theory, Complexity/Chaos Theory, Behaviourism, Sociocultural Theory and Activity Theory, producing a complicated theoretical foundation.

(7) From a cognitive perspective, it follows that language learning strategies are themselves learnable and teachable.

(8) A review of several well-known and somewhat contradictory classification systems leads to the conclusion that learning strategies are too diverse a phenomenon to be categorised in such a way as will be appropriate for all learners, in every situation, studying for any goal. It is recommended that if strategies need to be grouped for a particular research purpose, it should be done and justified on a case-by-case basis according to the individuals, targets and contexts involved.

It is important to establish these basic concepts before moving on to look at some fundamental questions which will be investigated in the next chapter.

1.9 Conceptual Areas for Further Research

As this chapter has attempted to demonstrate, there is still much work to be done in the area of basic concepts. Particularly urgent is the need to:

(1) achieve consensus regarding terminology, definition and theoretical principles, the absence of which currently creates a great deal of controversy

and confusion, hampers research initiatives, and leaves findings open to question;

(2) continue with studies to investigate the relationships between/among effective strategies, learning target, learning situation, strategy orchestration and individual variables;

(3) continue to discuss and refine the understanding of the complex theoretical underpinnings of the language learning strategy concept;

(4) experiment with useful ways of classifying strategies so that unwieldy numbers of items can be grouped in more manageable as well as theoretically and statistically justifiable ways, thereby facilitating meaningful interpretation of research data.

2 A Quantitative Perspective

2.1 Fundamental Questions

Even once we have dealt with some of the basic concepts, including terminology, definition, theoretical underpinnings and classification, some thorny fundamental questions remain. It is, for instance, by no means universally agreed that language learning strategies are related to successful language learning. So we need to ask:

- Is frequency of language learning strategy use related to successful learning?
- Is quantity of language learning strategy use related to successful learning?
- Are some strategy types more related to successful learning than others?
- Do strategy choices vary according to learner variables such as motivation, nationality, sex or age, and how are any individual variations related to successful learning?
- What are the relationships among situation, strategy selection and effectiveness?
- What are the relationships among learning target, strategy selection and effectiveness?
- Are a learner's strategies set in concrete and resistant to change, or do they develop over time?
- How do any strategy modifications relate to successful learning?
- Are strategies the cause or the effect of successful learning?

Each of these basic questions will be dealt with in turn in the course of this chapter.

2.2 Is Frequency of Language Learning Strategy Use Related to Successful Language Learning?

This question has given rise to a great deal of debate over many years. Green and Oxford (1995: 285) found that there was 'significantly greater overall use of language learning strategies among more successful learners' when they surveyed 374 Puerto Rican university students using the 50-item version of the *SILL*. In other words, the more proficient students used language learning strategies more frequently than less proficient students.

But by no means all studies have yielded such clearly positive results. Studies by Bialystok (1981), O'Malley *et al.* (1985), Huang and Van Naerssen (1987) and Ehrman and Oxford (1995) all failed to find a significant relationship between frequency of language learning strategy use and successful learning, although they managed to show relationships between effective learning and various types of strategies (such as metacognitive, functional practice or cognitive strategies; for more on strategy types, see Section 2.4).

There have also been studies which seem to cast doubt on the importance of language learning strategies. Porte (1988), for instance, interviewed 15 underachieving adolescent learners in private language schools in London and discovered that his 'poor' learners were using strategies very similar to those reported by 'good' language learners. A similar observation was made by Vann and Abraham (1990) during a study of two low-level Saudi Arabian women (Mona and Shida) studying on an intensive English programme in the USA. The researchers employed think aloud protocols and task product analysis to investigate strategy use by their two participants while completing four activities (an interview, a verb exercise, a cloze passage and a composition). Although Mona and Shida appeared to use a large number of strategies, providing 'counter evidence for the claim that unsuccessful learners are inactive' (Vann & Abraham, 1990: 177), the women's progress in language acquisition was slow, as evidenced by low TOEFL scores.

In the face of such inconsistent results, in order to investigate the relationship between strategies and successful language learning further, 348 international students studying English at a private language school in Auckland, New Zealand were surveyed (Griffiths, 2003b). There were both males (approximately one-third) and females (approximately two-thirds), ranging in ages from 14 to 64 and they came from 21 different nationalities. Participants were spread over seven levels from elementary to advanced (elementary, mid-elementary, upper elementary, pre-intermediate, mid-intermediate, upper intermediate, advanced). These levels were decided on the basis of a student's initial score on the Oxford Placement Test (Allan, 1995), plus an assessment of communicative ability by the school representative responsible for placement, and performance on class tests after placement.

The instrument used in the study was the 50-item version of the *Strategy Inventory for Language Learning* (*SILL* – Oxford, 1990). The *SILL* was chosen because of its comprehensiveness (Ellis, 1994), and because of claims that it is valid and reliable (Oxford, 1996b; Oxford & Burry-Stock, 1995). For further details, see Section 1.7.

The data were analysed using SPSS. The abbreviated strategy statements (for original, see Oxford, 1990) with the average reported frequencies of use for elementary (E) and advanced (A) students as well as across all students (All) can be seen in Table 2.1, where the strategies reportedly used highly frequently (average = 3.5 or above; Oxford, 1990) are shaded for emphasis. Overall average reported frequency of strategy use and the number of strategy items reportedly used at a high rate of frequency for elementary, advanced and all students are summarised at the bottom of the table.

As can be seen from the table, the overall average reported frequency of strategy use for all students ($n = 348$) was 3.2, and they reported using 12 strategies highly frequently (average = 3.5 or higher, as defined by Oxford, 1990). The average for advanced students ($n = 34$) was 3.4, and advanced students reported using 27 strategy items at a high rate of frequency. Elementary students ($n = 44$) reported an overall average frequency of strategy use of 3.1 and reported using only three strategy items at a high rate of frequency.

A statistically significant relationship was discovered between reported frequency of overall language learning strategy use and class level ($r = 0.27$, $p < 0.01$, Spearman). Although this relationship is not strong, it is more than would be expected merely by chance and suggests that around 7% of the variance in class level might be related to language learning strategy use. When it is considered how many variables there are which might conceivably interact with learning success (such as motivation, age, gender, nationality, etc., some of which will be dealt with later in the book), to find a factor which appears to account for as much as 7% is actually worthy of further interest.

Are strategies related to successful learning? – Frequency

This result indicates that frequency of language learning strategy use is positively related to successful language learning.

Table 2.1 Average reported frequency of *SILL* language learning strategy use for elementary (E) students (*n* = 44), advanced (A) students (*n* = 34), and all (All) students (*n* = 348) with overall average and number of strategies reportedly used highly frequently (average = 3.5 or above). Highly frequent items are shaded for emphasis

Sub-group	SILL	Statement (paraphrased for brevity)	E	A	All
Memory	1	I think of relationships	3.3	3.6	3.4
Memory	2	I use new words in a sentence	3.1	3.4	3.1
Memory	3	I create images of new words	3.3	3.0	3.2
Memory	4	I make mental pictures	3.1	3.4	3.0
Memory	5	I use rhymes to remember new words	2.2	2.4	2.4
Memory	6	I use flashcards to remember new words	2.6	1.8	2.3
Memory	7	I physically act out new words	3.0	2.1	2.6
Memory	8	I review English lessons often	3.3	2.5	3.2
Memory	9	I use location to remember new words	3.2	2.9	3.1
Cognitive	10	I say or write new words several times	3.4	3.6	3.4
Cognitive	11	I try to talk like native speakers	3.4	4.0	3.6
Cognitive	12	I practise the sounds of English	3.4	3.9	3.5
Cognitive	13	I use words I know in different ways	3.0	3.2	2.8
Cognitive	14	I start conversations in English	3.4	4.0	3.4
Cognitive	15	I watch TV or movies in English	3.2	4.1	3.5
Cognitive	16	I read for pleasure in English	2.5	3.4	2.9
Cognitive	17	I write notes, messages, letters, reports	2.5	2.7	2.8
Cognitive	18	I skim read then read carefully	2.9	3.5	3.1
Cognitive	19	I look for similar words in my own language	3.2	3.6	3.3
Cognitive	20	I try to find patterns in English	3.1	3.5	3.2
Cognitive	21	I divide words into parts I understand	2.8	3.7	3.1
Cognitive	22	I try not to translate word for word	2.3	3.5	2.7
Cognitive	23	I make summaries	2.5	2.9	2.8
Compensation	24	I guess the meaning of unfamiliar words	3.0	3.9	3.4
Compensation	25	When I can't think of a word I use gestures	3.6	3.9	3.7
Compensation	26	I make up words if I don't know the right ones	3.1	2.9	3.1
Compensation	27	I read without looking up every new word	2.5	4.1	2.8
Compensation	28	I guess what the other person will say next	3.1	3.3	3.1
Compensation	29	If I can't think of a word I use a synonym	3.1	4.6	3.7
Metacognitive	30	I try to find many ways to use English	3.4	3.7	3.5
Metacognitive	31	I use my mistakes to help me do better	3.1	4.0	3.5
Metacognitive	32	I pay attention to someone speaking English	3.5	4.5	3.9

(continued)

Table 2.1 (*Continued*)

Sub-group	SILL	Statement (paraphrased for brevity)	E	A	All
Metacognitive	33	I try to find how to be a better learner	3.2	3.6	3.6
Metacognitive	34	I plan my schedule to have time to study	3.0	2.7	3.0
Metacognitive	35	I look for people I can talk to in English	3.3	3.4	3.3
Metacognitive	36	I look for opportunities to read in English	3.0	3.3	3.2
Metacognitive	37	I have clear goals for improving my English	3.1	3.4	3.1
Metacognitive	38	I think about my progress in learning English	3.3	3.8	3.5
Affective	39	I try to relax when afraid of using English	3.3	4.0	3.3
Affective	40	I encourage myself to speak even when afraid	3.3	3.8	3.4
Affective	41	I give myself a reward for doing well	2.7	2.8	2.9
Affective	42	I notice if I am tense or nervous	2.9	3.0	3.1
Affective	43	I write my feelings in a diary	2.6	1.7	2.3
Affective	44	I talk to someone else about how I feel	3.0	2.5	2.9
Social	45	I ask others to speak slowly or repeat	3.7	4.3	3.9
Social	46	I ask for correction when I talk	3.0	3.5	3.2
Social	47	I practise English with other students	3.1	3.4	3.2
Social	48	I ask for help from English speakers	3.4	3.6	3.3
Social	49	I ask questions in English	3.3	4.1	3.6
Social	50	I try to learn the culture of English speakers	3.0	3.7	3.3
		Overall average reported frequency of strategy use	3.1	3.4	3.2
		Number of strategies reportedly used highly frequently	3	27	12

It should be noted, however, that although a significant relationship between overall frequency of strategy use and class level was found, there was no such relationship between class level and any of the *SILL* sub-groups (memory, cognitive, compensation, metacognitive, affective, social). This would appear to throw further doubt on the usefulness of grouping strategies in this way as already discussed under classification (Section 1.6).

2.3 Is Quantity of Language Learning Strategy Use Related to Successful Language Learning?

As we can see from Table 2.1, lower level students used fewer ($n = 3$) strategies at a high rate of frequency (according to Oxford's (1990) average = 3.5 threshold for highly frequent usage) than higher level students ($n = 27$). In other words, according to this study, higher level students used nine times as many strategies highly frequently as lower level students.

Are strategies related to successful learning? – Quantity

As can be seen from the table, in addition to reporting more frequent use of language learning strategies, advanced students reported frequently using many more strategies (nine times as many, in fact) than elementary students.

So how can we explain the apparent contradictions among the findings by Porte (1988) and Vann and Abraham (1990) and those reported in Section 2.2? In fact, the studies are difficult to really compare since the terms of reference are not the same, a problem which crops up again and again in this research area and renders much comparison meaningless. We have no way of knowing, for instance, whether Vann and Abraham's (1990) or Porte's (1988) active strategy users employed strategies at a similar rate of frequency to the elementary students described here, or whether they used strategies more or less often. The elementary students reported in this chapter, after all, also reported quite high frequency ratings, even if these ratings were not as high as those of the advanced students. Indeed, there were actually only two strategies out of the 50 in the questionnaire which were rated by elementary students in the low frequency area (average less than 2.5; Oxford, 1990). These were:

- Item 5: *I use rhymes to remember new words* (average = 2.2)
- Item 22: *I try not to translate word for word* (average = 2.3)

Apart from these two, all the rest were reportedly used moderately frequently (average = 2.5–3.4; Oxford, 1990) or highly frequently (average = 3.5–5.0; Oxford, 1990). See Table 2.1 to check these data.

Another key observation by Porte (1988) was that 'the majority of learners said that they used strategies which were the same as, or very similar to, those they had used at schools in their native countries' (Porte, 1988: 168). It would seem, then, that these low-level students were unable to select strategies which were appropriate for the situation in which they found themselves (discussed in Section 1.4.2). Furthermore, Porte (1988) comments, 'where these under-achievers' strategies differ from those of good language learners ... is in the fact that they may demonstrate less sophistication and a less suitable response to a particular activity'. In other words, they do not know how to choose strategies which are appropriate for the goal (this issue is discussed in Section 1.4.1). Vann and Abraham (1990) also conclude that, although their participants were active strategy users, 'they often failed to apply strategies appropriately to the task at hand' (Vann & Abraham, 1990: 191). In other words, they also did not choose strategies appropriate for their goals (see Section 1.4.1).

It must also be remembered that, although the results of the study described in Section 2.2 indicate that on average higher level students use a larger number of language learning strategies more frequently than lower level students, the *overall* statistics do not necessarily apply to every individual learner. There may be other factors which affect language learning success and which influence a student's choice of language learning strategies and their ability to use them effectively. For instance, although frequency and number of strategy use may be a factor in successful learning, learners may also need to be able to select and orchestrate *types* of strategies appropriate for their own individual needs, goals and situations.

And this leads us to the next fundamental question:

2.4 Are Some Strategy Types More Related to Successful Learning Than Others?

Although the results of the study reported previously in Sections 2.2 and 2.3 indicate that higher level students report using more language learning strategies significantly more often than lower level students, it is possible that not only quantity and frequency are important when considering the relationship between strategies and success in language learning. There are studies which suggest that strategy type must also be considered (e.g. Bialystok, 1981; Ehrman & Oxford, 1995; Huang & Van Naerssen, 1987; O'Malley *et al.*, 1985). However, studies which have attempted to investigate the relationship between language learning strategy type and success in language development have produced mixed results.

O'Malley *et al.* (1985) discovered that, although students at all levels reported the use of an extensive variety of learning strategies, higher level students reported greater use of metacognitive strategies (i.e. strategies used by students to manage their own learning). This led the researchers to conclude that the more successful students are probably able to exercise greater metacognitive control over their learning.

Bialystok (1981) and Huang and Van Naerssen (1987), on the other hand, came to a different conclusion. Both of these studies found that strategies related to functional practice were most associated with proficiency. Ehrman and Oxford's (1995) conclusion was different again. In this case the researchers discovered that cognitive strategies such as looking for patterns and reading for pleasure in the target language were the type of strategy most frequently used by successful students in their study.

Wong Filmore (1982) discovered the importance of social strategies (although she did not use this term) employed by good language learners. She reported that the good language learners in her study 'spent more time than they should have during class time socialising and minding everyone else's business ... they were constantly involved in the affairs of their classmates' (Wong Filmore, 1982: 163).

An examination of Table 2.1 suggests that strategies might fall into several groups: those favoured by lower level students, those used highly frequently across all levels, and those used highly frequently by higher level students in addition to those used highly frequently by all students. Griffiths (2003a,b) suggests that these groups might be labelled *base* strategies, *core* strategies and *plus* strategies.

2.4.1 *Base* strategies

If we look carefully at Table 2.1 (columns E and A), we can see that, with only nine exceptions, all *SILL* strategy items were reportedly used more frequently by advanced students than by elementary students. These nine exceptions are listed in Table 2.2.

Table 2.2 *Base* strategies used more frequently by elementary students (E) than by advanced students (A)

Sub-group	SILL	Statement (paraphrased for brevity)	E	A
Memory	3	I create images of new words	3.3	3.0
Memory	6	I use flashcards to remember new words	2.6	1.8
Memory	7	I physically act out new words	3.0	2.1
Memory	8	I review English lessons often	3.3	2.5
Memory	9	I use location to remember new words	3.2	2.9
Compensation	26	I make up words if I don't know the right ones	3.1	2.9
Metacognitive	34	I plan my schedule to have time to study	3.0	2.7
Affective	43	I write my feelings in a diary	2.6	1.7
Affective	44	I talk to someone else about how I feel	3.0	2.5
		Number of *base* strategies	9	

Although the validity of the *SILL* sub-groups has been questioned (e.g. Cohen & Dornyei, 2002; LoCastro, 1994), it is impossible not to notice that five (that is more than half) of the strategies in this group relate to memorisation. According to these results, then, memory strategies tend to be favoured by lower-level students.

There are also two strategies out of these nine (more than 20%) which relate to the management of feelings:

- Item 43: *I write my feelings in a diary*
- Item 44: *I talk to someone else about how I feel*

This compares with two out of 15 (only slightly over 13%) in the *plus* list (see Section 2.4.3).

Of course, the importance of affect in language learning has long been recognised (e.g. Krashen & Terrell, 1983) and more recently by writers such as Arnold (1999). The higher proportion of this type of strategy among those reportedly used more frequently by elementary students than by advanced students might possibly indicate higher anxiety levels among lower level students. These affective strategies typical of lower level students, furthermore, appear to involve rather solitary activities (writing a diary) or rather introspective interaction (talking about feelings), whereas those relating to the management of feelings in the *plus* list involve more outgoing attempts to relax, to communicate and to control nervousness concerning interaction with others.

Of the two remaining strategies reportedly used more frequently by elementary than by advanced students, only one might be considered to relate to the management of learning:

- Item 34: *I plan my schedule to have time to study*

This would seem to support O'Malley *et al.*'s (1985) finding that metacognitive strategies are more typical of higher level students (or, in this case, less typical of lower level students).

A 'compensation' strategy completes the list of nine *base* strategies:

- Item 26: *I make up words when I do not know the right ones*

Since it is quite possible that such a strategy is motivated more by a need to communicate than to learn and that it may well not result in learning, it might be considered that this is not really a learning strategy at all.

> ## Are some strategy types more related to successful learning? – *Base* strategies
>
> From these results, it would appear that lower level students tend to rely most heavily on *memorisation* as a basic language learning strategy type.

2.4.2 *Core* strategies

If we look again at Table 2.1, we can see that there is a core of 12 *SILL* strategies used highly frequently (average = 3.5 or higher; Oxford, 1990) across all students. These are listed in Table 2.3 and the frequency averages are highlighted in the 'All' column.

These 12 strategies reportedly used highly frequently across all students seem to form a core of strategies which have some elements in common with what Green and Oxford (1995: 289) call *'bedrock strategies'* (authors' italics), reportedly used at similar rates of frequency across all levels. Green and Oxford (1995) suggest that such strategies are not necessarily unproductive, but that they may 'contribute significantly to the learning process of the more successful students although not being in themselves sufficient to move the less successful students to higher proficiency levels'.

Table 2.3 *Core* strategies used highly frequently across all students

Sub-group	SILL	Statement (paraphrased for brevity)	All
Cognitive	11	I try to talk like native speakers	3.6
Cognitive	12	I practise the sounds of English	3.5
Cognitive	15	I watch TV or movies in English	3.5
Compensation	25	When I can't think of a word I use gestures	3.7
Compensation	29	If I can't think of a word I use a synonym	3.7
Metacognitive	30	I try to find many ways to use English	3.5
Metacognitive	31	I use my mistakes to help me do better	3.5
Metacognitive	32	I pay attention to someone speaking English	3.9
Metacognitive	33	I try to find how to be a better learner	3.6
Metacognitive	38	I think about my progress in learning English	3.5
Social	45	I ask others to speak slowly or repeat	3.9
Social	49	I ask questions in English	3.6
		Number of *core* strategies	12

It is interesting to note that this group of strategies does not include any that involve just basic memorisation, which made up the largest group of the *base* strategies. However, there are several strategies which require cognitive engagement with the target language:

- Item 11: *I try to talk like native speakers*
- Item 12: *I practise the sounds of English*
- Item 15: *I watch TV or movies in English*

This *core* group also includes two strategies which relate to pronunciation (Items 11 and 12). This type of strategy did not appear among the *base* strategies at all.

There is also one *core* strategy (Item 15) which relates to the use of resources (TV and movies). It is possible, of course, that these resources are too difficult for lower level students, and this may be the reason they do not appear among the *base* strategies.

Also interesting is the inclusion of two strategies relating to interaction among the *core* strategies:

- Item 45: *I ask others to speak slowly or repeat*
- Item 49: *I ask questions in English*

This is another strategy type which was altogether missing from the *base* strategies, possibly reflecting a lack of confidence among lower level students, an issue which will be further discussed later. These items also involve the functional use of language (asking for clarification, asking questions).

But it is metacognitive strategies relating to the management of learning which form the largest *core* strategy sub-group (almost half):

- Item 30: *I try to find many ways to learn English*
- Item 31: *I use my mistakes to help me do better*
- Item 32: *I pay attention to someone speaking English*
- Item 33: *I try to find how to be a better learner*
- Item 38: *I think about my progress in learning English*

As O'Malley *et al.* (1985) and Anderson (2008) might have predicted, these results underline the importance of metacognition in successful language learning.

Are some strategy types more related to successful learning? – *Core* strategies

It would appear that metacognitive strategies are a core ingredient of language learning strategy repertoires overall.

These *core* strategies are all included among the strategies favoured by higher level students. Advanced students, however, also report highly frequent use of a large number of other strategies in addition (therefore *plus*) to the *core* strategies, which would seem to suggest that the *core* strategies may be necessary but not sufficient for students at higher levels in language learning.

2.4.3 *Plus* strategies

The group of 15 *SILL* strategies reportedly used highly frequently (average = 3.5 or higher; Oxford, 1990) by advanced students (see Table 2.1, column A) in addition to the strategies reportedly used highly frequently across all students seems to characterise the higher level learners. These *plus* strategies appear to be the ones which set the higher level students apart from the lower level learners and account for more than 10% ($r = 0.33$, $p < 0.01$, Spearman) of the variance in class level. Although some might not consider 10% a large proportion, I would like to argue that, when it is considered how many factors there potentially are which might relate to learner success (such as nationality, age, gender, motivation, situation, etc.), to find a factor which accounts for a 10th of the variance in level is worthy of attention. These strategies are set out in Table 2.4. The *plus* strategy averages are highlighted in the 'A' column.

According to the *SILL*'s sub-categories, it can be seen from the table that 'cognitive' strategies form the largest *plus* strategy sub-group. However, it can also be seen from the table that these strategies are, in fact, somewhat miscellaneous, involving vocabulary, reading, writing, conversation, translation, affect, interaction, functions, ambiguity toleration and grammar. Given this diversity, we will examine these 15 strategies along somewhat different lines.

It is noteworthy that **strategies relating to interaction** with others feature strongly (more than 25%) among the *plus* strategies:

- Item 14: *I start conversations in English*
- Item 46: *I ask for correction when I talk*

Table 2.4 *Plus* strategies used highly frequently by advanced students (A) in addition to those used highly frequently across all students

Sub-group	SILL	Statement (paraphrased for brevity)	A	All
Memory	1	I think of relationships	3.6	3.4
Cognitive	10	I say or write new words several times	3.6	3.4
Cognitive	14	I start conversations in English	4.0	3.4
Cognitive	18	I skim read then read carefully	3.5	3.1
Cognitive	19	I look for similar words in my own language	3.6	3.3
Cognitive	20	I try to find patterns in English	3.5	3.2
Cognitive	21	I divide words into parts I understand	3.7	3.1
Cognitive	22	I try not to translate word for word	3.5	2.7
Compensation	24	I guess the meaning of unfamiliar words	3.9	3.4
Compensation	27	I read without looking up every new word	4.1	2.8
Affective	39	I try to relax when afraid of using English	4.0	3.3
Affective	40	I encourage myself to speak even when afraid	3.8	3.4
Social	46	I ask for correction when I talk	3.5	3.2
Social	48	I ask for help from English speakers	3.6	3.3
Social	50	I try to learn the culture of English speakers	3.7	3.3
		Number of *plus* strategies	15	

- Item 48: *I ask for help from English speakers*
- Item 50: *I try to learn the culture of English speakers*

The inclusion of four interactive strategies among those used highly frequently by higher level students would seem to suggest that interacting in the target language and with the target culture is important when learning a new language. This emphasis may well reflect an awareness of the communicative nature of language and also increased confidence by the higher level students in their ability to manage such communication. By their nature, these strategies also involve the skills of speaking and listening, and Items 46 and 48 also involve functions (asking for correction and asking for help).

Also well represented (20%) are **strategies relating to vocabulary**. For some years, emphasis on vocabulary was somewhat unfashionable (Nation, 1990), although there has recently been a renewed interest in the contribution made by vocabulary to academic success (Loewen & Ellis, 2001; Moir & Nation, 2002, 2008; Nation, 2008). As Wilkins (1972: 111) puts it:

Without grammar very little can be conveyed, without vocabulary nothing can be conveyed. If you spend most of your time studying grammar, your English will not improve much. You will see most improvement if you learn more words and expressions. You can say very little with grammar, but you can say almost anything with words.

The lexical approach to language learning (Lewis, 1993, 1997) has also revived the awareness of the importance of vocabulary in the language learning process (although the emphasis tends to have shifted away from the traditional vocabulary-list, discrete-word approach and towards word clusters and collocation). The inclusion in this group of strategies typical of higher level students of three vocabulary-related strategies would seem to support the idea that vocabulary is an important element of language development. In addition, Item 10 involves the skill of writing:

- Item 10: *I say or write new words several times*
- Item 19: *I look for similar words in my own language*
- Item 21: *I divide words into parts I understand*

Making up another 20% of the total *plus* strategies are three **strategies relating to the ability to tolerate ambiguity**:

- Item 22: *I try not to translate word for word*
- Item 24: *I guess the meaning of unfamiliar words*
- Item 27: *I read without looking up every new word*

This result would seem to support Naiman *et al.*'s (1978) inclusion of this type of strategy among the characteristics of the 'good' language learner who is able to develop strategies to cope with a 'degree of inherent uncertainty' (White, 1999: 450). The ability to tolerate ambiguity helps students manage 'the enormous linguistic uncertainty that ESL students face each day' (Ely, 1995: 87).

Also among those on the *plus* list are **strategies relating to the ability to come to terms with relationships and patterns** (which might be called language systems), the importance of which is emphasised by Naiman *et al.* (1978):

- Item 1: *I think of relationships*
- Item 20: *I try to find patterns in English*

The inclusion of these strategies among those used highly frequently by higher level students would seem to indicate the importance of developing strategies to recognise relationships between existing knowledge and new things that are learnt and to discover patterns in what is learnt and how this new knowledge fits into the overall language system (often called 'grammar'). Grammar is another area which went through a period of being unfashionable in the wake of the communicative revolution, but which has, in more recent years, been increasingly recognised for its potential contribution to language learning (e.g. Bysgate *et al.*, 1994; Ellis, 2006; Gass, 1991; Tonkyn, 1994).

According to Naiman *et al.* (1978) and Arnold (1999) it is also important to come to terms with the affective demands of learning a new language. Schumann (1975) drew attention in his classic study of an unsuccessful learner to the importance of affect in language learning. Krashen (e.g. Krashen, 1981; Krashen & Terrell, 1983) is another who stresses the importance of what he calls the 'Affective Filter', which he believes, under unfavourable conditions, can block language acquisition. This was Burling's (1981) experience of spending a year trying to learn Swedish while he was guest professor at a Swedish university: although intelligent and judging himself to be highly motivated, the affective difficulties he experienced left him feeling that his progress was unsatisfactory. My own experience of many years in the classroom leads me to believe that students underestimate the importance of affective considerations, and often do not want to admit to affective difficulties. According to the results of this study, higher level students report highly frequent use of **strategies for managing feelings and controlling emotions**, especially of fear, so that they remain relaxed and positive:

- Item 39: *I try to relax when afraid of using English*
- Item 40: *I encourage myself to speak even when afraid.*

A **strategy relating to reading** is also included in the list of *plus* strategies:

- Item 18: *I skim read then read carefully*

As well as relating to the toleration of ambiguity, Item 27 (*I read without looking up every new word*) is also a reading strategy. In addition, it is interesting to note that, with an average of 3.4, Item 16 (*I read for pleasure in English*) is only just under the high frequency threshold, which adds support to the possibility that reading in the target language is a useful language learning strategy, as discovered by Huang and van Naerssen (1987) and by Ehrman and Oxford (1995).

> ### Are some strategy types more related to successful learning? – *Plus* strategies
>
> According to the results of this study, higher level students make highly frequent use of *plus* strategies relating to interaction (speaking and listening), to function, to vocabulary, to writing, to the toleration of ambiguity, to language systems (grammar), to affect and to reading.

2.4.4 The *core-plus* repertoire

It should also be noted that, although there are no 'metacognitive' strategies or strategies related to pronunciation or to the use of resources such as TV or movies in the *plus* list, these types of strategies feature among the *core* strategies which are also used highly frequently by higher level students. In other words, we can see that according to these results, higher level learners, rather than keeping to a limited range of language learning strategies, make highly frequent use of a large repertoire of different strategy types, including those related to:

- vocabulary
- grammar
- pronunciation
- function
- reading
- writing
- listening
- speaking
- interaction with others
- tolerance of ambiguity
- affect
- management of learning
- use of resources (e.g. TV, movies)

Higher level students do not, however, make frequent use of memorisation strategies as lower level students do. These basic strategies seem to become unnecessary or inappropriate as students progress to higher levels.

These findings related to strategy use will be further exemplified in the interview reports in Chapter 3 and the pedagogical implications will be discussed in Chapter 4.

> ### Are some strategy types more related to successful learning? – The *core-plus* repertoire
>
> From these results, we can conclude that more successful learners do not limit themselves to a narrow range of strategies. On the contrary, they seem to go all out and choose an extensive array of activities in order to facilitate the achievement of their learning goals.

Clearly, however, it is in any practical way impossible for all students to employ all possible strategies. At some point, learners have to choose the strategies which are useful for themselves in preference to others. So next we need to consider the factors which influence strategy selection.

2.5 Are Learner Variables Related to Strategy Choice?

Although the discoveries reported so far regarding the relationship between language learning strategies and successful learning are interesting, no account has so far been taken of the effect of learner variables. It is possible, however, that the language learning strategies reportedly used on the road to proficiency may not be the same for all learners, and that learner characteristics may have a 'significant bearing on how learning proceeds' (Cohen & Dornyei, 2002: 170).

Learners, in fact, can vary greatly from each other in their approach to learning, and a multitude of factors may affect the way an individual processes information. As Ellis (1994: 472) comments, there is a 'veritable plethora of individual learner variables which researchers have identified as influencing learning outcomes'. Four factors which are often thought to have a strong influence on the way individual learners go about their learning are the variables of motivation, nationality, age and sex.

2.5.1 Motivation

Motivation has been shown to be related to successful language learning and to language learning strategy use (see Section 1.4.4). For instance, Oxford and Nyikos (1989) conducted a large-scale study of US college students and found that highly motivated learners used four out of five strategy categories significantly more frequently than less motivated learners. In turn, frequency of strategy use has been shown to be related to success in language learning (Green & Oxford, 1995; Griffiths, 2003a, 2003b, 2008a).

The 348 international students studying English at a private language school described earlier in this chapter (Section 2.2) provided a multiplicity of reasons motivating them to study English. Some were down-to-earth and practical (for instance, further education, future employment). Others were more personal (such as travel, friendships).

The motivation given by the largest single group ($n = 132$) for learning English was that they wanted to learn English in order to travel. Other personal reasons given varied from the romantic (for instance, 'I want to marry a New Zealander') to the sometimes sweeping ('I want to change my life'!). This group displaying predominantly personal motivation totalled 195.

The second largest group ($n = 115$) said they wanted to learn English for future employment and 58 said they needed English for further education. Many of those who wanted English to pursue educational opportunities overlapped with those wanting to learn in order to enhance their future job prospects, making a total of 153 for this group whose motivation appeared to be predominantly vocational.

Those who reported wanting to study English for further education and/or future employment (vocational, $n = 153$) scored a higher median for course level and a higher average for reported frequency of strategy use than those who gave wanting to learn English for travel and/or other personal reasons ($n = 195$) as their motivation. Furthermore, a much higher number of strategy items ($n = 22$) used at a high rate of frequency (rating = 3.5 or above; Oxford, 1990) was reported by those who gave vocational reasons as their motivation for learning English than by those who gave personal reasons ($n = 3$) as their motivation (see Table 2.5).

Statistically significant relationships were found between motivation and course level ($r = 0.26$, $p < 0.01$, Spearman) and between motivation and reported frequency of language learning strategy use ($r = 0.30$, $p < 0.01$, Spearman), with those studying for vocational reasons working at a significantly higher course level (median = 4, which is pre-intermediate) and reporting significantly more frequent use of language learning strategies (average = 3.3) than those studying for personal reasons, whose median course level was 3 (upper elementary), and whose average reported frequency of language learning strategy use was only 3.1.

From these results it would seem that those with educational or employment related reasons (vocational) for studying report more frequent use of language learning strategies and are more successful in their studies than those with less clearly focused reasons relating to personal

Table 2.5 Median course level, average reported frequency of language learning strategy use, and number of strategies reportedly used highly frequently according to motivation and across all students

Motive	Median course level (seven-point scale)	Average strategy frequency (five-point scale)	Number of highly frequent strategies
Travel/other (personal) ($n = 195$)	3.0 (upper elementary)	3.1	3
Education/employment (vocational) ($n = 153$)	4.0 (pre-intermediate)	3.3	22
All students ($n = 348$)	3.0	3.2	12

goals such as travel or friendships. Given that educational/employment goals might be considered extrinsic to the learner, something the student uses as an instrument to reach some further target, these findings might suggest that extrinsic/instrumental motivation types are more productive than the intrinsic/integrative types of motivation which drive those who want to travel or form friendships for their own personal satisfaction. In other words, although intrinsic motivation is often regarded as the 'optimal' (Ushioda, 2008: 21) kind of motivation, the results of this study suggest that it may not be as motivationally powerful as something which has more immediate and tangible rewards (such as a good job or higher salary).

On the other hand, we might argue that, for students to be motivated to work hard to qualify for a particular course of study or job, they must want it (be intrinsically motivated) in the first place. Put another way, extrinsic/instrumental motivation may only be effective if there is an underlying intrinsic drive, of which those who give 'future employment' or 'further education' as a reason for studying may not even be aware.

Motivation, then, is an extremely complicated phenomenon, which Oxford (2011b: 72) describes as 'dynamic and changeable, depending on internal and external influences'. Given the complexities, it may well not be possible to meaningfully categorise motivation according to the well-established instrumental–integrative or intrinsic–extrinsic continua, since the factors which motivate a learner are highly individual and complex. Nevertheless, we can say that, according to the results of this study, motivation is significantly correlated both with strategy use and with successful learning in terms of course level.

> ## Are learner variables related to strategy choice? – Motivation
>
> These data indicate that motivation is a significant factor in strategy use and successful language learning.

Individual and pedagogical perspectives on motivation will be dealt with in Chapters 3 and 4.

2.5.2 Nationality

As previously discussed in Section 1.4.4, nationality is often confused with the closely related concepts of culture (ways of behaving), ethnicity (relating to racial origin) and language. Since it is not always easy to assign individuals to particular cultural, linguistic or ethnic categories, nationality (what is on the student's passport) will be used as the grouping variable for the purpose of this study. Although nationality is often assumed to imply certain cultural, linguistic or ethnic characteristics, it should be remembered that this is not always the case.

When grouping the 348 students studying at a private language school for international students in Auckland, New Zealand according to nationality, Griffiths (2003b) discovered that 219 (63%) were Japanese, 61 (18%) were Taiwanese, 21 (6%) were Korean and 30 (9%) were European. The remaining 17 students (4%) were from various other Asian countries such as Thailand, Indonesia and Hong Kong. This group was not analysed further because the numbers were too low to make analysis statistically viable, leaving 331 participants in this analysis.

The Europeans were grouped together because no one European country was represented in sufficient numbers to form a statistically viable group on its own. The European group included Germans, Swiss, Czechs, Russians, Swedish, Danish and also South Americans such as Brazilians, Chileans, Columbians and Argentinians (included because they speak a European language). Although this is a very diverse group, it was considered that students from countries such as Germany and France, Sweden and Russia, Spain and Argentina are culturally and linguistically more similar to each other than, for instance, Germans and Koreans. They were, therefore, grouped together in the interests of creating a statistically viable unit.

When the data reported in Table 2.1 were analysed according to nationality, none of the differences among any of the Asian national groups (Japanese, Taiwanese, Korean) was found to be significant. The Europeans, however, were found to be working at significantly higher levels than the other groups of students, and they also reported significantly more frequent use of the language learning strategies as itemised in the *SILL* ($p < 0.05$, Mann–Whitney). These results are set out in Table 2.6.

Of particular interest is that European students reported highly frequent (average = 3.5 or higher; Oxford, 1990) use of four strategies which were not included in the *plus* strategies (see Table 2.4) used by students of all nationalities (Items 16, 35, 36, 47 – see Table 2.7).

It is worthy to note that of these four strategies:

- two relate to reading;
- two relate to interaction with others.

The European students' emphasis on reading is interesting because, although it can be difficult to get students to read in the target language, there are many who advocate the advantages to be gained from doing so. Grabe and Stoller (2011), for instance, point to the usefulness of reading to develop vocabulary and fluency and to promote motivation.

The Europeans' willingness to interact with other students is also interesting since it is not uncommon to find students reluctant to interact with other students as they do not think it is useful to converse with others whose

Table 2.6 Median class levels and average reported strategy frequencies according to nationality

Nationality	Median class level (seven levels)	Average strategy frequency (five-point scale)
Japanese ($n = 219$)	3 (upper elementary)	3.1
Taiwanese ($n = 61$)	4 (pre-intermediate)	3.2
Korean ($n = 21$)	4 (pre-intermediate)	3.4
European ($n = 30$)	5 (intermediate)	3.5
Overall	3 (upper elementary)	3.2

Table 2.7 *SILL* strategies reportedly used highly frequently (average = 3.5 or above; Oxford, 1990) by European students in addition to those in the *plus* list used highly frequently by advanced students of all nationalities

SILL	Frequency average	Statement (paraphrased for brevity)
16	3.9	I read for pleasure in English
35	3.7	I look for people I can talk to in English
36	3.7	I look for opportunities to read in English
47	4.0	I practise English with other students

English is imperfect. The European students in this study, however, seem to operate on a 'half a loaf is better than no bread' principle and are prepared to interact with other learners even if the interaction may be less than perfect.

It is, of course, possible that many factors might contribute to the higher average class levels of European students. It is conceivable, for instance, that:

- Similarities of language, culture and educational practices make it easier for Europeans to learn English than it is for non-Europeans.
- Since many European languages use the same or similar graphic conventions as English, whereas languages such as Chinese and Korean use a system of writing which is very different from English, this might add a whole extra layer of difficulty to the learning task for students from these backgrounds.
- The common vocabulary and similar grammatical systems which many European languages share with English might provide a point of reference for European students, whereas Asian students have no such advantage.
- Europeans (especially younger students) are typically educated to communicate ideas freely, whereas in other cultures (e.g. Japanese) students tend to be expected to show polite restraint at all times (Usuki, 2000), making it more difficult for students from these backgrounds to adapt culturally as well as linguistically.
- There may be cultural/linguistic bias in the items included in the *SILL*. Some languages, for instance, do not have the concept of rhyme, so students who speak these languages find Item 5: *I use rhymes to remember new words* very difficult even to understand.

Are learner variables related to strategy choice?– Nationality

Although a variety of factors may help to explain the higher median class levels attained by European students, a potentially important factor may be that European students report using language learning strategies significantly more frequently than other students. Especially interesting in this regard may be the group of four strategies relating to reading and interaction reportedly used highly frequently by European students which are in addition to the *plus* strategies used highly frequently by advanced students of all nationalities.

Although it may not be the only factor, the finding of a relationship between class level and reported frequency of language learning strategy use (as itemised in the case of this study in the *SILL*) suggests that an examination of the strategies used by the higher level Europeans might help to throw further light on how strategies might be used by other groups. Particularly deserving of note might be the four strategies (two relating to reading and two to interaction – see Table 2.7) which were found to be used highly frequently by European students in addition to the strategies used highly frequently by higher level students of all nationalities.

Individual and pedagogical perspectives on nationality will be dealt with in Chapters 3 and 4.

2.5.3 Age

The relationship between age and successful language learning has been quite extensively studied and theorised (see Section 1.4.4), and the relationship between successful language learning and language learning strategies has been demonstrated. It is, therefore, perhaps surprising to discover that there are 'very few studies' (Oxford, 1989a: 238) which attempt to explore the relationships among successful language learning, language learning strategy use and age. Although Oxford (1989a) comments that older learners appear to use more 'sophisticated' language learning strategies than younger learners, this is not explained in any detail.

In order to further explore age-related differences in language development and strategy use, the data reported in Table 2.1 was analysed according to age with the students being divided as closely as possible in half. The ages of the younger group ($n = 172$) ranged from 14 to 23 while the ages of the older group ($n = 176$) ranged from 24 to 64.

Younger students were found to be working at a slightly higher average class level (average = 3.6) than older students (average = 3.2), but the difference was not statistically significant (Mann–Whitney). The overall average reported frequency of language learning strategy use was the same for both groups (average = 3.2). (See Table 2.8).

These findings related to the effects of age on successful language learning will be further exemplified in the interview reports in Chapter 3 and a

Table 2.8 Average class level and average reported frequency of strategy use according to age and across all students

Age	Average class level (seven levels)	Average strategy frequency (five-point scale)
Younger ($n = 172$) (age = 14–23)	3.6	3.2
Older ($n = 176$) (age = 24–64)	3.2	3.2
All students ($n = 348$) (age = 14–64)	3.4	3.2

pedagogical perspective on age-related differences will be presented in Chapter 4.

Are learner variables related to strategy choice? – Age

Perhaps contrary to expectations, the difference in class level according to age was slight and not found to be significant (Mann–Whitney), and there was no difference in average reported frequency of strategy use between older and younger students.

2.5.4 Sex

The relationships among sex/gender, language learning strategies and successful language learning have been discussed in Section 1.4.4. When the data reported in Table 2.1 were analysed according to sex, there were 114 (32.8%) male students and 234 (67.2%) female students. As with the study by Green and Oxford (1995), the results of this study indicated that women reported using language learning strategies (average = 3.2) more frequently than men (average = 3.1). Women also had a higher average class level (average = 3.5) than men (average = 3.3). None of these differences, however, proved to be statistically significant (Mann–Whitney). These results are set out in Table 2.9.

Since women tend to be more motivated to learn language and to use learning strategies more frequently than men it would be reasonable to expect women to be more successful language learners than men, and many studies show a slight advantage for women (e.g. Gu, 2002; Sunderland, 2000). Ehrman and Oxford (1995), however, found no correlation between strategy use according to sex and successful language learning, nor was there a difference in performance between men and women 'by any measure' (Ehrman & Oxford, 1995: 81). Nyikos (2008: 78–79) consequently concludes:

Table 2.9 Average class levels and average reported frequency of strategy use according to sex and across all students

Sex	Average class level (seven levels)	Average strategy frequency (five-point scale)
Male (n = 114)	3.3	3.1
Female (n = 234)	3.5	3.2
All students (n = 348)	3.4	3.2

Are learner variables related to strategy choice? – Sex

In spite of the fact that these results indicated that females were on average working at a higher level and reported using language learning strategies slightly more frequently on average than males, the differences in class level and in strategy use according to sex were not found to be statistically significant (Mann–Whitney).

It is therefore crucial to emphasise once more that differences in language learning preferences between males and females, although in some cases statistically significant, tend to be slight, with far greater variation between individuals than between the sexes.

These findings related to the relationship between sex and strategy use will be further exemplified in the interview reports in Chapter 3 and the pedagogical implications will be discussed in Chapter 4.

2.6 Are Situational Variables Related to Strategy Choice?

Another important variable which should not be disregarded in any discussion of strategies is learning context (discussed in Section 1.4.2). Although the role of learning situation was long overlooked as a factor in language learning, its critical importance has been highlighted by writers such as Norton and Toohey (2001). Clearly, no human activity, including language learning, takes place in a vacuum, and learning environment may well have a marked influence on the strategies that learners are willing or able to choose. But which strategies are going to be useful?

In order to investigate the strategies which appeared to be most positively related to success in terms of higher class levels for international students studying in an English speaking environment (see Section 2.2 for details), the data presented in Table 2.1 were analysed on an individual strategy basis using a Spearman test of correlation. There were nine items whose reported frequency of use had a correlation of 0.200 ($p < 0.01$) or greater with class level. These items are set out in Table 2.10, along with the correlation coefficients.

In this native speaking learning environment, the findings reported here indicate that vocabulary is important for success in language learning in terms of higher class level. In particular, higher level students show lexical flexibility as demonstrated by being able to choose synonyms (Item 29).

Table 2.10 SILL strategy items most highly correlated (r > 0.200) with class level over all students (n = 348)

SILL	Statement (paraphrased for brevity)	R
29	If I can't think of a word I use a synonym	0.373**
32	I pay attention to someone speaking English	0.302**
27	I read without looking up every new word	0.271**
31	I use my mistakes to help me do better	0.240**
22	I try not to translate word for word	0.234**
16	I read for pleasure in English	0.221**
18	I skim read then read carefully	0.215**
24	I guess the meaning of unfamiliar words	0.215**
38	I think about my progress in learning English	0.208**

Notes: These correlations are all significant at the $p < 0.01$ level, as indicated by **

In other words, when higher level students find they need a word for a particular communicative function but they cannot think of it, they think laterally and are able to find a word with a similar meaning. Although it is possible to argue that frequent use of a strategy such as using synonyms is as much a product of proficiency as it is a contributing factor (since higher level students might be expected to have a larger vocabulary), it would seem sensible to suggest that students should be encouraged to be flexible in their lexical choices. This, in turn, implies that the larger the vocabulary they have at their disposal the more flexible they are able to be, so that vocabulary expansion is clearly important.

These results also indicate a positive correlation between metacognitive strategies such as paying attention (Item 32), learning from mistakes (Item 31) and monitoring progress (Item 38). Metacognitive strategies were discovered by O'Malley et al. (1985) to be typical of higher level learners, and Anderson (2008) also argues their importance. Indeed, for some time now it has been recognised that successful learners are able to self-regulate (Dornyei, 2005; Winne, 1995); that is, they are able to employ strategies of various kinds to manage their own learning, and are therefore less at the mercy of the situation in which they happen to find themselves than students who are not able to self-regulate. Without these kinds of strategies, as O'Malley et al. point out, students lack direction, and are likely to be less effective learners than those with well-developed metacognitive skills.

Higher level students also appear to be more able to manage uncertainty than lower level students. They avoid literal translation by not looking up every new word (Item 27) and avoiding word-for-word equivalents (Item 22).

They are willing to guess and to take risks when meaning is unclear (Item 24). The positive relationship between these kinds of strategies and class level accords with the finding by Naiman *et al.* (1978) that the ability to tolerate a degree of ambiguity is a characteristic of more proficient learners. These kinds of students tend not to immediately reach for a dictionary the moment they find a word they do not know, but use strategies such as working out meaning from context. Authority-oriented students may find this difficult to get used to, but good language learners seem to understand that not everything may always be totally understood, and they are able to live with this uncertainty until, perhaps, a later moment of enlightenment occurs.

The use of reading as a language learning strategy is also among the strategies most strongly positively correlated with class level. Higher level students report reading for pleasure (Item 16) significantly more frequently than lower level students. While reading, they more frequently use strategies such as skimming (Item 18) and avoidance of looking up unfamiliar words (Item 27). It is often not easy to get students to read in English. This may be partly because many students do not come from a learning environment where reading is emphasised, so that it is not an established behaviour, or it may be related to the contemporary emphasis on listening and speaking which has been in vogue since the communicative language teaching approach was introduced. The finding that reading is related to successful language learning accords with the findings by Huang and van Naerssen (1987) and Ehrman and Oxford (1995) that reading is a useful way to learn a target language. In fact, reading is a way to expand vocabulary, to obtain models of real language in use, and to obtain cultural insights. Furthermore, a book is always available whenever the student has time, can be revised at will, and is more within the reader's control than people, who may not always want to interact, who may get impatient with being asked to repeat, and who may ridicule mistakes leading to loss of confidence.

This study did not attempt to explore students' previous strategy use in their home environments (an interesting area for possible future research), and it should also be remembered that some researchers (such as Porte, 1988; Vann & Abraham, 1990) have concluded that even unsuccessful learners are frequent users of many language learning strategies. Nevertheless, the finding that frequency of reported language learning strategy use is significantly positively related to successful learning in terms of course level (see Section 2.2) might be interpreted as suggesting that, in addition to other possible factors, more frequent use of a large repertoire of language learning strategies might contribute to effective language learning for students studying in native-speaking environments.

Are situational variables related to strategy choice?

These results suggest that when learning in an unfamiliar environment, flexibility is important as well as the ability to manage the learning process and tolerate ambiguity. Willingness to develop vocabulary and read in the target language are also important.

Especially worthy of note are the correlations between success in language learning and strategies which relate to:

- lexical expansion and flexibility;
- the management of learning;
- the tolerance of ambiguity;
- reading.

Implications of these findings regarding the teaching/learning situation will be suggested in the chapter on pedagogical perspectives (Chapter 4).

2.7 Are Target Variables Related to Strategy Choice?

It would seem to be no more than stating the obvious to suggest that different strategies are more or less suitable depending on the learning goal. Students who want to expand their vocabulary, for instance, may write down new words they find in a notebook. Those who want to improve their grammar may look for patterns in what they read. Those who want to improve their speaking skills may listen to people talking on the bus, and so on. But how transferable are these strategies across targets, for students studying business or tourism, for instance? In fact there is very little research into goal-appropriate strategies.

Griffiths (2004) undertook a study of the strategies used by international students studying the Research Methods paper at Auckland Institute of Studies, a tertiary institute in New Zealand. There were 53 students in this class, most of whom were taking the class in order to prepare themselves for further study. Approximately 60% of the class were male and 40% female, and they were aged between 22 and 36 years old. They came from a variety of national backgrounds, including China, India, Indonesia and Fiji.

Students were asked to rate each statement on the *LSD* (*Language Skills Development*) survey (see Section 1.7 and Appendix for details) from 1 (very low) to 5 (very high) according to the frequency of use.

In order to avoid encroaching on students' lecture time, *LSD Questionnaires* were handed out to be completed in the students' own time and handed back at their convenience. Surveys were returned by 32 students from the Research Methods class.

The alpha co-efficient for reliability of the instrument across these students was 0.88, which is in the 'very acceptable' range according to Oxford and Burry-Stock (1995: 6). Overall reported frequency of *LSD* strategy use (40 items) was 3.4 and the average reported frequencies of the *LSD* strategy groups were:

Listening *LSD* strategies	average = 3.6
Speaking *LSD* strategies	average = 3.6
Reading *LSD* strategies	average = 3.4
Writing *LSD* strategies	average = 3.3

Reportedly, the most frequently used individual LSD strategy items were:

Reading 10: *I use a dictionary*	average = 4.1
Listening 2: *I use the media*	average = 3.9
Speaking 7: *I use gestures*	average = 3.9
Speaking 9: *I use similar words or phrases*	average = 3.9

At the other end of the scale, the least frequently used items were:

Writing 9: *I write a diary*	average = 2.3
Reading 8: *I make predictions*	average = 2.8
Reading 7: *I make summaries*	average = 2.9
Writing 10: *I get someone to proof read*	average = 2.9

Although the relationship between overall *LSD* strategy use and end-of-course results did not prove to be significant, a statistically significant relationship was found between reported frequency of reading strategies as a group and end-of-course results ($r = 0.430$, $p < 0.05$). This means that reading strategies account for around 18.5% of the variance in end-of-course results, or nearly one-fifth.

Of the *LSD* strategy items, those with a significant positive correlation with end-of-course results were:

Reading 1: *I read extensively for information* $(r = 0.361, p < 0.05)$
Reading 3: *I find reading material at my level* $(r = 0.709, p < 0.01)$
Reading 6: *I look for text organization* $(r = 0.408, p < 0.05)$
Speaking 9: *I use similar words or phrases* $(r = 0.402, p < 0.05)$

Although students report using listening and speaking strategies most frequently, it was reading strategies which proved to be significantly correlated with end-of course success. The individual strategy item most strongly correlated with end-of-course results was Reading 3 (*I find reading material at my level*), and there were also significant correlations with two other reading strategies, making reading by far the best represented of the groups in terms of relationship to positive outcomes. This result accords with the results of some other studies (e.g. Ehrman & Oxford, 1995; Griffiths, 2002, 2003a, 2003b; Griffiths & Parr, 2000, 2001b; Huang & van Naerssen, 1987), which emphasise the importance of reading when learning another language.

The finding that using a dictionary is reportedly the most frequently used of the strategy items in the questionnaire will probably come as no surprise to those who work in the field of teaching speakers of other languages (SOL). This frequently-used strategy, however, was not significantly correlated with end-of-course results, possibly because it is so commonly used across students of all levels, and not only by either higher or lower level students. At the other end of the scale, diary writing proved to be the least frequently used strategy (average = 2.3).

Out of the 32 students who completed the questionnaire, there were six who achieved an A pass, and three who were given a D grade in the final exam. The average overall reported frequency of *LSD* strategy use by the A students was 3.8, and by the D students it was 3.2, a difference which proved to be significant (Mann–Whitney, $p < 0.05$).

Reading *LSD* strategy use by the six A students averaged 3.9, and the average use of Reading Strategy 3 (*I find reading material at my level* – the single questionnaire item most strongly correlated with results) was 4.2. Compared with these figures, the average reported frequency of reading *LSD* strategy use by the three D students was 2.9, while average reported Reading Strategy 3 use was 2.3. The difference between reported frequency of reading strategy use by A students and D students was also significant (Mann–Whitney, $p < 0.05$).

After the publication of end-of-course results, the six students who achieved A passes were interviewed in order to explore the patterns of *LSD* use by individuals. These students mentioned a variety of strategies they used to develop their language skills, and all six regarded reading as a key strategy, using it as a source of new vocabulary and as a model of correct grammar and usage to be applied across language modes (reading, writing, listening, speaking). Reading was also considered valuable because the reader has more control over the language input than is the case when listening, when much of the control is with the speaker. Types of reading these students considered useful included newspapers, magazines, text books, novels and graded readers

Other strategies which the A students mentioned as useful for developing skills and coping with difficulties included:

- making friends with native speakers;
- talking to other non-native speakers in English;
- paying careful attention when English is being spoken;
- revision;
- listening to the radio (e.g. in the car);
- going to Church;
- going to the gym;
- talking to neighbours;
- being good humoured about making mistakes;
- lots of practice;
- preparation;
- watching TV;
- taking classes;
- talking to homestays.

Although they were not interviewed, it is interesting to note that the three students who got D passes reported more frequent use of the strategy Speaking eight (*I practise the target language with other students* – average = 3.3) than did the A students (average = 3.1). In the light of how commonly this strategy is encouraged in modern communicative classrooms, perhaps we should pause and consider the possibility that, while interactive activities may provide variety and help to maintain interest in a classroom, the degree to which they promote learning may be less certain, and should therefore be used with some caution as a teaching technique.

Further research with an instrument such as the *LSD Questionnaire* is required before it will be possible to comment with any authority on the relationship between language learning strategies and learning target. In the case of the study reported here, students were studying a Research Methods course, which might, by its nature, have been expected to require a lot of reading, thereby favouring those with well-developed reading strategies.

If we compare this study, however, with the report on strategy use according to environment in the previous section involving general English students, we can see that reading also features as a significant factor in this analysis. Does this suggest that reading is important when learning a new language irrespective of the specific learning target? This question awaits further investigation. Implications of these findings regarding learning target will be suggested in the chapter on pedagogical perspectives (Chapter 4).

Are target variables related to strategy choice?

In this study, students who gained A passes in a Research Methods course reported using reading strategies significantly more often than students who gained D passes and, in the course of the interviews, all of the A grade students mentioned using reading as a key strategy.

2.8 Do Strategies Change Over Time?

An important feature of strategies is that they are *'amenable to change'* (Wenden, 1991: 18, author's italics). However, measuring this change is not always easy and the vast majority of strategy research has looked at a sample of learners at a particular point in time rather than trying to measure changes over a period of time. According to Ellis (1994: 559), nevertheless, longitudinal studies are 'sorely needed' because of our incomplete understanding of the development of language learning strategy use and the relationship of this development to successful language learning.

The relationship between changes in strategy use and progress was investigated by Griffiths (2003b, 2006) by looking at students' reported frequency of language learning strategy use on entry to their language course and again three months later. Any changes in the reported frequencies were then compared with students' progress in terms of promotion through the levels of the school.

This study was conducted in the same private English language school as the study in Section 2.2 of this chapter, using the same placement procedures: the Oxford Placement Test (Allan, 1995) plus communicative interview. After placement, promotion through the levels of the school was determined by the results of regular weekly tests. These tests were based on the work covered in class during the week. If students scored well in the test (usually 75% or more), they would be offered the opportunity to go up to a higher level. Students who made good progress in their language learning might well be promoted quite frequently. In other words, levels of promotion over a given period of time was taken as an indication of progress in language learning in this environment.

There were 30 students with courses of 3 months or longer who completed an *ELLSI* (*English Language Learning Strategy Inventory*) questionnaire (for details see Section 1.7) on two occasions. Students were asked to rate each strategy item from 1 (very low) to 5 (very high) according to their perception of the frequency with which they used it (see Appendix). The first occasion was in the week of arrival at the school, when all students completed the questionnaire during the Study Skills class. The second occasion was three months later when they were approached by the researcher and asked to complete another questionnaire. Although three months is not a long time in language learning terms, the students in this school generally came for quite short courses, the minimum being only two weeks. Very few students enrolled for courses longer than three months, which was, therefore, the longest period of time over which a study could realistically be spread in this environment.

Participants' ages ranged from 16 to 32 with the majority (23 or 77%) being in their twenties. These 30 students came from a variety of national backgrounds (Korea, Japan, Taiwan, China, Vietnam, Thailand, South America). There were 11 (37%) males, and 19 (63%) were female. Students gave a variety of reasons for wanting to study, including improving their job prospects, needing it to further their education or using it for travel purposes.

Data from the *ELLSI*s were analysed for reliability, means, correlations and differences using *SPSS* (*Statistical Package for Social Sciences*). The alpha reliability co-efficient for the *ELLSI* was calculated at 0.87, which is in the range described as 'very respectable' by Oxford and Burry-Stock (1995: 7).

Viewed overall, for the 30 students who completed two *ELLSI*s at an interval of 3 months, the median ratings total for reported frequency of use on entry was 95.5. When re-surveyed three months later, the median was 106.5. The difference between the entry and the re-survey medians for language learning strategy frequency ratings use was, therefore, +11.

The entry and re-survey ratings totals for frequency of language learning strategy use for each of the 30 students are set out in Table 2.11 along with the changes in the totals between surveys and the number of levels of promotion. Overall medians are noted at the bottom of the table.

As can be seen from Table 2.11, in some cases the increase was quite dramatic. The ratings for student number 1, for instance, increased from 81 to 128, an increment of +47, or more than 50%. In some cases, however, the change was in a negative direction. The ratings for student number 30, for instance, went from 132 to 94, a decrease of −38. Promotion for these 30 students over that period of time ranged from 0 to 4 levels, with the median being 1 level.

Table 2.11 Entry and re-survey totals for reported frequency of language learning strategy use (*ELLSI*), with the change in reported frequency of strategy use between surveys and the number of levels of promotion

Student number	Entry totals	Re-survey totals	Entry/re-survey change	Levels of promotion
1	81	128	47	3
2	105	128	23	1
3	79	101	22	1
4	89	110	21	3
5	91	107	16	0
6	102	116	14	1
7	105	118	13	3
8	83	94	11	0
9	137	148	11	4
10	105	114	9	2
11	89	97	8	1
12	112	119	7	2
13	114	121	7	1
14	111	116	5	2
15	112	117	5	2
16	117	121	4	0
17	101	105	4	0
18	94	97	3	1
19	139	142	3	0
20	94	97	3	3
21	106	107	1	2
22	104	105	1	2
23	129	124	−5	1
24	104	96	−8	0
25	124	116	−8	0
26	101	90	−11	1
27	119	106	−13	0
28	138	113	−25	2
29	133	100	−33	0
30	132	94	−38	1
Overall median	**95.5**	**106.5**	**4.5**	**1**

> ## Do strategies change over time?
>
> These results indicate that the answer to this question is 'Yes'.

The pedagogical perspectives of this finding will be discussed in Chapter 4.

2.9 How Do Strategy Changes Relate to Progress?

Over the three months, there were five students who were promoted three or more levels. The median ratings increase for the frequently promoted group was +21, which is nearly five times the median entry/re-survey change overall. These results are set out in Table 2.12.

The largest increases in the entry/re-survey totals for the five students who were promoted three or more levels in the three months were reported for a group of 10 strategies:

Item 6:   *Watching TV in English*
Item 7:   *Revising regularly*
Item 10:   *Writing letters in English*
Item 14:   *Reading newspapers in English*
Item 16:   *Consciously learning new vocabulary*
Item 17:   *Keeping a language learning notebook*
Item 19:   *Noting language used in the environment*
Item 20:   *Controlling schedules so that English study is done*
Item 25:   *Listening to native speakers of English*
Item 29:   *Watching movies in English*

Table 2.12 Language learning strategy ratings totals on entry and when re-surveyed, with the change in ratings, levels of promotion, and median ratings change for the five students who made the fastest progress during the 3-month period

Student number	Entry totals	Re-survey totals	Entry/re-survey change	Levels of promotion
9	137	148	+11	4
1	81	128	+47	3
4	89	110	+21	3
7	105	118	+13	3
20	94	97	+3	3
Median	**94**	**118**	**21**	**3**

Interestingly, however, this frequently promoted group did not report increased use of all strategies. There were two strategy items for which reduced usage was reported:

Item 13:   *Using a dictionary*
Item 28:   *Making friends with native speakers*

The decrease in the frequency of dictionary use may well reflect on the one hand the tendency for higher level students to be more tolerant of ambiguity and therefore less inclined to reach for a dictionary when faced with words they don't know. It may also, of course, simply be a sign of a larger vocabulary which leaves fewer gaps needing to be looked up.

In the case of Item 28, it is not uncommon for students to find that making friends with native speakers is not as easy as they had hoped, since interaction with native speakers (such as shopkeepers, bus drivers, etc.) is often at a fairly superficial level. Furthermore, the native speakers they come across often have their own established relationships which restrict them from opening up to newcomers and, anyway, making friends takes time and international students are often only in the overseas learning environment for quite short periods.

Over the three months, there were nine students who were not promoted at all. The results for this group can be seen in Table 2.13. It is interesting to note that, of these nine students who made no progress in terms of promotion to higher-level classes, four (students 24, 25, 27, 29) actually gave lower ratings for frequency of strategy use over the 3-month period. Overall, the median change, although positive, was low: in fact, it was one-seventh of the change reported by the frequently promoted group (see Table 2.12).

The difference in the median ratings increase for the frequently promoted group (+21), and the median ratings increase for those who were not promoted at all (+3) was found to be significant ($p < 0.05$, Mann–Whitney). This suggests that perhaps the really important factor when it comes to the relationship between language learning strategy use and successful language learning may be not so much the actual frequency, but the degree to which a learner is prepared to take on new strategies and to expand existing strategy repertoires.

We might, for instance, compare student 1 and student 8 (see Tables 11, 12, 13), both of whom gave quite low initial ratings (81 and 83 respectively) on the *ELLSI*. Three months later, however, student 1 had increased this total to 128 (an increase of 47) while student 8 had only increased the total by 11 to 94. And whereas student 1 had been promoted three times, student 8 had not been promoted at all.

Another interesting group is the set of eight students whose re-survey ratings total was lower than the ratings total on entry. With only one

Table 2.13 Language learning strategy ratings totals on entry and when re-surveyed, with the change in ratings, levels of promotion, and median ratings change for the nine students who were not promoted at all during the 3-month period

Student number	Entry totals	Re-survey totals	Entry/re-survey change	Levels of promotion
5	91	107	16	0
8	83	94	11	0
16	117	121	4	0
17	101	105	4	0
19	139	142	3	0
24	104	96	−8	0
25	124	116	−8	0
27	119	106	−13	0
29	133	100	−33	0
Median	**117**	**106**	**3**	**0**

exception (student 28), students in this group were promoted only one level or not at all (see Table 2.14). Possible explanations of this phenomenon might be that students who reported using strategies frequently on arrival might be affected by others who were less strategic in their approach to their studies, by peer pressure, by a desire to fit in, by a need to adapt to the new culture in which they found themselves, or by the sudden absence

Table 2.14 Language learning strategy ratings totals on entry and when re-surveyed, with the change in ratings and levels of promotion for the eight students who reported a reduction in frequency of strategy use over the 3-month period

Student number	Entry totals	Re-survey totals	Entry/re-survey change	Levels of promotion
28	138	113	−25	2
23	129	124	−5	1
26	101	90	−11	1
30	132	94	−38	1
24	104	96	−8	0
25	124	116	−8	0
27	119	106	−13	0
29	133	100	−33	0
Median	**126.5**	**103**	**−12**	**0.5**

of the kinds of pressures they had at home. Another possible interpretation might be that the language learning strategies reported on arrival might not have been a realistic representation of actual strategy use, a recognised limitation of self-report data discussed at length by Gu *et al.* (1995), among others. It is possible that not all students report their strategy use reliably or using the same frames of reference: what is 'always or almost always' for one student might, for instance, be given a lower rating by another (Gu *et al.*, 1995). Furthermore, increases in reported strategy use might represent increased awareness rather, actually, than increased frequency.

Whatever the explanation for the decline in reported frequency of strategy use among these eight students, this group achieved only a very low rate of promotion (median $= 0.5$, which is half of the overall median, and considerably less than the progress achieved by some of the more successful students).

How do strategy changes relate to progress?

These findings indicate that, *overall*, the students who progressed most rapidly in terms of promotion through the levels of the school were those who reported the largest increases in the frequency of their language learning strategy use over the research period.

Care needs to be taken when interpreting these results because numbers are relatively low ($n = 30$), the time span relatively short (three months), and significance level not particularly high ($p < 0.05$). Nevertheless, it is noteworthy that the group of students who progressed through three to four levels during the three months reported a median increase of +21 in frequency ratings, which is seven times greater than the median increase of only three reported by students who remained at the same level throughout the three months.

It is important to bear in mind, however, that although this study found a positive relationship between increased reported frequency of strategy use and progress overall, this finding does not necessarily apply to every individual student. An examination of Table 2.11 reveals that not all students who achieved a high level of promotion also reported a large increase in their frequency of language learning strategy use. Student number 20, for instance, progressed through three levels in spite of reporting an increase of only +3 in the strategy frequency ratings total. Conversely, there were those like student number five who reported a relatively high entry/re-survey ratings change of +16 but who was not promoted at all during the 3-month period of the study.

Another interesting case is student number 28, who will be called Lee. Wanting to learn English 'for myself', she was initially placed at pre-intermediate level. Her initial frequency ratings total was very high (138) and she appeared to arrive with good intentions of making the best of her time abroad, giving ratings of five (always or almost always) to strategies such as *Talking to native speakers* and *Making friends with native speakers*. However, even in this first survey, completed in the first week of her course, Lee was complaining in notes which she added to the *ELLSI* questionnaire form that 'teacher doesn't talk to Asia student', that 'I want talking with native person for long time' and that 'I want to stay small [number of] students in my classroom'. A picture emerges of a rather inflexible and unhappy student who found it difficult to adapt to the realities of the situation in which she found herself. By the end of three months, Lee's frequency ratings total had decreased to 113. In her second survey, Lee complained that 'I cannot meet English person' and gave *Talking to native speakers of English* a rating of 2, and a rating of only 1 this time to *Making friends with native speakers*, with the implication in her comments that native speakers are difficult to talk to and unfriendly. Although she had been promoted to upper intermediate (two levels of promotion), a rate of promotion which is actually higher than the median (one level), the impression among those of us who knew her at the school was that she could have done better but for her negative attitudes which appeared to be reflected in the declining frequency she reported in language learning strategy use.

By comparison, student number 9, who will be called Taro, scored almost the same as Lee on the initial ratings total (137) and by the end of the three months he had increased this by +11 to 148. Taro was cheerful and outgoing and interacted enthusiastically with teachers and fellow students alike. By the end of the research period he had been promoted through four levels, the highest rate of promotion in the study.

Therefore, it is not possible to claim an uncomplicated linear association between rate of promotion and reported increment in language learning strategy use. Nevertheless, the results of this study do indicate that, in general, increased reported frequency of language learning strategy use is linked to progress, and that, overall, the most frequently promoted students are the ones who report the greatest increase in the frequency of their language learning strategy use over a period of time. Although this generalisation did not apply to every individual learner, a significant difference was found in promotion according to increased strategy use overall, reinforcing the idea that strategies are indeed a factor in successful language learning.

The pedagogical perspectives of these findings will be discussed in Chapter 4.

2.10 Which is the Chicken and Which is the Egg?

Although this chapter has provided answers to a number of fundamental questions regarding the language learning strategy concept, the whole question of cause and effect remains problematic. Merely because we can quote statistics to show that language learning strategies are *related* to class level does not mean to say that one causes the other, and we need to be very careful that this basic non-sequitur is clearly understood.

For instance, if higher level students use more reading strategies than lower level students, does this mean that the reading strategies lead to (cause) promotion, or is it that higher level students have a larger vocabulary which facilitates the employment of more sophisticated reading strategies? If higher level students are more likely to start conversations in English, does this strategy contribute to their increased proficiency, or does a higher level of proficiency provide the confidence required to initiate such interaction? Does avoiding literal translation and guessing unfamiliar lexis lead to higher levels of proficiency, or is it just easier for higher level students to use these strategies since they already have a well-developed linguistic base?

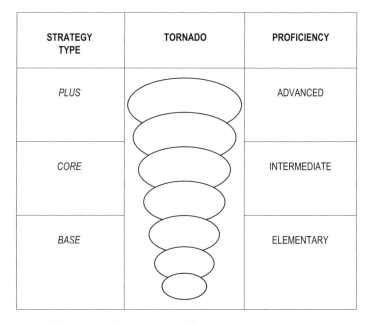

Figure 2.1 Model: Hypothesised Tornado Effect

I would like to suggest that the relationship is probably spiral, where enlarged vocabulary and other linguistic knowledge improves reading, confidence and interactive ability, which exposes the learner to more vocabulary and linguistic input, which makes comprehension and production even easier and more enjoyable, and so on in an ever augmenting spiral. This might be termed the Tornado Effect, a model of which might be represented as in Figure 2.1.

But this kind of non-linear effect is difficult to investigate, since, by its nature, one factor influences the other ad infinitum, creating a complex system, as discussed, for instance, by Larsen-Freeman (1997), and rendering it difficult if not impossible to definitively assign causality to any given effect. Nevertheless, to discover some means of studying such spiral phenomena would represent a major breakthrough in language learning strategy research.

2.11 Conclusion

The studies discussed in this chapter have hopefully contributed some answers to some fundamental questions. In particular:

(1)   Language learning strategies do appear to be related to success in language learning. According to the results of the study reported here, there is a significant relationship between language learning strategy use and class level, and advanced students report using many *more* language learning strategies significantly *more frequently* than elementary students.

(2)   Some types of strategies do appear to be more related to successful language learning than others. In particular, there is a *plus* group of 15 *SILL* strategy items which appears to account for more than 10% of the variance in class level. These strategies relate to interacting with others, to the functional use of language, to learning vocabulary, to tolerating ambiguity, to learning the systems of the target language (grammar), to managing affective states and to all four skills. In addition, the group of 12 *core* strategies (used highly frequently across all students), among which are a large number of metacognitive strategies as well as strategies related to pronunciation and the use of resources, are also reportedly used highly frequently by higher level students. In other words higher level students use a wide variety of strategies rather than just a limited range, although they tend not to frequently use the memory strategies which feature prominently among the *base* strategies favoured by elementary students.

(3) Some learner variables (such as nationality and motivation) do seem to be related to strategy choice and to class level, whereas others (such as sex and age) do not appear to be significantly related.

(4) Although there is not a lot of research investigating the relationship between strategy choice and learning context/environment, there are some indications that students are more likely to be successful if they read in the target language and are able to tolerate ambiguity and adapt their strategies to the situation in which they are currently studying.

(5) The relationship between language learning strategies and learning goal/aim is another under-researched area, but there are suggestions that reading in the target language may be useful across learning objectives.

(6) Strategies do appear to be capable of changing over time, with students sometimes reporting an increase, and sometimes a decrease, in language learning strategy use. On the whole, those students who most increase their language learning strategy use appear to be the ones who make the fastest progress.

(7) Cause and effect remain problematic in relation to language learning strategies: do strategies contribute to increased proficiency, or does increased proficiency influence strategy use, or is the relationship a spiral one, with one factor augmenting the other? It is suggested that this might be termed the 'Tornado Effect', but much more research is required before anything definitive can be said about this complex system.

We have already seen, however, that these generalisations, although useful when looking at the situation overall, do not apply to every individual student. The next chapter will look more closely at individuals and try to discover what we can learn from looking at how particular learners go about learning language.

2.12 Quantitative Areas for Further Research

The studies described in this chapter have produced some interesting findings, but there are still many unanswered questions, especially:

(1) More studies are still needed to confirm the **relationship between quantity/frequency of strategies and success in language learning**.

(2) More research is still needed to refine concepts of **strategy type**.

(3) The studies reported here give some indications of relationships which might exist between **strategies and the learner variables** of motivation, nationality, age and sex, but there are many other variables (such

as style, personality, beliefs, autonomy, aptitude, affect, identity, investment, and so on) which also have the potential to affect strategy selection but which remain under-researched.

(4) Studies of the relationship between **strategies and learning context
or learning goal** are very rare. Given that situational or target variables
have the potential to profoundly affect strategy choice and learning
outcomes, further studies are urgently needed.

(5) Another area which is conspicuous by its lack of published research is
that of **longitudinal studies** into strategy use to investigate strategy
development over time and how this is related to success in language
learning.

(6) If we accept an expanding spiral model of language learning strategy
development (the Tornado Effect), we need to develop some means of
researching **complex, non-linear phenomena**.

3   A Qualitative Perspective

3.1 The Individual Language Learner

Selinker (1972: 213) is emphatic when he states: 'a theory of second language learning that does not provide a central place for individual differences among learners *cannot* be considered acceptable' (author's italics). Although data such as those presented in Chapter 2 are interesting in terms of overall patterns, far from behaving according to some aggregated statistical model, individuals are uniquely engaged in their own infinitely variable world of human activity within the social context to which they belong, and preoccupied with their own personal goals. They are much more than 'a quantified collective' of statistics (Roebuck, 2000: 82).

The semi-structured interview was chosen as the most suitable for the present study because of its flexibility and because of the rich information which such interviews can produce (Dowsett, 1986). From among the international students studying English at a private language school in Auckland, New Zealand (for more details see Section 2.2), 26 were selected and invited to an interview which lasted about half an hour (Griffiths, 2003b). The interviewees were purposefully selected to be as representative as possible of the learner variables included in the study in terms of class level, sex, age and the major national groups.

In addition to the *Strategy Inventory for Language Learning* (*SILL* – Oxford, 1990), which students had already completed before the interview, an interview guide was used consisting of three main questions (regarding key strategies, learning difficulties and the effects of learner variables) designed to probe a student's strategy use and to explore some of the factors which interrelate with this strategy use. The interview guide (see Appendix) was designed to complement the *SILL*'s quantitative approach by adding a qualitative element in the form of individual opinions, attitudes, reactions or beliefs.

During the interview, the interviewer asked the student the questions on the guide and noted the responses for later summarising. In addition to providing direct answers to the questions, students were encouraged to elaborate on their answers by providing examples and personal insights, which were also noted by the interviewer. During the interview, the *SILL* responses were discussed. The students were asked about the strategies they had found most useful and about their development of strategies to deal with the difficulties they had found with learning English. Students were also asked whether they thought their nationality, their sex, their age or other factors affected their choice of language learning strategies and/or how they felt these factors affected others with whom they learnt. Any other interesting insights, such as their reasons for learning (motivation), were also noted.

Following the interviews, the notes were examined for useful insights into strategy use and 10 were selected for closer examination and detailed reporting. These 10 students were chosen to be as varied as possible in terms of proficiency, nationality, sex and age and also in terms of the success or otherwise they achieved during their courses (information obtained from their class teachers and from test results). The selected interviewees were also chosen because of the quality of the insights they provided during the interview and the degree to which these insights added something new to previous interviews (some tended to be rather repetitive of material obtained previously). Pseudonyms are used for these students in order to protect their privacy.

Using the notes and the *SILL* responses, learner profiles of the 10 selected interviewees were constructed. Learner characteristics (nationality, sex, age and other characteristics) were noted and the *SILL* results (average frequency, number of strategies rated 5, number of *base* strategies rated 5, number of *core* strategies rated 5, number of *plus* strategies rated 5) summarised. (The terms *base, core* and *plus* have been explained in Section 2.4). Achievement (in terms of examinations passed) was recorded or rate of progress (in terms of levels per month) calculated.

In addition, the interview notes were examined for qualitative insights which were also added to the profiles. In particular, any learning difficulties the students encountered (such as 'understanding native speakers' or 'cultural differences') were noted as well as the key strategies employed (the ones students identified as being important for themselves, such as 'consciously working to manage lack of self-confidence' or 'eating western food'). Interviewees' perceptions regarding the role on their language learning of individual differences such as nationality, sex, age or other factors were also included. Since motivation for learning was often mentioned, this was also added to the profile. All of this information was included in a written summary, as well as any comments and insights which helped to round out the learner as an individual and suggested possible answers to some otherwise puzzling questions, such as 'Why did Yuki make so little effort to learn?', 'Why did May choose to work at a level below her level of achievement?', 'Why did Lilly appear to lose motivation mid-course?', 'Why did Hiro want to study English in his retirement?', 'Why was Mikhail much less successful then Kira?' or 'Why did Kang refuse to eat Korean food while he was in New Zealand?'.

3.1.1 Nina

An examination of the interview data relating to how individuals reportedly use language learning strategies would seem to indicate general support for the findings from the survey data that the most successful students report frequently using a large number of language learning strategies. Nina, for instance, who gained an A pass in the high level CPE examination reported highly frequent use of many language learning strategies and was also able to add a number of key strategies of her own to the *SILL* items.

At 19 years old, Nina had already studied English for 9 years in her native Germany and had passed the Cambridge First Certificate (FCE) examination. She was, therefore, already at quite an advanced level on arrival. After sitting the Cambridge Advanced English (CAE) and the CPE examinations, Nina planned to return to Germany to study English at university in order to equip herself for a career in a field where her English would be useful.

The results of Nina's *SILL* indicated that she reported using language learning strategies highly frequently (average = 3.5) with 14 of the 50 items being given the maximum rating of 5 ('always or almost always'). Nina gave a rating of 5 ('always or almost always') to only one of the nine *base* strategies (reportedly used more frequently by less proficient students than by more proficient students), to three of the 12 core strategies (used highly frequently across all students) and to nine of the 15 *plus* strategies (reportedly used highly frequently by more proficient students). Of the *plus* strategies, three relate to vocabulary (Items 10, 19, 21), two relate to the ability to tolerate ambiguity (Items 24, 27) and one relates to reading (Item 18). Nina also gave a rating of 5 to Item 16 (*I read for pleasure in English*), reportedly used highly frequently by European students.

This pattern of strategy use suggests a student who makes good use of the strategies typical of higher level students, who is able to cope with a degree of uncertainty, and who is especially aware of the importance of vocabulary and the usefulness of reading in English. She has obviously grown beyond the *base* strategies, although she still uses location to remember new words. Nina's responses are summarised in Student Profile 1.

Student Profile 1: Nina

Learner characteristics
Nationality: German   Sex: female   Age: 19
Motivation: to study at university

SILL results and progress/achievement
Average reported frequency of use: 3.5
Number of strategies rated 5
    ('always or almost always'):   14
Number of *base* strategies rated 5:   1
Number of *core* strategies rated 5:   3
Number of *plus* strategies rated 5:   9
Achievement: passed CAE and CPE

Learning difficulties
• Speaking in English

Key strategies
• Talking to people in English to improve speaking skills
• Consciously working to manage lack of self-confidence
• Living in an environment where English is spoken
• Writing new language items down in a notebook

As a European, Nina said she felt she had an advantage over Asian students because of the similarities in the languages. As a woman, she felt that women are more likely to study language than men, who are more likely to be expected by others to study something practical. She felt that it was an advantage for her to be doing something others accepted as 'normal' rather than having to fight against the expectations of others. Nina did not feel, however, that either nationality or sex affected the strategies which were likely to lead to success. As for age, she commented that when she was younger she used reading as her main strategy (receptive), whereas now she was more aware of the importance of writing (productive).

During the interview, Nina said that a key strategy she used was always to write everything she learnt down since this helped to fix it in her mind and meant she could revise and learn it later (other students also commented on her penchant for this strategy). She had found talking to people in English the most useful strategy as a means to improving her speaking skills, an area in which she lacked confidence. She felt that the best way to overcome this difficulty with confidence was to stay in an environment where the language was spoken, preferably living with a native-speaking family (as she did), since this maximised opportunities for practice and meant that she had to make the effort to interact in English whether she felt like it or not.

Nina was such a competent student, it was easy to forget that confidence (as mentioned above) is an issue, even with someone like her. One day she arrived in class uncharacteristically flushed and flustered. When asked what was the matter she told us that, as she was walking to school and waiting to cross at the lights, a woman came up to her and asked how to get to the station. Trying to think how best to direct her, Nina said 'Um', and the woman immediately said, 'Oh, so you are a foreigner too!' This brief exchange really unsettled Nina and threw her into a tail-spin of self-doubt. 'I didn't say anything!' she exclaimed to us in class. 'Only "Um", and from that she could tell I was a foreigner!'

Although visibly affected by the encounter, it was not long before Nina had recovered from this ego-denting experience, as might, perhaps, have been expected from the high rating she gave to Item 40: *I encourage myself to speak English even when I am afraid of making a mistake*. It is difficult to be sure, however, whether the use of such a strategy might be a cause of language learning effectiveness, or whether the fact that Nina was already a successful learner gave her the underlying confidence to recover her composure and use such a strategy effectively. The issue of confidence is further discussed from a pedagogical perspective in Chapter 4.

3.1.2 Kira

Although, unlike Nina, he did not sit an examination to provide an external measure of success, Kira made the fastest rate of progress of the 10 selected interviewees in terms of progress through the levels of the school (two levels per month). Kira reported the highest average frequency of language learning strategy use (average = 3.8) and the highest number of strategies rated 5 ('always or almost always', $N = 19$). Of these, eight were core strategies, six were *plus* strategies and only one was a base strategy. It is also interesting to note that Kira gave a rating of 5 to all nine of the *SILL's* 'metacognitive' strategies. Although the validity of grouping the strategies in this way has been previously discussed in Section 1.6, it is nevertheless of interest that a student as successful as Kira opts so emphatically for the group of strategies which may relate to the ability to manage the learning process.

When 28-year-old Kira started his English language course he was placed in a mid-elementary class on the basis of the placement procedures adopted by the school (explained in Section 2.2). He said he wanted to learn English in order to obtain a new job and so that he could write English lyrics for songs which he could perform with the band he had in Japan. Although Kira had not studied English formally since leaving school and had 'forgotten much', even at an early stage in his course he was a very confident speaker and managed to use the knowledge he had very effectively, an ability which he put down to having worked in a duty free shop where he had to speak English to customers, and to having been in a band where he sang in English.

Like Nina, Kira was very focused: he knew what he wanted and he worked very hard. Staff members often mentioned having to evict him from the self-study room as they were going round the school locking up long after the majority of the students had gone. According to all the teachers who taught him, he was a delight to have in class, always participating keenly in classroom activities. He was also very popular among the students, having, among other things, organised a school soccer team which gave him status and a high profile and provided time out from direct study, which he used as a deliberate strategy to 'refresh myself'.

During his interview, Kira was very definite and specific about his key strategies, readily producing a long list. He said he watched TV as much as possible to practise listening and that he read newspapers. In order to reactivate the knowledge acquired in his school days, he spent 2–3 hours a day working on his grammar. In class he always sat next to the teacher, so that it was easy to ask questions, or next to the best speaker in the class, so that he could use the other student's knowledge to expand his own. He did homework and lesson revision every day and talked with his host family in the evenings. He used every opportunity to converse with native speakers such as taxi drivers and shop keepers and kept a special notebook in which he wrote sentences. Kira believed in writing full sentences in order to check the usage: isolated words and meanings he found insufficient. In order to give himself a break from study, at the weekends he played sport, which he considered beneficial.

According to Kira, the responsibility for learning was basically the students', who needed to make positive efforts to learn if they were to be successful. However, he believed a teacher could be very helpful, especially by creating a good atmosphere, by providing useful feedback, and by acting as a reference.

When he was young, Kira considered that he had not been a good student of English. However, when he was about six or seven years old he used to go to visit a friend of his mother's who spoke good English and she would play language games with him. He found this a lot of fun and, therefore, from an early age developed a positive attitude towards English, the importance of which is stressed by Stern (1975).

Kira made excellent progress, moving through six levels (mid-elementary to advanced) in a mere 3 months (two levels a month). Even allowing for the

---

Student Profile 2: Kira

Learner characteristics
Nationality: Japanese   Sex: male   Age: 28
Motivation: new job, songwriting

SILL results and progress/achievement
Average reported frequency of use: 3.8
Number of strategies rated 5
   ('always or almost always'):   19
Number of *base* strategies rated 5:   1
Number of *core* strategies rated 5:   8
Number of *plus* strategies rated 5:   6
Number of *base* strategies rated 5:   1
Progress: 2 levels per month

Learning difficulties
- Understanding spoken English   • Grammar
- Reading and writing

Key strategies
- Watching TV to practise listening
- Talking to native speakers
- Reading newspapers
- Writing sentences in a notebook
- Working specifically on knowledge of grammar
- Consciously manipulating position in the classroom
- Doing homework and revision regularly
- Providing for time out from study in order to refresh himself

---

possibility that some of this progress might have been the result of reactivating stored knowledge, this was a remarkable rate of promotion.

The consensus among his teachers was that Kira was a conspicuously excellent, hard-working student who was keen to participate in everything and who approached his studies with a consistently positive attitude which made him a pleasure to have in class. Kira had an outgoing personality and showed real leadership qualities among the other students while his disciplined approach to his learning earned everyone's respect and helped him to achieve an all-round excellence which is a rare accomplishment in such a short time. The possibility that some of this success might be related to

Kira's extensive repertoire of language learning strategies is suggested by the positive relationship which was discovered between reported frequency of language learning strategy use and proficiency.

3.1.3 Fernando

Another interviewee who made very good progress (1.2 levels per month) was Fernando, a 23-year-old from Argentina, which placed him in the 'European' category for the purposes of this study, since he spoke a European language (Spanish). At the beginning of his 5-month English language course, Fernando was placed at mid-elementary level. At this stage he struggled to communicate verbally in English and his grammar was especially weak. He was, however, extremely focused, determined and assertive; indeed, the term 'pushy' was used to describe him on more than one occasion. He had left a job to study abroad and had financed his own studies which he wanted to use to improve his job prospects. He was, therefore, very aware of what the course was costing him in monetary terms and there was an urgency about his determination to make the best of his time at the school which was not evident with many of the other students whose courses were often being paid for by parents or others. Highly motivated, therefore, to make the best use of his time and money, he agitated ceaselessly for promotion and decided to join a class working for the First Certificate in English (FCE) examination.

When Fernando's *SILL* questionnaire was examined, a high average reported frequency of strategy usage (average = 3.7; Oxford, 1990) was discovered and also a high number ($N = 18$) of strategies rated in the 'always or almost always' (rating = 5) category, of which eight were *plus* strategies (reportedly used highly frequently by advanced students but not by all students).

Fernando gave a rating of 5 to five of the *SILL*'s six 'social' strategies. Although the validity of the *SILL* sub-groupings has been discussed previously (Section 1.6), a student who opts so emphatically for this group of strategies might be expected to be very aware of the advantages of interaction when learning language.

The most difficult aspects of learning English, according to Fernando, were prepositions, understanding native speakers, and also working out the pronunciation of English words. Although English has a lot of vocabulary which is related to Spanish, he found that it is often not possible to work out the pronunciation from the written form as is usually the case with Spanish. However, he said he was not afraid to ask people if he was unsure of pronunciation and was prepared to learn from correction (although, in fact, he was often so busy talking that he would continue right over attempts to correct him!).

Student Profile 3: Fernando

Learner characteristics
Nationality: Argentinian   Sex: male   Age: 23
Motivation: better job

SILL results and progress/achievement
Average reported frequency of use: 3.7
Number of strategies rated 5
   ('always or almost always'):   18
Number of *base* strategies rated 5:   1
Number of *core* strategies rated 5:   7
Number of *plus* strategies rated 5:   8
Progress: 1.2 levels per month

Learning difficulties
- Prepositions
- Understanding native speakers
- Pronunciation

Key strategies
- Asking for help
- Learning language in chunks
- Speaking only in English
- Watching TV, especially for listening practice and pronunciation modelling
- Learning from correction
- Keeping a notebook

When asked what he found the most useful strategies, Fernando said he liked to learn language in related chunks rather than as isolated words, a strategy which he credited to a highly esteemed private teacher with whom he had studied in Argentina, and which was also prominent in Kira's strategy repertoire.

Other key strategies included keeping a notebook in which he recorded language items new to him (e.g. prepositional usage) and watching TV as much as possible in order to practise listening and as a model for pronunciation. When it was pointed out to him that his *SILL* questionnaire indicated that he reported very little use of 'memory' and 'cognitive' strategies and suggested that he might usefully consider using such strategies (e.g. writing letters, reading for pleasure) more often, Fernando expressed impatience with this advice and insisted that speaking English only was the most important learning strategy. His considerable charm certainly facilitated the exercise of this strategy by ensuring him a constant supply of eager (female) companions, with whom he no doubt spent the time speaking English constantly!¿

Fernando left the school from the advanced class, having moved through six levels in 5 months. This is a good rate of progress and due very much to his single-minded determination. He did not pass First Certificate, however, a failure which may well be at least partly attributable to the fact that he did not put nearly as much effort into the formal areas of his studies as he did into the communicative aspect (an observation made by his teachers and also able to be inferred from an examination of the types of language learning strategies he used, of which, as has already been noted, a high number were 'social' strategies). Although interactive strategies may be important (as evidenced by their inclusion among the types of *plus* strategies used highly frequently by higher level students), Fernando's lack of all-round success (such as was achieved, for instance, by Nina) suggests the possibility that it may also be important to balance different types of strategies so that all aspects of language development are given due attention.

3.1.4 Kim

Like Fernando, when 20-year-old Kim from Korea arrived for a 5-month English course, she was initially placed in a mid-elementary class. These two students have several points of similarity and also some interesting differences, so they are interesting to compare and contrast with each other.

Kim had come to study English in order to improve her job prospects and to have a 'better life' and she had worked for 8 months as a teacher and librarian in order to earn the money for her course. She worked hard and made steady progress. She was a good student in class, participated well in all activities and was not especially demanding in terms of promotion – she was promoted purely on her results, without the kind of pressure other more 'pushy' students, such as Fernando, sometimes exerted.

An examination of her *SILL* results showed a high average reported frequency of language learning strategy use (average = 3.7; Oxford, 1990) and also a high number of strategies ($N = 18$) used in the 'always or almost always' (rating = 5) category. Coincidentally, both the reported strategy average and the total number of strategies rated 5 are the same as Fernando's. Unlike Fernando, however, who gave ratings of 5 to five 'social' strategies, Kim gave ratings of 5 to five 'metacognitive' strategies. Although the validity of dividing strategies in this way has been previously discussed (Section 1.6), the choice of such different types of strategies might suggest rather different types of learners: Fernando being highly sociable and keen to use interaction with others to improve his English, Kim being more aware of the need to control her own learning.

Kim said she found idioms especially difficult when learning English and she felt that Europeans had an advantage here because 'their thinking is closer to English – they can guess'. English vocabulary was also a problem. In spite of the Korean education system's well-developed method for teaching vocabulary in lists, Kim found it difficult to distinguish between the many words in English which mean almost the same thing. English grammar was similarly problematic, since it is 'completely different' from Korean and she found the unfamiliar conventions of English (such as word order) hard to get used to. Kim had found it necessary to pay conscious attention to these areas of English, writing idioms, vocabulary and grammar in a notebook as she came across them and consciously learning them later. Other key language learning strategies she said she had found useful were watching TV and using tapes in the self-study room to improve her listening skills, as well as reading magazines, newspapers and stories, which she found helped her writing as well as her ability to read. Kim said she put a lot of time into her study, believing: 'We must study steadily and with patience.'

Kim also tried to speak to her host family or non-Korean friends at school as much as possible in order to improve her speaking and listening skills, with which she lacked confidence because in Korea her lessons had been textbook based and she had had no access to English speakers. She said she did not concern herself too much with strategies relating to feelings because 'it is important to keep your mind on your work and not to worry too much about feelings'. As might have been expected from Kim's emphasis on 'metacognitive' strategies in the *SILL*, she believed in taking charge of her own learning. As she put it: 'The teacher leads, but learning is up to the student.'

Kim was well thought of by all her teachers and the other students. She left the school planning to continue at an English school in Korea and to go back to university to study accountancy. She was such a quiet, steady worker that it was actually a surprise, at the end of her 5-month course, to discover that she had gone all the way from mid-elementary to advanced (six levels), a rate of progress which matched Fernando's.

It is encouraging to discover that, in spite of European students' higher average class levels, Asian students can progress as rapidly. The possibility that appropriate language learning strategies may be related to Kim's excellent progress is suggested by the positive correlation which was shown by the results of the data analysis to exist between reported frequency of language learning strategy use and class level.

Student Profile 4: Kim

Learner characteristics
Nationality: Korean   Sex: female   Age: 20
Motivation: better job, 'better life'

SILL results and progress/achievement
Average reported frequency of use: 3.7
Number of strategies rated 5
   ('always or almost always'):   18
Number of *base* strategies rated 5:   1
Number of *core* strategies rated 5:   8
Number of *plus* strategies rated 5:   7
Progress: 1.2 levels per month

Learning difficulties
- Idioms
- Grammar
- Vocabulary

Key strategies
- Writing language items (especially idioms, vocabulary, grammar) in a notebook and consciously learning them
- Watching TV and listening to tapes to practise listening skills
- Reading newspapers, magazines, stories to improve reading and writing
- Putting a lot of time into study
- Speaking English to the homestay family and non-Korean friends

3.1.5 Mikhail

Compared with these four students (Nina, Kira, Fernando and Kim) who all gave high frequency ratings to many strategies and who all made excellent progress, Mikhail, who gave only nine strategies a rating of five and whose average reported frequency of strategy use was below the high-frequency threshold, progressed through only 0.6 levels per month. Mikhail was a 24-year-old Russian who, like Kira, was initially placed in a mid-elementary class. When interviewed 10 months later, he had been working in the advanced class for some weeks. His promotion to this level, however, had not been without reservations on the part of myself and of the various teachers he had met along the way.

Mikhail was very ambitious and keen to achieve the status of being in a higher level class. Over the months he managed to become very fluent and able to communicate what he needed to say with little difficulty. Those of us who knew him better, however, realised that this surface fluency often disguised the fact that his underlying grammatical competence by no means kept pace with his communicative competence. When listened to with more than conversation-level care, Mikhail's utterances would be discovered to be liberally sprinkled with extremely suspect structures, such as 'Twenty-oneth of January', 'One month and half of holiday', 'When I have been in elementary class I study quite hard', and so on. However, in line with the philosophy behind the currently fashionable communicative approach to language teaching and learning, that the most important aspect of language is the ability to use it to communicate, Mikhail was promoted as he desired and essentially in line with his verbal communicative ability.

The weaknesses in grammatical competence were even more evident in Mikhail's written work. His own awareness of this was suddenly and rather uncomfortably brought home to him in his last week at school when he sat an IELTS (International English Language Testing System) practice test prior to sitting the exam itself the following week. Needing to get at least a level 6 in order to fulfil his (and his parents') ambition to enter university the following year, he was dismayed to discover that the practice test indicated a level considerably below what he needed.

According to his reported use on the *SILL*, Mikhail did not employ language learning strategies highly frequently (average = 3.2; Oxford, 1990). Mikhail gave only nine of the *SILL* items a rating of 5 ('always or almost always'). Of these nine, three (30%) are grouped in the *SILL* under the category of 'compensation' strategies, or strategies employed to make up for missing knowledge. Of the *plus* strategies reportedly used highly frequently by higher level students he gave a rating of 5 to only three, of which two related to the tolerance of ambiguity and one to the need to relax!

When asked whether he could suggest any reasons for the rapid progress he had made in his verbal communication skills, Mikhail said that he felt that watching TV (especially American comedy) and talking to friends (especially English-speaking friends) had been more important than formal study.

Mikhail complained that English grammar, especially the tense system, was difficult to come to terms with. As for strategies he might use to overcome the problem he rather dubiously suggested checking a grammar book, but then said he would be more likely to consult a friend.

Student Profile 5: Mikhail

Learner characteristics
Nationality: Russian   Sex: male   Age: 24
Motivation: further study/social

SILL results and progress/achievement
Average reported frequency of use: 3.2
Number of strategies rated 5
   ('always or almost always'):   9
Number of *base* strategies rated 5:   0
Number of *core* strategies rated 5:   5
Number of *plus* strategies rated 5:   3
Progress: 0.6 levels per month

Learning difficulties
• Grammar (especially tenses)

Key strategies
• Watching TV
• Talking to friends in English
• Consulting friends for answers to language questions

Ostensibly, further education was Mikhail's main reason for learning English – he was studying to be a lawyer. However, he himself did not consider this a particularly urgent motivation; he was doing it mainly to please his parents. For himself, he needed English mainly for social purposes such as drinking and going to parties. It was clear that for Mikhail, having a good time was his major reason for learning English, a motivation reminiscent of Wes's in the well-known study by Schmidt (1983). The problem for Mikhail seemed to be that the language required to survive well in the limited contexts of the language school and the parties he attended left him with a false sense of his own ability, the deficiencies in which suddenly became vividly apparent when he had to sit the IELTS examination, at which time all the terrifying spectres of parental expectations also suddenly resurfaced.

Faced with the probability of failing the qualification he needed to enter university and satisfy his parents, Mikhail said he wished he had put more work into building up his underlying knowledge base of English by consciously studying English grammar and vocabulary to underpin his admittedly considerable gains in fluency. Rather than blaming himself, however, Mikhail attributed his lack of success to the school and his teachers for failing to impose sufficient discipline!

In fact, when Mikhail sat the IELTS exam he actually scored only 4.5, well below the level he needed for university, and he had to endure the indignity (as he felt it) of being enrolled by his parents in a foundation programme which involved working on his English for another year before he was able to go on to university.

3.1.6 Yuki

Even less conspicuous than Mikhail by her progress as a language learner (0.25 levels per month) was Yuki, who, according to the *SILL*, reported the lowest average frequency of language learning strategy use of the interviewees (average = 2.1) and the lowest number of strategies rated 5 ('always or almost always', $N = 0$). When 44-year-old Yuki started her English language course, she had already been in New Zealand with her children on a visitor's visa for a year. Wanting to stay with her children, rather than having to return to Japan, leaving her children behind, she applied for a student visa, which meant that she was obliged to attend school. On the Oxford Placement Test (Allan, 1995) she scored 81, which is categorised as a 'minimal user' and she was placed in the lowest class.

For some time Yuki's attendance was very erratic. She or her children were often sick and she 'moved my house' four times. She was not easy to interview because she found it difficult to understand the questions and, when she understood, found it difficult to express what she wanted to say in English. The English she could manage was frequently extremely ungrammatical: 'I can't express myself very well English'.

After being warned of the possible consequences of breaching the conditions of her visa, Yuki's attendance became more regular. After 4 months she was moved to a mid-elementary class, and 3 months later to an upper elementary class. Her ability to communicate remained very low, however, often requiring the services of the Japanese counsellor to translate. The results of the monthly tests were also unspectacular. After nearly a year at the language school, and after nearly 2 years living in an English-speaking environment, Yuki was still only in the upper elementary class.

The most difficult aspects of learning English for Yuki were speaking and writing (production skills). She thought that using the telephone and writing long sentences might be useful strategies to help with these difficulties, although she said she did not actually use either of these. From a Japanese perspective, she found English grammar difficult, but was unable to suggest strategies for dealing with the difficulty.

Student Profile 6: Yuki

Learner characteristics
Nationality: Japanese   Sex: female   Age: 44
Motivation: children's education

SILL results and progress/achievement

Average reported frequency of use:	2.1
Number of strategies rated 5 ('always or almost always'):	0
Number of *base* strategies rated 5:	0
Number of *core* strategies rated 5:	0
Number of *plus* strategies rated 5:	0
Progress:	0.25 levels per month

Learning difficulties
• Speaking and writing
• Grammar

Key strategies
• *Reading easy books in English*

The only key strategy Yuki was aware of using was reading easy books in English. Yuki thought English was difficult to learn because 'my mind is blank', a condition which she put down to her age. Her motivation was her children's education, and she attended an English language school only because she needed a student visa. As such, her motivation to learn English appeared low and her progress was minimal.

3.1.7 Hiro

Although Yuki believed she was too old to learn English, she was far from the oldest student in the school. Hiro was a 64-year-old Japanese man who came to spend a month studying English. His entry test indicated that he was at pre-intermediate level, and he studied at this level throughout the month he spent at the school. He said he had spent seven years studying English, but 'that was a long time ago' during the war, when he believed he had been handicapped because there were no books, no paper, and he was taught by non-native speakers.

In spite of his age, Hiro was extremely well liked and respected by the younger students and he got on with them extremely well. As an older

Japanese person, however, especially as an older man, interacting with younger students (who in many cases were a lot more communicatively competent than he was) was fraught with cultural difficulties. They could not display superiority without being, in their terms, impolite, and he could not appear to be inferior without losing face in a way that they would all have found socially very difficult. Hiro was, therefore, acutely aware of the need, as an older learner, to develop effective strategies to cope with the social difficulties of interacting with students much younger than himself. One such strategy he used was to busy himself with his notebook when he found classroom communicative activities too threatening.

Student Profile 7: Hiro

Learner characteristics
Nationality: Japanese   Sex: male   Age: 64
Motivation: hobby/fun

SILL results and progress/achievement
Average reported frequency of use: 3.3
Number of strategies rated 5
   ('always or almost always'):   11
Number of *base* strategies rated 5:   0
Number of *core* strategies rated 5:   4
Number of *plus* strategies rated 5:   6
Progress: in the same class for the
                                            month he was at the school

Learning difficulties
- Grammar   • Vocabulary

Key strategies
- Reading newspapers   • Listening to radio and songs
- Watching movies   • Speaking only the target language
- Recording grammar and vocabulary in a notebook
- Learning language from the environment (e.g. posters, signs)
- Remembering new vocabulary by connecting it with something memorable
- Using 'face-saving' techniques such as avoiding threatening situations by becoming absorbed with note taking

---

This 'opting out' strategy, however, created some problems with classroom dynamics. His teacher was concerned that Hiro spent quite a lot of class time recording new grammar and making long lists of vocabulary in his notebook, and even complaining that the class was not given enough 'new' grammar and vocabulary. The teacher felt that vocabulary acquisition strategies such as these were not as useful as, for instance, interacting with other students and practising using the vocabulary they already knew.

The teacher also felt defensive at the suggestion that Hiro was perhaps discontented with her teaching. She reported that, although generally a delightful student, Hiro had a tendency to be a little rigid and formal in his approach to his learning. Understandable given his age and background, this was almost the only negative comment ever made about Hiro during his time at the school.

In addition to the avoidance and note-taking strategies already noted, Hiro said he found the most useful strategies for learning English were reading newspapers, listening to the radio and songs, going to movies, and noting language from the environment such as posters and signs. He felt it was useful to speak only the target language and to try to remember new vocabulary by connecting it with something memorable. As an example of this he mentioned remembering the word 'notorious' by connecting it to a politician who gained notoriety by paying an exorbitant price for a pair of silk boxer shorts.

As reported on the *SILL* questionnaire, Hiro did not employ language learning strategies at a high rate of frequency (average = 3.3; Oxford, 1990). He gave a rating of 5 to 11 of the SILL items, six of which were plus strategies (used highly frequently by higher level students but not by all students).

When asked his reasons for learning English Hiro said it was just a hobby. He felt that this was a good motivation for learning English, since being relaxed and unworried about the outcome would help him to automatically employ strategies to help him learn more effectively, such as picking up natural language from the environment. As he delightfully put it:

I have worked hard all my life. Now I am going to have some fun!

Although his course was too short for any firm conclusions to be drawn regarding rate of progress, and even though there was no difference in reported frequency of language learning strategy use between older and younger students, Hiro's case points to some interesting possible implications regarding the use of language learning strategies (such as 'face-saving' strategies) by the older learner, and suggests some possibly fruitful areas for further research especially designed to investigate age-related differences in strategy use.

3.1.8 May

In general, when students report a high average frequency of language learning strategy use there is also a high number of strategies used highly frequently. However, this is not always the case. May, for instance, reported highly frequent language learning strategy use (average = 3.6; Oxford, 1990) according to the *SILL*, but the numbers of strategies rated as 5 (used 'always or almost always') were relatively low ($N = 5$). An examination of her responses reveals an unusually high number of items rated 4 ('usually') compared with the others, which has the effect of increasing the average in spite of a low number of strategies used 'always or almost always'. This might possibly be an example of the 'highly valued modesty' referred to by Gu *et al.* (1995: 3) as typical of Asian students, creating a tendency to use the middle of a scale rather than the extremes.

At 35 years old, May was older than average for the school. On the results of her intake test, she was initially placed at pre-intermediate level when she arrived from Taiwan for a 6-month English course. In spite of her greater age, her cheerful, obliging personality meant that she fitted into her classes among generally much younger students without obvious difficulty. Indeed, her mature attitudes were an asset to the class and much appreciated by her teachers. Prior to leaving Taiwan she had worked for a trading company and hoped that better English would improve her job prospects, although she also wanted to travel and 'change my life'.

The most difficult aspect of learning English, according to May, was listening and speaking. The main reason for this, she said, is that the schooling system she was used to was very formal, with large classes and so 'we learned just reading and writing'. Even the reading and writing which she had learned in school presented problems for May. Her native language, of course, uses Chinese ideographs for writing which bear little or no relationship to the pronunciation, unlike languages such as Korean where there is a phonic correspondence with the written form of the word. Consequently, when asked to read English aloud from a text (such as a newspaper) in class, May often struggled to work out words she did not already know or even to produce an accurate version of words she did know (for instance, she might read 'complex' for 'complexity', 'learn' for 'learned', 'read' for 'reading', and so on).

For May, the complications of English grammar and the size and complexity of English vocabulary were also a challenge. Especially problematic was the tense system. Compared with Taiwanese verbal concepts, usually consisting of just one form with tense expressed by an adverbial ('I go yesterday', 'I go now', 'I go tomorrow'), she found the contortions of English tense structures extremely difficult to master. Added to this, the vast array of synonyms in English, all meaning more or less (but not quite) the same thing, was also a constant anxiety.

Another problem was gender differentiation, which does not exist in Chinese languages as it does in English. This helps to explain why Chinese students can say 'she' when talking of a man and be quite unaware of the incongruity. The fact that English speakers often find this kind of mistake amusing and are likely to laugh can be a problem in itself because of the Asian fear of 'losing face'. This was something May said she had learnt: it is natural to make mistakes, and she tried not to be afraid of doing so.

According to May, cultural differences manifested themselves not just in what people did but in how they thought: 'They have different logic', as she put it. Although I came back to this rather intriguing statement several times during the interview, attempts to get her to explain what she meant or to provide examples proved fruitless, perhaps in itself an example of our 'different logics'. I, as a European, expected to be able to analyse and rationalise such a statement. For May, the insight itself was enough. Perhaps, though, her anxiety over cultural differences might help to explain the rating of 5 that she gave to the strategy *I try to learn the culture of English speakers*.

May's reported strategies for coping with her many difficulties in learning English included making conscious efforts to maximise her exposure to English. She went to movies, watched TV, listened to tapes and went on school activities to increase her opportunities to meet native speakers. When she went to restaurants and cafes she listened to the English being spoken around her and tried to 'copy their sentence'. She tried to make friends with non-Taiwanese, endeavoured to learn 'many vocabularies' and tried not to worry about making mistakes.

At the end of 6 months May had progressed from pre-intermediate to advanced (four levels). At this point she decided not to go back to Taiwan and enrolled spasmodically at the school. She decided, however, that she did not want to have to cope with the anxiety of working at advanced level and so asked to be put back to upper intermediate, explaining: 'I am tired. I have been here a long time. I don't want to pressure.'

In fact, it was probably true that upper intermediate was a more suitable level for May, since, although communicatively she had become very competent (even on the phone, which most English language students find very difficult), and although, when she studied, she could do well in tests (according to which she was promoted), her grammar remained unreliable to say the least and she did not seem to have the will to work on it as would have been necessary for the improvements needed in this area.

Student Profile 8: May

Learner characteristics
Nationality: Taiwanese   Sex: female   Age: 35
Motivation: job/travel/change

SILL results and progress/achievement

Average reported frequency of use:	3.6
Number of strategies rated 5 ('always or almost always'):	5
Number of *base* strategies rated 5:	0
Number of *core* strategies rated 5:	3
Number of *plus* strategies rated 5:	2
Progress:	0.66 levels per month

Learning difficulties
- Listening and speaking
- Cultural differences
- Grammar (especially tenses and sex differentiation)
- Vocabulary (especially synonyms)

Key strategies
- Listening to and copying native speakers
- Making non-Taiwanese friends
- Working consciously to expand vocabulary
- Trying not to worry about mistakes
- Maximising exposure to English, for instance, by going to movies, watching TV, listening to tapes and going on school activities

---

So May stayed for another 6 months, sometimes at school, sometimes not, but picking up a lot of English just from being in a native-speaking environment. However, her unwillingness to push herself meant that she never quite got to be as good as she might have been, and the interference from her own language meant that her spontaneous utterances remained full of grammatical inaccuracies right to the end when, by way of explaining why she was finally going home, she told me: 'My uncle she want me come back Taiwan'!

3.1.9 Kang

While May, even with a high reported average frequency of strategy use, failed to make particularly good progress, Kang, with less than highly frequent average reported strategy usage (average = 3.2; Oxford, 1990) and the lowest number ($N = 3$) of *SILL* strategy items rated 5 except for Yuki, still managed to make good progress (one level per month). Like Yuki, Kang was in his forties, but apart from their age, they could hardly have been more different.

When the 41-year-old Korean first arrived, he was initially placed in the lowest elementary class. At this point, Kang's knowledge of English was negligible, although he was evidently fluent in Japanese, so was not inexperienced as a language learner.

Although he had left his wife and young children in Korea and obviously missed them, Kang settled single-mindedly to his work. Like Kira, he spent long hours in the self-study room revising lessons, doing homework and listening to tapes, especially pronunciation tapes, which was the area he found most difficult.

An interesting theory that he had was that pronunciation is affected by the food we eat, because different kinds of foods require different movements of the mouth and tongue. Accordingly, while abroad, he eschewed his traditional Korean diet (a major sacrifice!) and ate local food instead, a strategy aimed at helping him to get his mouth around the sounds of English.

Although, according to his *SILL*, Kang did not make highly frequent use of language learning strategies, he nevertheless mentioned quite a list of key strategies during his interview, including listening to the radio, watching TV and going to the movies. Kang said he consulted a text book for vocabulary, sentence structure and grammar, and used a notebook to write down language he picked up from signs, notices and advertising. He kept a dictionary with him at all times and listened to people talking around him.

Unlike some other students who believed that 'good' or 'bad' teaching was responsible for their success or otherwise, Kang accepted realistically that some teachers are going to be better than others, and that some teachers' styles may affect the way some students learn. Therefore, he believed, students must change their attitudes and strategies if they are to make the best of the teacher and succeed. This acceptance of the responsibility for his own learning was another characteristic he shared with Kira and with fellow Korean, Kim.

Although age is often considered to be a disadvantage when learning language, Kang was more successful than many of the much younger

---

Student Profile 9: Kang

Learner characteristics
Nationality: Korean   Sex: male   Age: 41
Motivation: better job and better lifestyle for his family

SILL results and progress/achievement
Average reported frequency of use: 3.2
Number of strategies rated 5
    ('always or almost always'):   3
Number of *base* strategies rated 5:   2
Number of *core* strategies rated 5:   1
Number of *plus* strategies rated 5:   0
Progress: 1.0 levels per month

Learning difficulties
• Pronunciation

Key strategies
• Revising lessons   • Doing homework   • Listening to tapes
• Eating western food   • Watching TV   • Listening to the radio
• Going to the movies   • Using a dictionary
• Listening to people   • Adapting to the
    talking   teacher
• Using a textbook for vocabulary, sentence structure and grammar
• Noting language from signs, notices and advertising in a notebook

---

students with whom he studied. By the end of his 7-month course Kang was working in the advanced class, although difficulties remained with typical Korean pronunciation problems such as r/l and f/p discrimination, in spite of 7 months of Western tucker! It is possible that previous language learning experience (Japanese) may have played a part in Kang's success. He was also able to detail a wide repertoire of language learning strategies which he used, in spite of not reporting a high frequency of strategy usage on the *SILL* items.

Asked why he thought he had made such good progress, Kang replied, 'My heart is 100% want to learn'. He wanted to learn English in order to improve his job prospects so that he could provide better opportunities for his family. This strong motivation showed itself in the consistent focus which he brought to his work, in the disciplined and thorough way he went about his study and in his keen awareness of the importance of strategies for learning.

3.1.10 Lily

Motivation, however, is not necessarily constant, as was exemplified by Lily. When Lily arrived from Switzerland with her husband, they planned to immigrate. She was 26 years old and her native language was Swiss German. She had been a primary school teacher in Switzerland, and she wanted to improve her already very good English in order to get a position as a teacher and to strengthen her eligibility for immigration. She therefore enrolled in a class studying for the CPE, a very high level examination close to native-speaker standard. In the same class as Nina, Lily began the course as a very hard-working student, focused on her goal. In fact, she scored higher than Nina on the initial placement test. She was cheerful and positive in class, keen to participate in all activities, meticulous with her homework, and also willing to use her skills as a teacher to support other students.

According to her *SILL*, Lily reported using language learning strategies at a high level of frequency (average = 3.7; Oxford, 1990). She also used a large number ($N = 15$) of strategies 'always or almost always' (rating = 5). She gave a rating of 5 to nine of the *plus* strategies (strategies reportedly used highly frequently by advanced students but not by all).

Communicating in spoken English, Lily believed, was the most important strategy since it provided the opportunity for repetition which her experience as a teacher had indicated was important for learning. As she put it: 'You only learn something when you do it several times.'

Lily found grammar, especially tenses, the most difficult aspect of learning English, and she believed that German speakers generally found the English tense system difficult because the patterns of German tenses are different from those of English. She believed in consciously studying grammar and looking up points she was unsure of, but said she found it difficult to bring the theory and the use together. A personal difficulty which she had was that she lived with her husband and also Swiss flatmates, so inevitably the tendency was to speak Swiss German at home. She felt this placed her at a disadvantage compared with other students (such as her classmate Nina) who lived in an English-speaking environment.

According to Lily, if a high level of proficiency was the goal, it was important not to translate word for word, but to develop a 'feeling' for the language. She acknowledged that this was easier for Europeans, whose languages were often related to English, than for Asian students who were often more dependent on dictionaries because their languages were too different from English to make it possible for them to guess when unsure.

Another key strategy she reported using was reading in English, often voluminous novels. She said she found books more useful than TV because the reader had more control over a book and a book could be reviewed as required. Lily believed that how much students learnt depended on how much they wanted to learn (that is, their motivation) and on the intensity of their desire to succeed, which would affect their choice of strategies.

In the light of the last comment, an interesting change occurred in Lily about half way through the course. At this point she and her husband decided to apply for permanent residence, so suddenly she urgently needed proof of her English level. With the CPE exam still some weeks away, she decided to sit for IELTS, an examination which can be sat at short notice with the results available in about a fortnight. After some hasty tuition in IELTS techniques she got 8.5, which put her close to native-speaker level (the top score being 9).

Student Profile 10: Lily

Learner characteristics
Nationality: Swiss   Sex: female   Age: 26
Motivation: immigration

SILL results and progress/achievement
Average reported frequency of use: 3.7
Number of strategies rated 5
   ('always or almost always'):   15
Number of *base* strategies rated 5:   1
Number of *core* strategies rated 5:   4
Number of *plus* strategies rated 5:   9
Achievement: obtained 8.5 in IELTS
                                              and passed CPE

Learning difficulties
• Grammar (especially tenses)

Key strategies
• Communicating in spoken English   • Repetition
• Consciously studying grammar   • Reading in English
• Not translating word for word

Lily was delighted with her IELTS result, but when the permanent residence application was declined she was bitterly disappointed. She was less cheerful and positive in class and she often complained of being tired. The written work she handed in had more errors than previously, possibly indicating less time and attention spent on homework, and when she made an error she was more likely to repeat it rather than learn from her mistakes. She rarely asked questions in class, and if she were asked a question she was much more likely than previously to answer incorrectly.

To really add to the difficulties Lily appeared to be having at this time, her mother came out from Switzerland about 2 weeks before the Proficiency exam. Lily became very homesick and lacked focus on her studies right at this critical time. She got a C pass in CPE, which was satisfactory, especially in such a high-level exam, but in the light of her initial level and the 8.5 she got in the IELTS exam, she might have been expected to do better. (As previously stated, Nina, whose score was lower than Lily's on the initial placement test, got an A pass.)

There is a postscript to the story, however. Lily came in to see me at school about 18 months later. She had a new baby in a pram and looked glowingly contented. She told me that after finishing her course she had had several relief teaching jobs before she became pregnant. A few days previous to her visit she and her husband had finally been given permanent residence. When the baby was older she was planning to apply for a teaching position, so she was looking forward positively to the future. She was, in fact, back to her old, cheerful, positive self, and her English was excellent! I am not sure I want to go so far as to seriously suggest having a baby or immigrating as good strategies for learning English, but Lily's case would seem to support Gardner and MacIntyre's (1993) proposal that attitudes interact with strategies to affect success in language learning.

3.2 What Can We Learn From the Interviews?

In order to facilitate the comparison of one student with another, the *SILL* results of the 10 selected student interviewees are set out in Table 3.1. Items rated 5 are shaded for emphasis. For abbreviated strategy statements, refer to Table 2.1, or for full *SILL* statements, refer to Oxford (1990). The *base* strategies reportedly used more frequently by elementary students than by advanced students are marked '–' in the '*SILL*' column. The core items which were reportedly used highly frequently (average = 3.5 or above; Oxford, 1990) across all students are marked 'c' in the '*SILL*' column. The *plus* items reportedly used highly frequently by advanced students in addition to those

Table 3.1 Reported frequency ratings of language learning strategy use according to the *SILL* by interviewees 1–10 with progress in terms of levels per month

SILL	Nina	Kira	Fernando	Kim	Mikhail	Yuki	Hiro	May	Kang	Lily
1+	4	3	4	3	3	2	4	3	2	5
2	3	5	5	5	3	2	3	3	3	4
3–	2	5	1	4	4	2	3	4	4	4
4	2	5	3	3	4	2	3	3	3	4
5	1	3	1	3	3	2	3	3	2	2
6–	1	2	3	1	1	3	3	2	2	2
7–	1	2	3	1	1	2	2	2	4	1
8–	3	4	4	5	1	3	3	3	4	3
9–	5	3	4	3	4	2	4	4	4	3
10+	5	5	1	4	3	2	3	4	3	4
11c	5	5	1	5	5	3	3	4	4	5
12c	4	5	4	4	4	2	3	4	2	4
13	3	3	4	4	3	2	3	4	3	3
14+	5	4	4	5	4	2	2	4	3	5
15c	5	3	4	5	5	3	5	3	4	5
16+	5	2	3	5	4	3	3	4	4	5
17	5	4	3	4	1	2	2	2	3	3
18+	5	3	5	5	3	2	5	4	4	3
19+	5	3	4	4	4	2	5	4	2	4
20+	3	5	3	3	4	2	5	4	4	4
21+	5	3	1	3	1	2	3	3	4	4
22+	3	2	5	3	4	2	2	4	1	5
23	2	3	3	4	5	2	3	4	4	3
24+	5	4	2	4	5	2	5	3	2	5
25c	4	4	5	5	3	2	2	4	4	3
26–	4	4	3	3	4	2	4	2	4	3
27+	5	3	5	5	5	2	5	2	1	5
28	3	4	5	2	4	2	5	3	2	2
29c	5	4	5	5	5	2	4	5	4	4
30c	3	5	4	3	4	2	4	3	3	4
31c	4	5	5	5	4	2	4	4	4	4
32c	3	5	5	5	5	2	5	5	4	4
33c	3	5	5	5	4	2	5	4	4	3
34–	2	5	5	3	1	2	4	4	3	5
35+	3	5	4	3	1	2	3	4	3	3

(continued)

Table 3.1 (*Continued*) Reported frequency ratings of language learning strategy use according to the *SILL* by interviewees 1–10 with progress in terms of levels per month

SILL	Nina	Kira	Fernando	Kim	Mikhail	Yuki	Hiro	May	Kang	Lily
36+	3	5	4	5	1	2	3	4	3	5
37	4	5	4	5	2	2	3	4	2	5
38c	4	5	3	4	5	2	5	4	5	3
39+	4	5	5	2	5	2	5	4	2	4
40+	5	5	5	3	2	2	4	5	4	3
41	3	2	3	3	3	2	1	1	2	2
42	2	4	3	3	3	2	2	3	2	4
43−	1	1	1	2	1	2	1	4	5	1
44−	2	3	2	1	4	2	1	4	5	3
45c	4	4	5	3	4	2	4	5	4	5
46+	3	3	5	2	1	2	4	4	2	3
47+	4	3	5	5	4	2	1	4	3	5
48+	3	3	5	4	3	2	4	4	3	4
49c	4	5	5	5	4	2	4	4	3	5
50+	4	4	3	5	3	2	4	5	4	5
Av.	3.5	3.8	3.7	3.7	3.2	2.1	3.3	3.6	3.2	3.7
No.	14	19	18	18	9	0	11	5	3	15
Base	1	1	1	1	0	0	0	0	2	1
Core	3	8	7	8	5	0	4	3	1	4
Plus	9	6	8	7	3	0	6	2	0	9
Ach/ prog	CPE	2.0	1.2	1.2	0.6	.25	0	.66	1.0	CPE

used highly frequently across all students are marked ' + ' in the '*SILL*' column.

At the bottom of the table there is a summary of the following key statistics:

Av.   the average reported frequency of *SILL* strategy use

No.   the number of *SILL* strategies rated 5 (always or almost always)

Base   the number of *base* strategies rated 5

Core   the number of *core* strategies rated 5

Plus   the number of *plus* strategies rated 5

Ach/prog   the achievement in terms of exams passed or the rate of progress in levels per month

3.2.1 Strategy use

It should be noted that the six students who progressed through one or more levels per month or who passed their examinations (Nina, Kira, Fernando, Kim, Kang, Lily) were all able to identify key strategies they used to address the difficulties they were having with learning English. Nina, for instance, lived in an environment where English was spoken in order to work on her difficulties with speaking in English. Kira read newspapers to improve his ability to read in English. Fernando asked for help when he could not understand native speakers. Kim used a notebook to record idioms so that she could review them later. Kang ate Western food to help with pronunciation. And Lily made a conscious effort to learn the problematic rules of English grammar.

Compared with these students who were all successful in terms of progress made or exams passed, Mikhail was only able to tentatively suggest as a key strategy asking a friend to help with grammar difficulties, and the only key strategy suggested by Yuki (reading easy books in English) did not address the difficulties of which she was aware (speaking and writing in English and learning grammar). Although Hiro said he recorded grammar and vocabulary in a notebook in order to help him with his difficulties with these areas of English, these strategies were perhaps not always used appropriately, since they often appeared to be employed in order to avoid interacting with other members of the class. May's case is somewhat different in that, although she reported using quite a list of strategies to cope with her difficulties, the main problem seemed to be a lack of real motivation to succeed in learning English.

If the key strategies reportedly used by the six students who progressed through one or more levels per month or who passed their exams (Nina, Kira, Fernando, Kim, Kang, Lily) are brought together, the following list emerges:

- *Watching TV/movies*
- *Reading newspapers/magazines, novels/stories*
- *Listening to tapes/radio/people talking*
- *Working through text books*
- *Using a dictionary*
- *Using the teacher*
- *Noting language in the environment (e.g. signs)*
- *Revising*
- *Learning in an English-speaking environment*
- *Doing homework*
- *Manipulating position in class*

- *Organising time out*
- *Learning from correction*
- *Keeping a notebook (e.g. for vocabulary)*
- *Spending a lot of time studying*
- *Repetition*
- *Talking to people in English*
- *Asking for help*
- *Consciously working on grammar*
- *Learning language in chunks*
- *Not translating word for word*
- *Consciously working on lack of self-confidence*

Kang's strategy of eating Western food, although it was made in all seriousness, was not included in this list, since it seemed rather too idiosyncratic to be the kind of strategy other students might like to copy, and also since there was little evidence that it had produced the desired results (that is, an improvement in pronunciation).

Of these key strategies, some are represented in the *SILL* (for instance, watching TV, reading in English), but many others are not included in the *SILL* (such as manipulating position in class, learning language in chunks, organising time out, working on self-confidence). The existence of what Lunt (2000) calls 'non*SILL* strategies' serves, as she points out, to emphasise the individuality of learners, and to remind us that, although we can learn a lot from an overall perspective by using an instrument such as the *SILL*, language learning strategy use at the individual level may not always be reflected in the overall view, as this list of key strategies demonstrates.

Many of the key strategies relate to the use of resources (TV, tapes, movies, people, the environment, newspapers, magazines, stories, novels, radio, text books, dictionaries, the teacher). Very few such strategies are listed in the *SILL*. The higher level students, however, appear to be very aware of the need to use available resources as a strategy to learn more effectively.

Strategies

The data obtained from these interviews accord with the findings in Chapter 2 and reinforce the idea that, in general, successful students frequently use a large repertoire of strategies of various types.

In general, then, it would seem that the successful students in this study reported the use of a large repertoire of frequently used strategies of various types. Another aspect of strategy use which is not easy to assess is how this repertoire is used together, or orchestrated. As Anderson (2008: 101) comments, 'effective strategy use does not occur in isolation ... [it is important to] ... integrate the use of various strategies in a positive way'. Although it is intuitively easy to agree with this comment, attempts to group strategies together, for instance, by means of factor analyses of the *SILL* and the *English Language Learning Strategy Inventory* (*ELLSI* – Griffiths, 2003b), have not proved very useful (see Section 1.7). It almost seems as though effective strategy orchestration is such an individual phenomenon, which is also dependent on situational and target factors, that attempts to quantify it are not very productive. However, since it is an important question, especially in the light of students who do not appear to be able to do it well (e.g. Porte, 1988; Vann & Abraham, 1990), further research would seem to be warranted.

The pedagogical implications of this conclusion will be discussed in Chapter 4.

3.2.2 Motivation

Motivation has been discussed at some length in relation to successful language learning and strategy use in Section 1.4.4. As might have been predicted from the quantitative results reported in Chapter 2, an examination of the interview data suggests that success in language learning is linked to motivation, as discovered also by Politzer and McGroarty (1985), Ehrman and Oxford (1989) and Oxford and Nyikos (1989) and considered at some length by Dornyei (2001) and Ushioda (2008). As Cohen and Dornyei (2002: 172) comment: 'Motivation is often seen as the key learner variable because without it, nothing much happens. Indeed, most other learner variables presuppose the existence of at least some degree of motivation.'

The students who progressed by one or more levels per month during the time of their courses (Kira, Fernando, Kim, Kang) and Nina (who gained an A pass in the CPE) were unwavering in their focus on their studies and wanted to learn English either for further study and/or future employment. All of them except Kang reported a high average frequency of *SILL* strategy use, a high number of strategies rated 5, and a high number of *plus* strategies (explained in Chapter 2). Even Kang, as has already been discussed, reported a high number of key language learning strategies of his own.

Compared with highly focused and successful students like Nina, Kira, Fernando, Kim and Kang (whose motivation for learning English was essentially vocational), Yuki used her English study as a means of staying with her children, May wanted it to 'change her life' and for Hiro it was a 'hobby'. Although she passed her exam, Lily's motivation wavered during her course, which may well have been reflected in her lower than expected grade in the CPE, and Mikhail's motivation, like that of Wes (Schmidt, 1983), was essentially social, and therefore lacked the dimension of urgency which characterised the more successful students.

Motivation

Results of the individual interviews accord with previous findings (Section 2.5.1) that motivation is an important factor in successful language learning and is likely to be reflected in strategy use.

The pedagogical implications of this conclusion will be discussed in Chapter 4.

3.2.3 Nationality

Nationality has also been discussed as a possible factor in successful language learning and strategy use (see Section 1.4.4) and was mentioned as a possible factor in language learning by Kim, Nina and May. Kim, from Korea, felt that Europeans had an advantage, not only because the languages are similar but also because the 'thinking' is similar. Nina, from Germany, agreed that she had an advantage when learning English because of the similarities of the languages. May provided a number of examples of the difficulties Chinese students may encounter when learning English, and she displayed first-language interference to the end.

Nationality

An important finding from the interviews indicates that, although European students appear to have an advantage over Asian students when learning English, Asian students can be very successful learners of English, especially if they are well motivated and frequently employ well-developed strategy repertoires.

Nevertheless, the interview data indicated that, although European students appear to have an advantage over Asian students when learning English, some Asian students manage to study English to a high level of proficiency, a successful outcome possibly related to the patterns of language learning strategies employed. This is highlighted particularly by comparing Kim from Korea and Fernando from Argentina. They were initially placed at the same level (mid-elementary) for a course of the same length (5 months). They reported the same frequency of strategy use (average = 3.7) and the same number of strategies rated 5 ($N = 18$). They both finished their courses at advanced level. Although she was Asian and he was European, and although there were differences in the types of strategies they reported using, their rates of progress and overall strategy patterns were remarkably similar.

The pedagogical implications of this conclusion will be discussed in Chapter 4.

3.2.4 Age

Although often considered a significant factor in successful language learning (for more details, see Section 1.4.4), an analysis of the quantitative data reported in Section 2.5.4 revealed no statistically significant differences for class level or reported frequency of language learning strategy use according to age. However, there were indications from the interview data that older students might go about their learning in ways which are qualitatively different from the approaches employed by younger students. For Hiro, for instance, saving face in front of younger students was obviously important in terms of his status within the class and how comfortable both he and they felt in the classroom. As a result, he needed space to apply his own strategies. Kang's strategy patterns were highly idiosyncratic, reflecting, perhaps, the way his strategy repertoire and thinking had developed over the years; however, his strategies were largely effective for him, even if not reflected in standard strategy inventories.

Age

Although age is often believed to reduce language learning ability, the interviews reinforce the findings in Chapter 2 that well-motivated and strategically active older learners can learn language successfully.

Although there are some interesting possibilities for research in this area (especially given an ageing student population reported by many learning institutions in many places), generally the failure to discover significant differences in proficiency according to age supports Ehrman and Oxford's (1990: 319) conclusion that there is 'optimism for older learners'. Certainly, students like Kang demonstrate that it is possible for older learners to learn very effectively.

The pedagogical implications of this conclusion will be discussed in Chapter 4.

3.2.5 Sex

The question of the role of sex differences in successful language learning and strategy use has also been discussed in Sections 1.4.4 and 2.5.4. Although contrary to much common belief, the results of the quantitative analyses in Chapter 2 regarding language learning achievement and strategy use indicated that there were no significant differences according to sex.

Sex

The qualitative data from the interviews also accords with the quantitative questionnaire data from Chapter 2 that there does not appear to be any real difference in language learning ability according to sex for motivated and strategically active learners.

Indeed, sex does not really seem to be an issue with most students, and the only one of the interviewees who mentioned it was Nina, who commented that most people felt that learning language was 'normal' for a woman, and she felt this was an advantage since she did not have to fight other people's prejudices.

This is not entirely to say, of course, that male and female students are equal in a classroom. Sunderland (1998), for instance, notes that girls are much quieter in mixed classrooms than boys (again, contrary to much common belief). Nevertheless, these social differences do not seem to be reflected in achievement or strategic behaviour.

The pedagogical implications of this conclusion will be discussed in Chapter 4.

3.2.6 Style

Although learning style was not directly investigated in the course of the study reported in this chapter, an examination of the interview data suggests considerable differences in the style preferences of the individual learners. Fernando, for instance, was highly interactive and sociable, whereas Kang spent long periods of time revising and doing homework on his own. Hiro was another with a somewhat solitary learning style, often focused on his notebook, a characteristic preference that may possibly have been related to his age. Nina, Kim and Lily were rather introspective in their style and they all used reading as an effective means of obtaining language input, whereas Kira (who didn't really enjoy reading) preferred sport and other activities for interacting with native speakers as a means of promoting his knowledge of English. But these learners were all successful, underlining the fact that learning style is a very individual matter.

Learning style

Although learners appear to favour certain types of activities according to their learning style, no particular learning style appears to be more likely to lead to success than any other.

The essential conclusion would seem to be that students should be allowed to study according to the style with which they feel comfortable and which produces the best results for themselves.

The pedagogical implications of this conclusion will be discussed in Chapter 4.

3.2.7 Personality

Personality is a specialised area which the data reported in Chapter 2 do not really address in any detail or by using any instrument designed to focus on personality characteristics. Furthermore, no in-depth personality testing was done to complement the interviews.

Personality

Somewhat contrary to expectations, Ehrman (2008) discovered that introverted personalities were the most successful learners in her study. Nevertheless, although personality might have some effect on strategy choice, overall there does not seem to be any particular personality which is more strongly typical of good language learners than others.

On a superficial level, however, it is interesting to note that the best language learner in terms of the highest level of achievement (an A pass in the CPE) was Nina, who had quite a shy personality, although not unfriendly. Kang and Kim also kept to themselves, but nevertheless made very good progress in their language learning. None of these three excellent learners would be considered an extrovert according to the common understanding of the term. Nevertheless, other successful learners, such as Kira and Fernando, appeared to be quite extroverted, and used strategies such as playing sport and speaking to others in English to improve their language abilities. Highly sociable Mikhail, however, was not highly successful in spite of his outgoing and highly sociable personality. It is possible, of course, that external behaviour in the cases of these students might not accurately reflect the inner characteristics underlying them.

In fact, there is not enough data from the interviews to enable any firm conclusions to be drawn regarding the interviewees' personalities, but the relationships among personality, strategies and success in language learning remain an interesting area for further research. For the moment, observations from the interviews would seem to accord with Ehrman's (2008) conclusion that good language learners are not limited to a particular personality type.

The pedagogical implications of this conclusion will be discussed in Chapter 4.

3.2.8 Autonomy

Autonomy is another area which neither the data reported in Chapter 2 nor the interviews address in detail. Nevertheless, if we examine the data with a view to investigating possible indications of autonomy, there are a few interesting observations which might be used to suggest further research.

Kira, for instance, believed that students need to make a positive effort if they are to be successful. Kira was a very active strategy user, especially the metacognitive strategies itemised in the *SILL*.

Autonomy

The interviews would seem to suggest that, in general, successful learners are autonomous and capable of regulating their own learning and that they use strategies in order to do this.

Kim also believed that learning is basically up to the student, who should study 'steadily and with patience'. The highly frequent ratings that she also gave to many of the *SILL*'s metacognitive strategies suggest that she believed in taking charge of her own learning.

Kang was another who believed that students must not be overly dependent on the teacher but must adapt attitudes and strategies if they are to learn successfully. As has already been noted, although Kang did not report highly frequent use of the *SILL* strategies, he could identify a large number of strategies of his own.

All three of these students exercised autonomy and accepted responsibility for their own study. They regulated their own learning, and all three were successful in terms of progress through the levels of the school.

In contrast, Yuki infrequently used very few strategies. In terms of volitional competence, she might be described as displaying learned helplessness since she believed she was too old to learn language, a condition which she saw as beyond her control. She made more or less no apparent effort to accept responsibility for her own learning, and it would seem possible that this lack of autonomy might be a contributing factor to her minimal progress in language learning.

The pedagogical implications of this conclusion will be discussed in Chapter 4.

3.2.9 Beliefs

Although the interviews did not examine learner beliefs directly, it is notable that Yuki, who was the most unsuccessful of the interviewees, believed she was too old to learn language, and she made minimal use of language learning strategies. Did this negative belief contribute to her lack of success? This question becomes especially relevant when it is considered that, although Yuki blamed her age, Kang, who was of a similar age, used many quite idiosyncratic strategies and did well in spite of his age. And even Hiro, who was considerably older, actually did quite well, and would probably have done even better with more time. In other words, it may well have been Yuki's beliefs about her age rather than age itself which were the problem.

Beliefs

Although beliefs are a relatively stable learner characteristic, it would seem that successful learners are able, at least to some extent, to adapt their beliefs to the requirements of their situation and to adopt effective strategies accordingly. In addition, they need to believe in themselves as equal to the learning challenge and also they need to believe that the learning task is worthwhile.

The pedagogical implications of this conclusion will be discussed in Chapter 4.

3.2.10 Aptitude

An examination of the interviews reported in this chapter does not really seem to throw much light on the question of aptitude. We have no way of knowing, for instance, whether Nina did well because of natural ability, or whether Yuki did not succeed because of aptitude deficiencies. Intuition would suggest that the main reason Nina did well was because she wanted to, and that the reverse is true of Yuki. But then, maybe natural aptitude contributed to Nina's motivation and may also have affected her choice of strategies? Further research using some aptitude measure as a baseline is required before anything at all conclusive could be said on this subject.

Aptitude

Although, intuitively, aptitude might be a strong predictor of success in language learning, the ability to measure the construct reliably remains problematic and, anyway, application of such measurements continues to be highly controversial. As a result, the relationship between aptitude and strategies remains under-researched.

The pedagogical implications of this conclusion will be discussed in Chapter 4.

3.2.11 Affect

As can be seen from the numerous sub-headings under the topic of affect, there has been considerable interest in the concept over the years. In spite of this, affect is often invisible when it comes to discussions of effective language learning. Of the *plus* strategies, only two relate to affect (Item 39: *I try to relax when afraid of using English* and Item 40: *I encourage myself to speak even when afraid*).

In the case of the interviews reported in this chapter, affect was mentioned directly only twice. Kim reported that she did not worry too much about feelings since it was more important to 'keep your mind on your work'. Kira, however, was more aware of the need to attend to his affective needs and to relax by playing sport. This is an interesting area, but more research is required in order to explore which of these positions is more realistic (perhaps Kim actually does employ more strategies to manage her affective states than she entirely realises) or productive in terms of learning outcomes.

Of the interviewees, it is perhaps May, who chose to work at a level below the one to which her test results entitled her, who most clearly demonstrates the effects of **anxiety**. The effect of positive attitudes can be seen in the cases of Nina, Kira, Fernando, Kim, Hiro and Kang, while Mikhail's and Yuki's negative attitudes may well have contributed to their lack of success.

In this study, the successful students (for instance, Kira, Kim, Kang) believed in their ability to control their own learning. Yuki, however, **attributed** her failure to her age, a factor which was beyond her control.

If we think of the interviews in this study, perhaps the one which most strongly suggests a possible relationship between **empathy** and successful learning might be Lily. When Lily thought her immigration application was likely to be successful, at which point we might hypothesise that her desire to empathise with the citizens of her new country and the language they spoke would have been high, she was outstandingly successful in her exam (*IELTS*). After the rejection of her application, however, when empathy levels might well have been lower, she was less successful.

Of the interviewees, there were two who mentioned the issue of **inhibition** directly. Fernando said he was willing to learn from correction (although, in fact, he often did not listen to corrections when they were offered). May said she tried not to be afraid of losing face when she made mistakes (although, by implication, she was worried about losing face, which may have contributed to her preference for working at a lower level than she was capable of – she was less likely to make mistakes there).

In terms of **self-concept**, Nina judged herself to be lacking in **self-confidence**, especially in relation to her speaking skills. She was, nevertheless, a highly successful student, both before and during the course, which may well have provided her with underlying **self-esteem** and positive **self-image**.

Affect

Affect has long been recognised as an important factor in successful language learning, and many facets of the affect phenomenon have been identified and investigated, including anxiety, attribution, empathy, inhibition and various dimensions of self-concept. Two affective strategies are included among the *plus* strategies, suggesting that, although learners may not always want to acknowledge, or even be aware of, the role of affect in their learning, affect is, nevertheless, important to successful learning.

Although **self-efficacy** was not directly researched in the current study, it is probably reasonable to assume that the successful interviewees believed they could do it. Yuki, however, did not believe she could do it, and she didn't. Some interesting question marks, however, might hang over the likes of Mikhail and May. If they had been asked whether they would be successful, I hypothesise that Mikhail would have said 'yes', whereas May would have said 'no'. And yet Mikhail was not successful, although May could have been if she had been willing to invest more effort. This potential gap between self-perceptions of efficacy and the actual level of achievement might be an interesting direction for further research.

The pedagogical implications of this conclusion will be discussed in Chapter 4.

3.2.12 Identity

Obviously, uniqueness of identity applies to all of our interviewees. They all had their own reasons for being at the school, their own personalities, backgrounds and dreams for the future. We could probably say that, for those who were successful in their studies, they saw English as contributing positively to their sense of identity, whether that was in the area of improved job status and/or income (Nina, Kira, Fernando, Kim), as a successful provider for a family (Kang), as a respected elder member of the school (and probably wider) community (Hiro), or as a successful immigrant (as Lily ultimately succeeded in becoming). It should also be noted, however, that patterns of strategy use were far from identical among these successful learners, leading, perhaps, to the conclusion that strategy use is determined by individual identity.

Of those who were not successful students, Yuki's identity was not tied up with being a successful learner of English: she was a Japanese housewife and mother and that was all she wanted to be. As for Mikhail, his identity as a 'party animal' was central to his sense of self and to his beliefs about what made life worthwhile: having to learn English was really just a nuisance which exacerbated his hangovers. Neither Yuki nor Mikhail were highly frequent strategy users.

May was more ambivalent about her identity, which might help to explain the somewhat unusual pattern of her strategy use, according to which, although she reported using strategies highly frequently (average = 3.6), only five strategy items were given the maximum rating of 5 (always or almost always). In fact, May really wanted to 'change her life', in other words, to adopt a new identity, different from the office worker persona that she brought with her from Taiwan. In the end, however, she had to go back, and this appeared to affect the level of investment that she was prepared to put into her studies.

Identity

A learner's identity is constructed from a potentially vast array of variables, a number of which have been dealt with in this chapter. It would seem possible that this complex identity structure might contribute to determining individual strategy use.

The pedagogical implications of this conclusion will be discussed in Chapter 4.

3.2.13 Investment

As previously noted, Yuki and Mikhail, the least successful of the interviewees, had low levels of strategic investment. Most of the others reported high levels of strategic activity, although it should be remembered that both Hiro and Kang used strategies which were not listed on the *SILL*.

Investment

Investment in language learning refers to the amount of time, attention and effort a learner is prepared to 'spend' learning language. The level of reported strategy use may well be a useful indicator of the extent of a learner's willingness to invest in the language learning enterprise.

The pedagogical implications of this conclusion will be discussed in Chapter 4.

3.3 Conclusion

The findings from the quantitative data reported in Chapter 2 indicated that higher level students reported highly frequent use (average = 3.5 or above; Oxford, 1990) of a large number of language learning strategies, and that they may favour the use of certain types of strategies. An analysis of the qualitative interview data indicates that:

(1) Most of the students who progressed to higher class levels or who passed the exams for which they were preparing reported a highly frequent

overall average use of language learning strategies and gave ratings of 5 ('always or almost always') to a large number of language learning strategies of different types, including many of the *plus* strategies (see details of Nina, Kira, Fernando, Kim and Lily earlier in this chapter).

(2)   There were, however, individual exceptions to this general finding. Kang, for instance, made very good progress during his course in spite of not reporting highly frequent use of the language learning strategies itemised in the *SILL*, while May failed to make particularly good progress despite highly frequent reported language learning strategy use (these individual cases have been discussed earlier in this chapter).

(3)   A variety of factors emerged from the interview data as possible contributors to an explanation of these varying levels of reported language learning strategy use and differing rates of progress of which motivation may well be the strongest.

The qualitative interview data, then, *generally* supported the quantitative findings but also indicated that each learner is unique, suggesting that attempts to apply overall truths to individuals must be made with extreme care. This, of course, is the reality that teachers face on a daily basis: a class full of individuals, each with his/her own needs.

3.4 Qualitative Areas for Further Research

The interviews reported here have produced some interesting findings which supplement the quantitative data reported in Chapter 2. However, there are also a number of areas needing further research. In particular:

(1)   When it comes to the relationships among language development, language learning strategy use, and third factors, there are many underexplored areas, including the influence of:
• learning style
• personality
• beliefs
• autonomy
• aptitude
• identity
• investment
• affect (including anxiety, attribution, empathy, inhibition, self-concept)

All of these areas require further research.

(2) As listed here, many of the key strategies which learners report using are rather general and ill-defined. *Doing homework,* for instance, could cover a range of behaviour, each of which might be considered a strategy in its own right. The same might be true of *Using a dictionary, Keeping a notebook,* and so on. Although time did not permit a more detailed examination of the use of these strategies in the context of the interviews, they might well be worth further research.

(3) The data reported in Chapters 2 and 3 have looked at frequency, number and type of strategies and how they interact with a range of other learner, situational and target variables. However, the question of how students orchestrate such a repertoire of strategies and use it to learn effectively remains underexplored.

4 A Pedagogical Perspective

4.1 The Place of Strategies in Overall Theories of Teaching

Although it is widely accepted that language learning strategies are a factor in successful language learning (e.g. Chamot, 2008; Cohen, 1998, 2011; Cohen & Macaro, 2007; Griffiths, 2008a; Macaro, 2006; Oxford, 1990, 2011b; Rubin, 1975; Wenden, 1987a), many questions remain with regard to:

- how strategies fit into the overall picture of language teaching theory as it has evolved over the years;
- strategy instruction;
- teachers' perceptions;
- how to promote learner confidence;
- how to deal with learner, situational and target variables;
- how to train teachers to conduct strategy instruction effectively.

Over the years, various methods have attributed more or less importance to the role of learners in their own learning. The basic assumption underlying the Grammar-Translation method, for instance, tended to be that if learners simply learned the structure (grammar) and the lexis of the new language and translated from one language into the other, they would, as a matter of course, learn the target language. In this structuralist view, there was little consideration given to the contribution that students themselves might make to the learning process (Richards & Rodgers, 1986). Although considered outdated by many contemporary educators, Grammar-Translation remains a common approach to the teaching and learning of language right up to the present.

Faced both with dissatisfaction with the structuralist Grammar-Translation approach, which tended to produce 'communicatively incompetent graduates' (Griffiths, 2011: 302), and an urgent need for fluent speakers of other languages during the war, a new method was developed known as the Army Method. Since this method was actually very successful at the time, after the war it was adapted for peacetime use and became known as Audiolingualism. Based on behaviourist principles that all behaviour (including language) is a habit (Watson, 1930), which is formed by means of stimulus, response and reinforcement (Skinner, 1957), Audiolingual techniques depended heavily on drills and repetition. According to this view, there was, if anything, even less importance accorded to the students' role than there had been under Grammar-Translation. Under Audiolingualism, students' efforts to regulate their own learning were viewed with suspicion, since they might make mistakes which, if not immediately corrected, were likely to become fossilised. Given such dire potential consequences, learners' strategies were not encouraged or even tolerated.

In a well-known review of Skinner's (1957) book, Chomsky (1959) attacked behaviourist theories and promoted a cognitive view of language development whereby learners use what he called a language acquisition device (LAD) to learn language and to generate rules regarding the language they are in the process of learning. According to a cognitive perspective, learners are capable of thinking through the language learning process until they gain the knowledge they require to achieve understanding of the new language system. Although Audiolingualism continued for some years, and still survives in language laboratories and classrooms in the form of drilling and repetitive exercises, it never really recovered from Chomsky's attack.

From a cognitive perspective, language learners are seen as much more than mere passive receptacles for linguistic patterning by means of the stimulus, response and reinforcement that had underpinned the Audiolingual method. The effect of Audiolingual techniques of rote learning, repetition, imitation, memorisation, drilling and pattern practice was to minimise the importance of explicit learning strategies employed in the language learning process (Stern, 1992; see Allen & Harley, 1992). Although some strategies such as *repeating vocabulary until it becomes automatic* might be considered basically behaviourist, most learning strategies require a much more cognitively engaged learner.

As noted above, a major principle of Audiolingualism related to error correction. According to a behaviourist view, errors must be dealt with by means of immediate correction in order to avoid fossilisation. Corder (1967), however, published a very influential cognitive view of learner errors which viewed the error phenomenon as an indication of the learner's progress in thinking through what Selinker (1972) later called *interlanguage*.

This developing awareness of the importance of cognition in language learning led to the interest in the strategies used by 'good language learners' in the mid- to late 1970s (e.g. Naiman *et al.*, 1978; Rubin, 1975; Stern, 1975).

However, at much the same time as the strategists were developing their ideas along a cognitive paradigm, Krashen (1976, 1977, 1985) proposed his five hypotheses (the Acquisition/learning Hypothesis, the Monitor Hypothesis, the Input Hypothesis, the Affective Filter Hypothesis and the Natural Order Hypothesis). In these (especially the Acquisition/Learning and Monitor Hypotheses) he postulated that language is best acquired by means of natural communication, the way children acquire their first language. Children, of course, do not learn their first language by means of vocab lists or grammar rules; therefore, Krashen argued, conscious learning has limited usefulness in the process of language development which must be naturally acquired by means of communication, a philosophy which was developed into the Natural Method (Krashen & Terrell, 1983). According to Krashen's view, therefore, strategies have a minimal role to play in language development, for which all that is required is sufficient comprehensible input: that is, input which is a little above the learner's current level of competence, often expressed by the formula I + 1.

Krashen's ideas have often been strongly criticised over the years (e.g. Gregg, 1984) and others have suggested modifications. Pienemann (1984, 1985, 1989), for instance, argued that language can be taught when the learner's interlanguage approaches the point where the target structure would be acquired in a natural setting (Teachability Hypothesis). Swain (1985) suggested the Output Hypothesis as a complement to the Input Hypothesis, arguing that comprehensible input alone is insufficient for learners to become competent in a target language, and that language production is also necessary. And Long (1996) proposed the Interaction Hypothesis, acknowledging the importance of comprehensible input, but suggesting that learning is more effective when learners must use the input to communicate.

Of course, the emphasis on language as communication had first been introduced into the literature by Hymes (1972), who published an article promoting an important theoretical principle which he called *communicative competence*. This is the ability to use language to convey and interpret meaning, later divided by Canale and Swain (1980) and Canale (1983) into *grammatical competence* (which relates to the learner's knowledge of the vocabulary, phonology and rules of the language), *discourse competence* (which relates to the learner's ability to connect utterances into a meaningful whole), *sociolinguistic competence* (which relates to a learner's ability to use language appropriately) and *strategic competence* (which relates to a learner's ability to employ strategies to compensate for imperfect knowledge).

This communicative view of language development contributed to the impetus for the now widely used communicative approach to language teaching and learning (CLT), according to which language is acquired in the process of using it to interact with others and employing it for communicative functions (e.g. Littlewood, 1981, 2012; Richards, 2006; Spada, 2007; Widdowson, 1978; Wilkins, 1976). Language development, therefore, becomes essentially a sociocultural phenomenon, a view developed by writers such as Lantolf (2000) and Pavlenko and Lantolf (2000) and is developed by means of social mediation within a cultural context (Vygotsky, 1978, 1987). The emphasis on social interaction led to the development of a widely used branch of CLT known as task-based language (TBL) teaching, based on the idea that language is learnt most effectively by engaging students in communicative activities which approximate those they might be required to perform in real life, such as going to the supermarket, renting a flat or planning a holiday (e.g. Ellis, 2003; Nunan, 2004). Given its communicative focus, strategies in a CLT paradigm tend to focus on interactive activities such as *seeking out conversation partners* and, possibly, strategies to remember anything learnt from communicative encounters for future occasions (such as *writing new vocabulary in a notebook*).

The development of language learning theory alongside teaching theories can be seen diagrammatically in Table 4.1. It is interesting to note from the table that, in spite of the fact that it has never been underpinned by any sort of theory (Richards & Rodgers, 1986), Grammar-Translation has survived while Audiolingualism has come and largely gone, and while cognitive and communicative theories have developed alongside it. From the table we can also see that in recent years theories of language development have tended to move away from dogmatic positions of right and wrong, and to be more willing to recognise the potential merits of a wide variety of possible methods and approaches, sometimes termed 'eclecticism' (e.g. Tarone & Yule, 1989) or postmethod (e.g. Kumaravadivelu, 2001). Although eclecticism has been criticised as 'resulting in a hodgepodge of conflicting classroom activities assembled on whim rather than upon any principled basis', effective eclecticism requires effort and places a great deal of responsibility on the teacher (Tarone & Yule, 1989: 10).

The increased interest in eclecticism is reflected in comments such as that by McLaughlin *et al.* (1983) who remind us of the story of the blind men and the elephant and then conclude that learning a target language is 'a complex phenomenon and there are many legitimate points of view. The trouble begins when one starts to claim that a particular point of view is the total one' (McLaughlin *et al.*, 1983: 156).

An important corollary which follows logically from placing language learning strategies within a largely cognitive theoretical paradigm is that, not

Table 4.1 Timeline for the development of structural, audiolingual, cognitive and communicative paradigms in language teaching

Year	G-T	Audiolingual	Cognitive	Communicative
1930	G R	Watson: Behaviourism		
1957	A M	Skinner: Verbal Behaviour		
1959	M		Chomsky: Review of Verbal Behaviour	
1967	A		Corder: The significance of Learners' Errors	
1972	R		Selinker: Interlanguage	Hymes: Communicative Competence
1975			Rubin & Stern: Good Language Learner Studies	
1976				Wilkins: Notional Syllabuses Krashen: Acquisition-learning Hypothesis
1977				Krashen: Monitor Hypothesis
1978			Naiman et al.: The Good Language Learner McLaughlin: Criticism of the Monitor Model Bialystok: Theoretical Model	Vygotsky: Mind in Society Widdowson: Language as Communication
1981				Littlewood: Communicative Language Teaching

Year		
1983		Canale: Four Dimensions of Communicative Competence
1984	**T** Pienemann: Teachability Hypothesis	
1985	**R** O'Malley et al.: Cognitive, Metacognitive, Social Categories	Swain: Output Hypothesis
1990	**A** Oxford: Language Learning Strategies	
	N O'Malley & Chamot: Learning Strategies in SLA	
1991	**S** Wenden: Learning Strategies for Autonomy	
1996	**L**	Long: Interaction Hypothesis
1998	**A** Skehan: A Cognitive Approach	
	T Cohen: Strategies in Learning and Using	
2000	**I**	Lantolf: Sociocultural Theory in SLA
2006	**O** Macaro: Revising the Theoretical Framework	
2007	**N** Cohen & Macaro: Learner Strategies	
2008	Griffiths: Strategies and Good Language Learners	
2011	Oxford: Teaching and Researching LLS	
	Cohen: Strategies in Learning and Using (2)	

ECLECTICISM

only are learners able to bring cognition to bear on their learning processes, but that the strategies themselves are also able to be learnt and, furthermore, that teachers are able to facilitate strategy development. In other words, from a cognitive perspective, language learning strategies are learnable and teachable.

In actual fact, although this sounds straightforward enough in principle, the learnability/teachability dimension of language learning strategies has proved not to be quite so straightforward in practice.

4.2 Strategy Instruction

It was anticipated by pioneering researchers such as Rubin (1975) that discoveries regarding how successful students learn could be used by other students to learn more successfully. From the beginning, therefore, the pedagogical perspective has been seen as the essential *raison d'être* underlying debates on and research into the language learning strategy concept. Or, as Gu (1996: 1) colourfully puts it: 'Research on language learning strategies (LLS) started off with the Robin Hoodian good will of breaking the secret behavioural codes of successful language learners and sharing them with the unsuccessful ones.'

Viewing language learning as a cognitive skill allows for the possibility that language learning ability can be improved and that language learning strategies can themselves be learnt (O'Malley & Chamot, 1990). This focus on learning how to learn was seen by Bruner (1960) as essential for the transfer of learning from one situation to another. Ellis and Sinclair (1994) devoted a book to the subject, while Nisbet and Shucksmith (1984: 4) describe the skill of learning as 'the most important skill of all'.

The possibility that knowledge gained about learning strategies might be made available to other students to help them to learn more effectively has been a major underlying tenet of much of the research and writing on language learning strategies. The idea that teachers should be concerned not only with 'finding the best method or with getting the correct answer' but also with assisting students in order to 'enable [them] to learn on [their] own' (Rubin, 1975: 45) was, at the time it was written, quite revolutionary. However, an important component of language learning strategy theory is the belief that language learning strategies are *'teachable'* (Oxford & Nyikos, 1989: 291, authors' italics) and that learners can benefit from coaching in learning strategies (e.g. Cook, 1991; Larsen-Freeman, 1991).

According to this view, the teacher's role expands from being mainly concerned with imparting knowledge to including the facilitation of learning by raising awareness of strategy options and providing encouragement and opportunities for practice so that students might be assisted towards the goal of managing their own learning. This idea is sometimes seen as a threat by teachers (e.g. Grundy, 1999). However, the new role of facilitator, counsellor and resource person can be an empowering one for both teacher and student (Cotterall & Crabbe, 1999; Harmer, 1995; Pemberton, 1996; Voller, 1997).

However, although a cognitive view of language learning suggests that language learning strategies are teachable (O'Malley & Chamot, 1990), and although there are those who argue that strategy instruction is an important part of the teacher's role (e.g. Oxford & Nyikos, 1989), the principle of the teachability of language learning strategies is by no means universally accepted. According to Rees-Miller (1993: 679), for instance, attempts to train learners to use learning strategies more effectively have produced 'only qualified success'. As evidence of this claim, she gives details of less than totally successful attempts at learner training, including studies by O'Malley (1987) and by Wenden (1987b). Possible reasons suggested by Rees-Miller (1993) for this lack of success in teaching strategies include the student's age, educational background, life experience, curriculum demands, varying cognitive styles, and the incompatibility of student and teacher beliefs regarding how to learn language. She also suggests that 'the behaviours defined as exemplary of successful learning strategies practised by good language learners may be based on cultural models that are not universal' (Rees-Miller, 1993: 684). Given the level of unresolved debate which surrounds the issue of the teachability of language learning strategies, Rees-Miller questions whether the time spent raising awareness of strategy use might not be better spent directly teaching language, at least until the situation has been clarified by further research.

Strategy instruction

Although, according to cognitive theory, language learning strategies are learnable and teachable, much controversy remains over the issue of strategy instruction.

4.3 Previous Research Into Strategy Instruction

Although long acknowledged as necessary and important, strategy instruction remains an under-researched area. Manchon *et al.* (2007), for instance, report that studies of strategy instruction make up only 10% of their corpus of strategy studies. Nevertheless, over the years there have been some.

In an attempt to investigate the effectiveness of language learning strategy instruction on language learning, O'Malley (1987) randomly assigned 75 students to one of three instructional groups for listening, speaking and vocabulary acquisition skills. In these groups, they received training in: (1) metacognitive, cognitive and socioaffective strategies; (2) cognitive and socioaffective strategies; or (3) no special instruction in language learning strategies (control group). A significant difference was discovered in favour of the treatment groups for speaking, but not for listening, while the control group for vocabulary actually scored slightly higher than the treatment groups. O'Malley (1987) explains this unexpected finding as being due to the persistence of familiar strategies among certain students, who continued to use rote repetitive strategies, and who were unwilling to adopt the strategies presented in training, especially when they knew they would be tested within only a few minutes.

Wenden (1987b) describes an intensive English programme which included a language learning strategy component at an American university. The students were described as 'very advanced' (Wenden, 1987b: 164), of various cultural backgrounds and with varied reasons for learning. A questionnaire revealed that less than 50% of the students thought that the strategy training had been useful. Wenden (1987b: 164) concluded that 'learner training was not considered relevant in its own right'. In fact, some of the students were so resistant that one of the classes was discontinued after only three weeks. This result supports Naiman et al.'s (1978: 225) belief that 'long lectures on strategies, or even lengthy discussions on the subject, would [not] be particularly profitable'.

Carrell et al. (1989) investigated the effects of metacognitive strategy training on ESL reading. Their research involved 26 students who were divided into three groups. Some of the participants were graduates, others undergraduates. They came from various linguistic backgrounds and were of differing ages and of both sexes. The researchers discovered that, in the context of their study (at the Center for English as a Second Language at Southern Illinois University), metacognitive strategy training was effective in enhancing reading ability by speakers of other languages. These results accord with O'Malley et al.'s (1985) conclusions regarding the importance of metacognitive strategies.

The effects of the teaching of cognitive and metacognitive strategies on reading comprehension in the classroom were also investigated by Tang and Moore (1992) using three recent adult immigrants to New Zealand. The researchers concluded that, while cognitive strategy instruction (title discussion, pre-teaching vocabulary) improved comprehension scores, the gains were not maintained upon the withdrawal of the treatment. Metacognitive strategy instruction, on the other hand (involving the teaching of self-monitoring strategies), appeared to lead to improvements in comprehension ability which were maintained beyond the end of the treatment.

In a classroom-based study in Hong Kong which aimed to research whether learner strategy training makes a difference in terms of knowledge, skills and attitudes, Nunan (1995) involved 60 students in a 12-week programme 'designed to help them reflect on their own learning, to develop their knowledge of, and ability to apply learning strategies, to assess their own progress, and to apply their language skills beyond the classroom' (Nunan, 1995: 3). The programme was based on a bank of tasks which belonged to four categories: general aspects of learning, different modes of learning, developing macroskills (reading, writing, listening, speaking) and language systems (pronunciation, vocabulary, grammar, discourse). Students also kept journals, from which Nunan (1995: 8) concluded that 'strategy training, plus systematic provision of opportunities for learners to reflect on the learning process, did seem to lead to greater sensitivity to the learning process over time'. Nunan recommended that language classrooms should have a dual focus, teaching both content and an awareness of language learning processes. However, as Nunan (1995: 1) comments, research in this area is still 'relatively uncommon, and results are rather mixed'.

A study of strategy use by four independent learners, carried out by Simmons (1996) over a period of six weeks at an Australian university, consisted of a series of intensive individual training sessions aimed at raising awareness of cognitive and metacognitive strategies. At the end of the period, Simmons concluded that students had increased the number and variety of their strategy use and were more aware of the strategies which suited themselves as individuals. Simmons (1996: 75) suggests that 'making the learning process more transparent' is important in the interests of empowering students to direct their own learning.

After studying a group of language students who were participants in a strategies-based instructional programme at the University of Minnesota, Cohen (1998, 1999) concluded that the programme had made a positive difference in speaking performance. Cohen summed up the pedagogical implications of his findings as indicating that language learning strategies should be both explicitly taught in the classroom and embedded in daily tasks.

In a study of the effects of strategy instruction on writing skills, Macaro (2001) studied the effects of intervention on two teenage British learners of French. When he compared the students' pre-intervention written work with their post-intervention output, Macaro concluded that their writing had improved, which he attributed in part to the planning, composing and checking strategies that they had learned to use.

At a college in Japan, 210 students were divided into two groups for reading instruction (Ikeda & Takeuchi, 2003). The treatment group included 73 high-proficiency and 23 low-proficiency students (total $N = 96$), while the control group included 82 high-proficiency and 32 low-proficiency learners (total $N = 114$). Classes were held for 90 minutes once a week, and during this time explicit strategy instruction in reading was conducted for 20 minutes. Although the researchers found no increase in frequency of strategy use among the low-proficiency students, increased frequency in strategy use was found among the high-proficiency members of the treatment group, and this increase was retained when students were retested 5 months later.

In order to study the effects of strategy instruction on vocabulary acquisition, Eslami Rasekh and Ranjbary (2003) divided 53 Iranian college students of EFL into a control group ($N = 26$, who were taught according to the regular curriculum) and a treatment group ($N = 27$, who were instructed in metacognitive strategies such as how to deal with unfamiliar words in context). According to the researchers, the group which received the strategy intervention showed significantly higher gains in vocabulary than the control group.

In a 12-week oral communication course, Nakatani (2005) divided 62 female students into two groups. One group ($N = 28$) received metacognitive strategy instruction, while the control group ($N = 34$) were taught according to normal communicative methods. According to the findings, the group which received strategy instruction significantly improved their speaking test scores, while improvements in the control group were not significant.

Oxford and Lee (2007: 117) describe grammar strategies as 'the second Cinderella' because of the relative lack of attention they have attracted. Bade (2008: 178), however, discovered that her 14 mature and motivated students enrolled for a 20-week course to better equip them to live and work in New Zealand expressed 'an overwhelming desire to be taught grammar'. Bade concluded by listing a number of useful cognitive and metacognitive strategies which the study had identified.

At the University of Ottawa in Canada, Vandergrift and Tafaghodatari (2010) investigated the effectiveness of listening strategy instruction with 106 students of French. The 60 students in the experimental group were given instruction in how to apply predicting, planning, monitoring, evaluating and problem-solving strategies while listening. Although taught by the same teacher, the 46 students in the control group were not given any strategy instruction. On the final assessment, the experimental group was found to significantly outperform the control group.

Such a mixed bag of results relating to the effectiveness of language learning strategy instruction and how best to go about it is difficult even to summarise. These results seem to indicate successful instruction for some types of strategies but not for others; success for strategies relating to some skills, but not for others; success for some students but not for others; and success in some situations, but not in others.

There is obviously still a considerable amount of work to be done in the area of research into how best to go about instruction in language learning strategy use. Nevertheless, according to Nunan (1995), although the effectiveness of strategy training remains uncertain, there is enough evidence of a positive relationship between language learning strategies and proficiency to suggest that further research is warranted.

> ### Previous research
>
> Previous research into strategy instruction has produced very mixed results and much research remains to be done to clarify questions of instructional effectiveness and the teacher's role in the process.

4.4 Strategy Instruction Programmes

Although strategy instruction has been far from uncontroversial (e.g. Rees-Miller, 1993), over the years a number of programmes have been designed with the aim of instructing students in the use of language learning strategies. Among the best known and most widely used are:

4.4.1 Cognitive Academic Language Learning Approach (CALLA)

CALLA was one of the first strategy-based instruction programmes, developed by Chamot and O'Malley (1986). As O'Malley and Chamot (1990: 190) explain, 'the focus of *CALLA* is on the acquisition and use of procedural skills that facilitate academic language and content learning'. In order to facilitate this acquisition, *CALLA* uses a three-dimensional approach:

* content instruction;
* academic language development;
* direct instruction in learning strategies.

The *CALLA* programme is based on several important propositions:

- mentally active students are better learners;
- learning is more effective with learning strategies;
- learning strategies can be taught;
- learning strategies can be transferred to new tasks.

Included in the *CALLA* instructional programme are 20 strategies, including:

- metacognitive strategies (such as *advance organisation, organisational planning, selective attention, self-evaluation, self-management*);
- cognitive strategies (such as *grouping, note-taking, summarising, deduction, imagery, elaboration, inferencing*);
- socio-affective strategies (such as *questioning for clarification, co-operation, self-talk*).

Promoted as a 'bridge to the mainstream' (Chamot & O'Malley, 1987: 227), *CALLA* employs a recursive instructional sequence of preparation, presentation, practice, self-evaluation and expansion, which was further expounded in the *Learning Strategies Handbook*, published by Chamot *et al.* (1999).

4.4.2 Learning to Learn

According to Ellis and Sinclair (1994), learner training aims to help learners consider the factors that affect their learning and discover the learning strategies that suit them best. *Learning to Learn English* aims to provide a systematic course that enables students to become more effective learners and take on greater responsibility for their own learning.

The programme is divided into two stages. The first involves preparing the student for learning and considers a number of questions (Ellis & Sinclair, 1994: v):

- What do you expect from your course?
- What sort of language learner are you?
- Why do you need or want to learn?
- How do you organise your learning?
- How motivated are you?
- What can you do in a self-access centre?

Section 2 works directly on developing language knowledge (including vocabulary and grammar) and skills (reading, writing, listening, speaking), each of which is organised according to a seven-step procedure (Ellis & Sinclair, 1994: v–vi):

- How do you feel about …?
- What do you know about …?
- How well are you doing?
- What do you need to do next?
- How do you prefer to …?
- Do you need to build up your confidence?
- How do you organise your …?

Learners and teachers can select the skills and strategies they need and plan their own route through the materials, and they can also make use of materials designed to encourage learner reflection such as a needs analysis chart, a self-assessment scale and a motivation graph.

The *Learning to Learn* course can be used either in conjunction with a regular language course or presented as separate learner training sessions.

4.4.3 Strategies-based instruction (*SBI*)

One of the foremost proponents of *SBI* has been Andrew Cohen and his team at the University of Minnesota. Cohen (1998) describes a study in which 55 intermediate-level language learners were divided into a control group and an experimental group which received SBI. The researchers (Cohen *et al.*, 1998) concluded that an increase in strategy use was linked to improved performance for the experimental group.

In more recent years, *SBI* has been integrated with styles to become styles- and strategies-based instruction (*SSBI*). The Centre for Advanced Research on Language Acquisition (CARLA) website lists a systematic approach to *SSBI* which involves:

- *Strategy preparation* – when learners' existing strategy knowledge is assessed;
- *Strategy awareness-raising* – when students are made aware of strategy possibilities;
- *Strategy training* – when students are instructed in strategy use;
- *Strategy practice* – when students are encouraged to try out their strategy repertoires;
- *Personalisation of strategies* – when students evaluate how well their strategies are working for themselves.

In order to conduct *SBI*, Cohen (2011: 115) suggests that teachers may need to adopt a number of different roles, including:

- *Catalyst for learners' self-diagnosis* – by making students more aware of strategies they might potentially employ;
- *Learner facilitator* – by explicitly or implicitly instructing learners in the use of strategies;
- *Coach* – by working with individual learners to develop their strategy repertoires;
- *Coordinator* – by overseeing the learners' study programmes and assisting with any problem areas;
- *Language learner* – by putting themselves in the role of a language learner, sharing the language learning experience, thereby establishing empathy with the learners;
- *Researcher* – by checking and analysing the progress of instruction.

Strategy instruction programmes

A number of strategy instruction programmes have been designed over the years, three of which are outlined here. *CALLA* is designed for an academic environment, *Learning how to Learn* is a stand-alone course which can be integrated with course content, and *SBI* has, in recent years, become an essentially internet-based programme. Although the focus and delivery of these three programmes is different, they all have in common that they aim to develop students' awareness of strategy options and their ability to use strategies effectively.

Underlying strategy-based instruction is the premise that 'language learning will be facilitated if students become more aware of the range of possible strategies that they can consciously select' (Cohen, 2011: 116).

4.5 Teachers' Perceptions

It may seem surprising that, although teachers are 'pivotal in the enterprise of teaching and learning' (Freeman & Richards, 1996: 1), their perspectives are often ignored in language teaching and learning research. In fact, as Richards (1996) reminds us, teachers are individuals as much as their students are, and teacher practices and perceptions are critically important because these factors often influence the effectiveness of the teaching/learning process.

The question of teacher perceptions becomes even more important in the light of research which suggests that teachers' and students' perceptions are often divergent. Nunan (1988), for instance, reports on a study where students and teachers were asked to rate 10 classroom activities (conversation practice, explanations to class, vocabulary development, pronunciation practice, error correction, language games, using pictures/films/video, listening to/using cassettes, student self-discovery of errors, pair work) according to their perceived importance. In only one case (the importance accorded to pronunciation practice) were student and teacher ratings the same. In other cases, the differences between student and teacher perceptions were often dramatic, especially with regard to error correction (which students rated 'very high' and teachers rated 'low') and in the ratings accorded to student self-discovery of errors and pair work (which students rated 'low' and teachers rated 'very high').

Other research suggests that teachers are often not aware of their students' learning strategies (e.g. O'Malley et al., 1985), and that teachers' assumptions about their students' strategies are often not correct (Hosenfeld, 1976). Indeed, it has been shown that teachers may hold beliefs regarding their students' strategy usage which are quite contrary to what their students report, as Griffiths and Parr (2001a) discovered. In this study, which used the *Strategy Inventory for Language Learning* (*SILL* – Oxford, 1990), 569 international students of English in Auckland, New Zealand were asked to rate the 50 items of the questionnaire according to frequency of use. The data were later analysed for frequency of use according to the categories of the *SILL* (memory, cognitive, compensation, metacognitive, affective, social). Thirty teachers also filled out a questionnaire on which they ranked the *SILL*'s categories from 6 = most frequent to 1 = least frequent according to which ones they believed their students used most often. The results are summarised in Table 4.2.

According to the results, teachers believed their students used memory strategies most frequently, while the students rated memory strategies as least frequently used. Students, however, actually reported social strategies as most frequently used, whereas teachers rated them only third in terms of the frequency with which they believed their students made use of them.

In fact, as can be seen from Table 4.2, there are points at which student and teacher perceptions are almost exactly the inverse of each other, especially with respect to memory strategies. Indeed, the only point at which teachers' and students' perceptions almost coincide is with affective strategies, which students ranked second to lowest (ranking = 2) and teachers ranked lowest (ranking = 1).

Table 4.2 Student and teacher rankings of frequency of use of the *SILL* categories (note that 6 = most frequent, 1 = least frequent)

	Teacher rankings	Student rankings
Memory	6	1
Cognitive	5	3
Compensation	2	4
Metacognitive	3	5
Affective	1	2
Social	4	6

Leaving aside the question of which sets of perceptions might be 'right' or 'wrong', such lack of awareness, incorrect assumptions and mismatches between student reports and teacher beliefs have the potential to affect what goes on in the classroom in quite negative ways since mutual understanding would seem to be a precondition of good student–teacher relationships. It would therefore seem to be important to discover more about how teachers' perceptions of language learning strategy use relate to reported strategy practices by students in order that such information might be used to inform classroom practice.

Therefore, at an international language school in Auckland, New Zealand, the *English Language Learning Strategy Inventory* (*ELLSI*) questionnaire (for details see Section 1.7 and Appendix 2) was given to 131 students. At the same school, 34 teachers were also given an adapted version of the *ELLSI* (see Appendix 4) which asked them to rate the strategy items according to degree of perceived importance (Griffiths, 2003b). After completion, data from the surveys were analysed and the results of the students' and teachers' *ELLSIs* compared in order to explore the degree to which the strategies which teachers reported considering important matched the strategies which students reported using.

The students who participated in this study (*N* = 131) reported an average frequency of strategy use over all *ELLSI* items of 3.1, and they reported high frequency use (average = 3.5 or above; Oxford, 1990) of seven of the 32 *ELLSI* items (Items 1, 2, 12, 13, 17, 25 and 26).

For their part, teachers reported ascribing a high level of importance to language learning strategies (overall average = 3.6), and they reported regarding 17 of the 32 strategy items (that is, more than half) as highly important (using the same average = 3.5 threshold used in other areas of the study).

The average levels of importance ascribed to language learning strategies by teachers are presented in Table 4.3 alongside the average reported frequencies

Table 4.3 Average levels of importance ascribed to language learning strategies by teachers (T), and average reported frequency of strategy use by students (S), with number of high importance/frequency items

ELLSI	T	S	Statement (paraphrased for brevity)
1	3.3	3.8	Doing homework
2	3.9	4.0	Learning from the teacher
3	4.6	3.4	Learning in an environment where the language is spoken
4	3.6	2.7	Reading books in English
5	2.4	2.6	Using a computer
6	3.2	3.1	Watching TV in English
7	3.8	3.1	Revising regularly
8	2.6	3.4	Listening to songs in English
9	3.5	2.1	Using language learning games
10	3.2	2.2	Writing letters in English
11	1.8	2.2	Listening to music while studying
12	4.4	3.5	Talking to other students in English
13	3.1	4.2	Using a dictionary
14	3.4	2.4	Reading newspapers in English
15	3.7	3.4	Studying English grammar
16	4.0	3.3	Consciously learning new vocabulary
17	3.8	3.5	Keeping a language learning notebook
18	4.8	3.4	Talking to native speakers of English
19	3.9	2.8	Noting language used in the environment
20	3.1	2.7	Controlling schedules so that English study is done
21	3.0	2.7	Pre-planning language learning encounters
22	3.7	3.2	Not worrying about mistakes
23	3.2	2.3	Using a self-study centre
24	4.2	3.2	Trying to think in English
25	4.4	3.8	Listening to native speakers of English
26	4.4	3.6	Learning from mistakes
27	3.2	3.3	Spending time studying English
28	4.2	2.8	Making friends with native speakers
29	3.2	3.2	Watching movies in English
30	3.3	2.8	Learning about the culture of English speakers
31	3.4	2.8	Listening to the radio in English
32	3.7	1.9	Writing a diary in English
	3.6	3.1	Overall average level of importance/frequency
	17	7	Number of high importance/frequency items

of strategy use across all students. The averages which indicate a high level of ascribed importance by teachers (average = 3.5 or above) are shaded for emphasis in the 'T' column.

Strategies reportedly used highly frequently by students are shaded for emphasis in the 'S' column. The overall average levels of importance or frequency and the number of items considered highly important by teachers (T) or reportedly used highly frequently by students (S) are summarised at the bottom of the table.

According to the results of the survey, the 17 strategies regarded as highly important by teachers included five of the seven strategies which students across all levels reported using highly frequently:

- Item 2: *Learning from the teacher*
- Item 12: *Talking to other students in English*
- Item 17: *Keeping a language learning notebook*
- Item 25: *Listening to native speakers of English*
- Item 26: *Learning from mistakes*

Perhaps unexpectedly, though, teachers do not report *doing homework* (Item 1) as highly important, although it is reportedly used highly frequently across all students. More predictably, teachers do not rate *using a dictionary* (Item 13) highly, although students report using it highly frequently.

When the students were divided into higher level ($N = 58$) and lower level ($N = 73$) groups, the higher level students were found to be using eight strategies at a high rate of frequency in addition to the seven high-frequency strategies used across all students. These were:

- Item 3: *Learning in an environment where the language is spoken* (higher level average = 3.5, lower level average = 3.3)
- Item 6: *Watching TV in English* (higher level average = 3.5, lower level average = 2.8)
- Item 8: *Listening to songs in English* (higher level average = 3.7, lower level average = 3.2)
- Item 15: *Studying English grammar* (higher level average = 3.6, lower level average = 3.3)
- Item 16: *Consciously learning new vocabulary* (higher level average = 3.7, lower level average = 2.9)
- Item 18: *Talking to native speakers of English* (higher level average = 3.6, lower level average = 3.2)
- Item 27: *Spending time studying English* (higher level average = 3.5, lower level average = 3.2)

- Item 29: *Watching movies in English* (higher level average = 3.6, lower level average = 2.9)

Since these eight strategies were reportedly used more frequently by higher level students than by lower level students, they should, perhaps, be considered for the possible contribution they might be making to the students' higher level of success. A possible area of concern, therefore, might be that teachers consider only four of these items highly important (Items 3, 15, 16, 18). Of the four items highly rated by higher level students which teachers do not consider highly important, three (Items 6, 8 and 29) relate to the use of readily available resources (TV, songs, movies). Perhaps in the light of their highly frequent reported use by high-level students it might be useful for teachers to reconsider the level of importance ascribed to this kind of strategy, especially since these resources are such an easy, obvious and inexpensive way for students to increase their exposure to English. On a purely practical level, it is a pity to waste resources which are so readily available, so intrinsically motivating and so easy to incorporate into classroom activities with relatively little preparation or equipment.

As for the lower level group ($N = 73$), with only four exceptions, their ratings were lower than those of the higher level group. These exceptions were:

- Item 11: *Listening to music while studying* (higher level average = 2.2, lower level average = 2.3)
- Item 13: *Using a dictionary* (higher level average = 4.1, lower level average = 4.2)
- Item 22: *Not worrying about mistakes* (higher level average = 3.1, lower level average = 3.2)
- Item 23: *Using a self-study centre* (higher level average = 2.2, lower level average = 2.4)

Of these, teachers rate only one (Item 22) as highly important. This possibly reflects teachers' awareness of the need to encourage the communicative use of language and a desire to promote fluency, which can suffer if students are overly concerned about correctness (Brumfit, 1984). Nevertheless, teachers should also be reminded that students appear to be able to learn from mistakes (Item 26) and they should remain aware of the importance of attention to detail and to correct use of language. Although teachers often do not want to discourage students by over-correction, especially where mistakes do not affect communication, if students are never corrected, they may continue using incorrect forms, unaware of their own errors which then become fossilised. Many students, furthermore, expect correction, and may feel that their teaching has been inadequate if they find (perhaps at a later date) that they have not been made aware of errors. The point of balance between under-correction to promote fluency and over-correction which may affect confidence is not always an easy one for teachers to find, and may depend on many factors, including students' personalities, motivation levels, learning styles, ages or affective states.

Also interesting, especially in light of the money which is often spent on self-study centres, is the discovery that lower level students report using such a resource more frequently (average = 2.4) than higher level students (average = 2.2), a phenomenon also noted by Cotterall and Reinders (2000), while teachers rate self-study centres (Item 23) in the neutral-to-important range (average = 3.2). Perhaps the inference from this discovery might be that the most important function of a self-study centre may be to get students to a point where they no longer need it. Viewed in this light, the evidently less frequent use of the centre by higher level students becomes a measure of success: perhaps the main function of a self-study centre (where a staff member is usually available to assist as required) may be to support students until they have developed strategies to cope on their own beyond the centre, rather than fostering long-term dependence.

Teachers' perceptions

A number of studies have shown that teachers' and students' perceptions of language learning strategy use vary widely. In Griffiths' (2003b) study, however, the teacher–student gap was not so wide, leaving optimism for the development of greater accord between student and teacher in the classroom.

According to the *ELLSI* (Griffiths, 2003b), then, teachers regard language learning strategies as very important, rating more than half of the items (17 out of the 32) as highly important (average = 3.5 or above), including all but two of the strategies (relating to homework and the use of dictionaries) reportedly used highly frequently across all students. This result would seem to imply that, according to the results of this study, teachers and students are generally 'on the same wavelength' when it comes to reported student practices and teacher perceptions of importance. This is an encouraging discovery because of its implications for a good accord between students and teachers in the area of strategic behaviour and its potentially positive consequences in terms of classroom dynamics.

4.6 The Classroom Experience

At the school where the study reported in Chapter 3 was carried out, students new to the school were involved in a Study Skills class about mid-way through their first week. The idea of the class was to raise awareness of how to study effectively and thereby maximise the benefit students might obtain from their time at the school. The one-off class seemed to be quite successful, so it was decided to offer a Study Skills class on a regular weekly basis, at a time (Wednesday afternoon) when regular weekly option classes operated. These classes were offered for a month, at the end of which time they would be offered again or discontinued, depending on demand (Griffiths, 2003b).

Materials used for the Study Skills class included commercially available texts such as Ellis and Sinclair (1994) and Willing (1989) as well as teacher-generated materials, some of which involved further exploration of the items of the *ELLSI* such as:

- When do you use a dictionary?
- What kind of dictionary?
- When should you NOT use a dictionary?

During the period when the class was running, attendance was recorded and student and teacher feedback informally noted in order to assess the effectiveness of this approach to language learning strategy instruction.

Quite a large number of students ($N = 12$, the maximum number of students allowed in a class) initially chose the special Study Skills option class, designed to run for a month, when it was offered on Wednesday afternoons. However, although initially enthusiastic, by the end of the month the drop-out rate was high and few of the students were actually attending the class. Informally asked why they were not attending class, students reported that after two or three weeks there was nothing new, and they would rather be learning grammar or vocabulary or practising skills (the foci of some of the competing classes). They did not perceive the class as useful on a long-term basis and therefore either didn't attend or asked to change class.

Teachers who taught the class reported finding it difficult to find or create interesting materials which students would find relevant and useful, and reported being discouraged by the lack of student interest. In the light of this rather negative feedback, the class was not re-offered the following month.

The classroom experience

By no means all classroom attempts to teach strategies have been successful. A less-than-successful one is described here.

So what went wrong here? If this is not a useful way to conduct strategy instruction, how should strategy instruction be carried out?

4.7 HOW Should Strategy Instruction Be Conducted?

In spite of critical appraisals of learner training in language learning strategies such as in the article by Rees-Miller (1993), and in spite of some less than spectacularly successful attempts at strategy training, such as those reported by O'Malley (1987), Wenden (1987b) and Griffiths (2003b), there are many others (e.g. Chamot & Rubin, 1994; Cohen, 1998; Nunan, 1995; Wenden, 1991) who can point to successful efforts at teaching strategies. Brown (2001), however, points out that there is still a great deal of uncertainty regarding HOW such instruction should be conducted.

Rubin (1987) suggests that an important element of strategy instruction is the raising of students' **awareness** of language learning strategy options. If students know the alternatives they have available, she argues, they are in a better position to make informed choices.

According to Oxford (1989a), **practice** is an important ingredient of strategy training. If the new strategies of which students have been made aware are rehearsed, they will become automatic and stored in a student's individual strategy repertoire to be called on as needed.

Wenden (1991) and Graham (1997) suggest that strategy training needs to be **explicit**. If students do not clearly understand what they are doing and why, they will not transfer the new strategies they have learnt beyond the immediate task to new ones. Students can be shown, for instance, how to break down words they do not know into recognisable units. The word 'insubordinate', for example, can be divided into in = not, sub = lower, ordinate = order/rank – therefore an adjective for one who does not behave according to his/her lower rank. Many students have never been shown how to carry out this simple exercise and are not aware that it is even possible. Yet such a simple strategy can unlock the mysteries of some quite intimidating vocabulary. Other well-known techniques include the *Keyword* method (Atkinson, 1975), in which a new word is associated with a familiar word which sounds similar, and the *Linkword* method developed by Gruneberg (1987), which involves linking words in the first and target language to construct a picture in the mind. Oxford (1990) identifies many other language learning strategies such as using flashcards or semantic mapping (creating a diagram with the key concept connected by lines or arrows to related concepts).

In addition to explicit instruction, others argue that strategy instruction should also be **implicit** (e.g. Cohen, 1998; Harris, 2001). That is, strategy instruction needs to be embedded into regular classroom activities and practised. However, it needs to be done in such a way that it is not seen as just a waste of time and a distraction from the real task of learning new language.

In other words, it would seem that effective strategy instruction should aim to raise learner awareness of strategy choices and provide opportunities to practise by means of both explicit and implicit instruction.

If strategy instruction is going to be embedded into the regular classroom activities, clearly it has to be compatible with whatever else is going on in the learning situation. As discussed under theoretical underpinnings in Chapter 1, audiolingual techniques, with their emphasis on rote memorisation and automatic responses, do not really sit comfortably with the idea that learners can use strategies to engage cognitively with their own learning. Neither do Krashen's (1976, 1977) Monitor and Acquisition/Learning Hypotheses, which promote the idea that conscious learning is of little value in the process whereby language develops by means of natural communication, fit easily with strategy theory which suggests that learners can promote their own language development by being cognitively active. Another factor which may need to be considered is the role of the learners' L1, which may affect interactive strategies, especially in monolingual classes.

However, although principles such as audiolingual behaviourism and the acquisition/learning nil interface position were once rigidly held, contemporary language teaching has tended to become much more eclectic. Language learning strategies have the potential to form a useful ingredient in modern eclectic syllabi and can be used compatibly with a wide variety of different methods and approaches including some of the less widely known and adopted such as Total Physical Response (Asher, 1969), The Silent Way (Gattegno, 1963), The Natural Approach (Krashen & Terrell, 1983) and Suggestopaedia (Lozanov, 1978). However, an important condition for this to be successful is teacher awareness. In turn, teacher cognition begins at the teacher training stage. In other words, teacher trainers and teacher training institutions need to acknowledge the critical importance of strategy instruction if any real progress is to be made in this direction (see Section 4.13).

How should strategy instruction be carried out?

From an examination of the existing literature and of successful strategy instruction programmes, it would seem that effective strategy instruction includes four main elements:

(1)   Raising <u>awareness</u> of available strategies from which students can make informed choices which suit their own individual characteristics, situations and learning goals;
(2)   <u>Explicit</u> teaching of strategies so that students can transfer new strategies they learn to different learning tasks;
(3)   Strategies need to be <u>implicitly</u> embedded in the content so that HOW they are trying to learn does not divert time and attention from WHAT they want to learn;
(4)   Students need to be given maximum opportunities to <u>practise</u> the strategies they have learnt until they become automatic.

4.8   WHAT Should Be Included in Strategy Instruction?

Content of strategy instruction programmes may vary according to student needs, situational constraints or target requirements. However, in general, it is possible to suggest some key features.

Although the importance of frequency of language learning strategies has been questioned (e.g. Purpura, 1999), indications from the study reported in Sections 2.2 and 2.3 suggest that, overall, the frequent use of a large number of language learning strategies is reported by higher level learners. This finding would seem to indicate that, in general, more is indeed generally better when it comes to reported frequency of language learning strategy use.

Within this generalisation, however, it is possible that not only the overall reported frequency (quantity), but also the type (quality) of language learning strategies chosen may be important, since certain types of strategies (such as strategies relating to interaction or to vocabulary, and so on) appear to be typical of more proficient students. Griffiths (2003b) identified three basic types of strategies, which all need to be considered from a pedagogical point of view:

4.8.1 *Base* strategies

It would be easy to jump to the conclusion that the nine *base* strategies – because they are favoured by elementary students (see Section 2.4.1) – do not help to promote language learning and should therefore be discouraged. However, it is also possible that these strategies typical of lower level students might form a base which, with practice and confidence, underpins the kind of strategy structure more typical of higher level students. If this were the case, these *base* strategies could be shown to serve an important function in helping to lay the foundations of language learning and supporting students while confidence develops. The findings reported in Chapter 2, however, would seem to suggest that students who continue year after year to employ strategies such as rote memorisation of long texts in the belief that this will somehow improve their language ability could learn much more effectively if they were willing to utilise strategies more typical of higher level students.

This is not necessarily to say, of course, that memorisation is not a useful strategy if used appropriately. It may well be necessary, especially in the early stages of learning a new language, to remember certain basic vocabulary, for instance, and some fundamental rules of grammar for putting the vocabulary together. However, these findings would seem to indicate that memorisation is utilised less frequently as students move on to higher levels. This suggests, perhaps, that memorisation is a lower order strategy and may possibly be an example of the less sophisticated use of strategies by lower level students noted by both Porte (1988) and Vann and Abraham (1990). Logically, therefore, students who wish to progress to higher levels in their language learning might be well advised to move on from these basic strategies as soon as they can cope with the kinds of strategies more typical of higher level students.

The discovery of this group of strategies reportedly used more frequently by elementary students than by advanced students raises questions regarding pedagogical practice: is it useful for teachers to encourage students (as they commonly do) to write diaries (Item 43), to review their lessons (Item 8), or to plan their schedules (Item 34), when research indicates that the use of these strategies is more typical of lower level students? Or is it possible that strategies such as these have their usefulness early on the road to proficiency and only become a problem if they are retained past the point where they are useful, perhaps if students become fixated on one or other of them to the exclusion of others (for instance, students who spend most of their time in their rooms reviewing lessons or writing diaries at the expense of spending time talking to host families or watching TV)?

Because these *base* strategies may well have their usefulness early in the language learning process, care is recommended regarding how their use is discouraged or even forbidden (as sometimes happens in language classrooms). Nevertheless, it would seem reasonable to suggest that students should probably be encouraged to move on from them and to develop strategy patterns more typical of higher level students.

4.8.2 *Core* strategies

Prominent among the group of *core* strategies (see Section 2.4.2) used highly frequently across all students are metacognitive strategies relating to students' ability to manage their own learning. Teachers sometimes find the idea that students can manage without them somewhat threatening (e.g. Grundy, 1999), but the fact that students can to some extent autonomously regulate their own learning does not obviate the need for the teacher. It merely changes the emphasis of the teacher's role from authority figure to facilitator, a shift which can, in fact, be very rewarding (e.g. Harmer, 1995).

Also included among the *core* strategies are items relating to interaction, to pronunciation, to the use of resources and to the functional use of language. It would seem that, as students begin to progress from the lower levels of language, they need to develop the ability to use the language to deal with the real world and with other people. Teachers need to be willing to assist in this process if effective learning is to occur.

4.8.3 *Plus* strategies

The discovery of a group of *plus* strategies (see Section 2.4.3) that are reportedly used highly frequently by higher level students but not by all students suggests the possibility that they are a group of activities which might be employed by students in general to promote more effective language learning. The possibility that these are strategies which teachers might usefully encourage students to use more frequently in order to 'enhance their success record', as Rubin (1975: 42) puts it, has exciting pedagogical implications.

It appears, for instance, that good language learners tend not to be the ones who demand 'the answer', and are constantly checking with their dictionaries for exact meanings: they are able to develop strategies to cope with a 'degree of inherent uncertainty' (White, 1999: 450). Strategies for managing ambiguity are used by higher level students as a means of maintaining continuity of learning in the face of imperfect knowledge. It is, of course, difficult to be sure whether strategies to tolerate ambiguity promote proficiency, or whether the additional confidence which comes with increased proficiency enables students to more easily compensate for the smaller gaps in their knowledge. One way or another, since these strategies seem to be typical of higher level students, it would seem to make sense for teachers to encourage all students to work towards adding them to their strategy repertoires as soon as they are able to cope.

Another strategy type which occurs among those used by higher level students relates to reading. Getting students who are speakers of other languages to read in English is not always easy. For many years the importance of reading when learning a language was unquestioned, but in recent years the perceived usefulness of reading in the target language has diminished (Bowler & Parminter, 1992). Reading in the target language, however, can be motivating, it can provide access to culture and it can expand students' language awareness (Lazar, 1993). The inclusion of reading-related strategies among those used highly frequently by the most proficient group of students would seem to add support to the belief that reading is important when learning a new language and should be encouraged by teachers.

Possible ways of promoting the use of reading as a language learning strategy among students might include encouraging students to make use of self-access libraries and/or setting up special interest classes focused on reading, conversation and/or the sharing of resources. My own experience is that once students have got over the initial reluctance that there often is to read in English, and once they have been guided towards suitable materials (such as graded readers) which they can read with reasonable ease at their level, they often become quite 'hooked' on reading and will continue enthusiastically under their own initiative. An awareness of the resources available and how to obtain or access them is often all that is necessary to get students to use readily available materials in English. A certain amount of effort by teachers or self-access staff often has to go into getting them to this point, however, and there may be resistance.

I clearly remember one student, for instance, who, after I had been extolling the virtues of reading to improve English ability, proudly bought me an enormous volume of Shakespeare which he was working at translating page by page, painstakingly writing the words in his own language above the English lines. When I tried to suggest that I did not think this was a particularly useful strategy, and that he would be better to choose something more enjoyable in modern English which would provide him with expressions that he could use in everyday conversation, he was adamant that he was finding this activity very helpful. In fact, I never did succeed in convincing him otherwise, and every now and then he would come and ask me about a passage that he was finding troublesome. I sometimes wonder if he is still labouring to translate 'to be, or not to be', 'out, damned spot' or 'lend me your ears', and what his English is like these days!

The *plus* strategies are, in fact, a very varied group, including a number of interactive strategies such as Item 14: *I start conversations in English*. Lack of confidence often inhibits the use of these kinds of strategies, since students may be afraid of looking foolish and may require a great deal of patient reassurance on the part of the facilitator. Topics of conversation should not just focus on the conversation class itself. In my experience, the most useful items discussed in such groups often revolve around what has happened outside, such as a failed attempt to purchase an item in a store. Other students may be able to contribute useful ideas about what went wrong, what should have been said or done, and how to avoid the problems next time. A great deal of humour and support can be generated by such discussions, hopefully leading to future successful encounters and increased confidence.

4.8.4 Orchestration

Strategy orchestration is a complex phenomenon. According to Anderson (2008: 101):

> Effective strategy use does not occur in isolation. Often we discuss the use of a strategy as if it happens all by itself. Understanding the interdependency of strategy use while engaged in a language learning task is an important learning experience. Being metacognitively aware of strategy use allows good language learners to integrate the use of various strategies in a positive way.

Since strategies are not isolated phenomena, the ability to use strategies effectively in combination with each other, in groups or clusters, is an important skill. It is a skill which the poor language learners whom Porte (1988) and Vann and Abraham (1990) report as active strategy users appeared not to have: although they used many strategies, they were unable to select strategies appropriate for their current learning situation and to use them effectively in combination.

From a pedagogical perspective, however, strategy orchestration is not an easy skill to teach. This is because the particular combination of strategies which will suit a given student is highly individual, and may vary according to numerous factors such as age, nationality, gender, affective states, and so on. It is also contextually dependent, and may vary according to the specific situation in which the learner is working or living: the same learner may not use the same strategies in a different environment. The combination will also differ according to the learning goal: strategies which work well for a General English course may or may not work as well for an exam or Business English course. In other words, it is not possible to provide a pre-set formula for effective orchestration. Each learner needs to experiment for him/herself to determine the combination which produces the best results given the unique blend of individual, situational and target variables. Nevertheless,

---

What should be included in strategy instruction?

There are numerous possibilities for what should be included in strategy instruction, but an effective programme should include awareness of:

(1) *Base* strategies – these are the strategies which form the foundation of students' strategy use and provide a base for further development as the student becomes more proficient;

(2) *Core* strategies – these strategies are at the centre of a student's strategy repertoire and consist predominantly of metacognitive strategies which enable students to manage, control or regulate their learning;

(3) *Plus* strategies – these are the strategies which seem to characterise higher-level students, which become available to them as they become more proficient, and which in turn promote greater proficiency;

(4) Orchestration – this is a skill which students develop to harmonise their strategy repertoires in ways which maximise their ability to learn.

---

discussion of the orchestration issue may well be helpful to assist students to work through the possibilities and arrive at a harmonious outcome.

4.9 The Issue of Confidence and the Tornado Effect

The issue of confidence mentioned at various points in the book (e.g. Sections 1.4.4 and 3.1.1) brings up the vexed question of cause and effect regarding the relationship between language learning strategies and proficiency. Does a strategy such as *not looking up every new word*, for instance, help to develop proficiency and, if so, should dictionaries be totally banned from all classrooms? Or is it just that more proficient students have a wider vocabulary and are therefore able to use confidently the knowledge they have as a framework to enable them to work out what they do not know? Would removing dictionary support from less proficient students help them to develop high proficiency-related behaviour, or would it simply remove a useful tool which they need at that point in their language development while the foundations of the new language are still being laid?

These are difficult questions akin to the age-old riddle about the chicken and the egg: which comes first? Perhaps it is useful to view cause and effect in this field not so much as linear but as a spiral, where language learning strategies may help to develop proficiency (for instance, by increasing vocabulary), which affects language learning strategy choice (for instance, with a wider vocabulary, students will be able to read newspapers with ease), which may further increase proficiency (they will come across even more vocabulary, as well as idioms and other authentic expressions), and so on in a hopefully ever enlarging spiral (the Tornado Effect? – see Section 2.10). If this is the case, since the analysis of the data indicates that some language learning strategies are reportedly used more frequently by more proficient students than by others (for instance, looking for patterns, learning the culture) perhaps teachers might usefully conclude that the strategies which are more typical of higher level students are goals to be aimed for and encouraged where appropriate, although care should be taken that their use is not imposed whether students are ready or not.

The Tornado Effect

The Tornado Effect concept rests on the hypothesis that strategy development is spiral (like a tornado) rather than linear. It suggests that, as proficiency and confidence increase, more and more strategies become accessible to the learner, increasing exponentially in strength into a powerful force for learning. Teachers should know how to harness the potential for learning which the Tornado Effect presents.

4.10 Learner Variables

Since learners vary according to factors such as motivation, nationality, sex and age, learner variables need to be taken into account when considering language learning strategy instruction. This is because strategies which are appropriate for some may or may not be suitable for others.

4.10.1 Motivation

From a pedagogical point of view, although Cohen and Dornyei (2002) suggest that teachers can actively address the issue of student motivation in order to increase the effectiveness of instruction, and although at times teachers may feel guilty that unmotivated students are somehow their fault, the indications are that the students whose interview data is reported in Chapter 3 succeeded or not on the basis of the motivation which they brought with them into the classroom situation. Whether or not it is within a teacher's power, or whether it is reasonable for teachers to be expected to motivate students like Mikhail and Yuki to learn language when, in fact, they have little or no intrinsic motivation to do so remains an area for ongoing research.

Motivation, however, has been found to be related to the reported frequency of language learning strategy use which, in turn, is related to course level. It would therefore certainly seem reasonable to expect that anything a teacher might be able to do in terms of increasing students' motivation may well bear dividends in terms of successful learning.

4.10.2 Nationality

Although there are some studies which have reported on differences in strategy use according to nationality (e.g. O'Malley, 1987; Politzer & McGroarty, 1985), generally research in this area is scarce. The finding of significant differences in class level and in the reported frequency of language learning strategy use between European students and students of other nationalities (see Section 2.5.2) is potentially an important one in terms of suggesting strategies which all students might be encouraged to use in order to learn more effectively.

Of the four strategies in the *SILL* study that European students reported using more frequently than other students, two related to reading (Items 16 and 36) and two related to interacting with others in English (Items 35 and 47), while Items 16 and 36 also relate to the use of resources and Items 35 and 36 also relate to the management of learning (see Table 2.6). Although it would be naïve to suggest that encouraging students of all nationalities to expand their use of the types of strategies which are reportedly used by European students would necessarily lead to increased proficiency for all students, it is possible that awareness of these results might be of interest to other national groups and that this knowledge might help them to make informed choices regarding their own strategy usage.

4.10.3 Age and sex

In spite of popular beliefs and some previous research evidence which might have led to contrary expectations (as already discussed in Section 2.5.3 and 2.5.4), no significant differences were discovered in proficiency or in reported frequency of strategy use according to either age or sex. Average reported frequency of strategy use was remarkably similar for both men and women and identical for both older and younger students. Although female students were working at slightly higher levels on average than male students, and younger students were working at slightly higher levels than older students, these differences were not found to be significant.

In spite of these overall findings, however, on an individual level Hiro's comments regarding the need for 'face-saving' strategies as an older learner were illuminating, and Kang's repertoire of idiosyncratic key strategies raises questions regarding the degree to which the ability to evolve such a set of strategies may be typical of the successful older learner. From a pedagogical point of view, it is important that classroom procedures are sufficiently flexible to allow for students such as Hiro to be comfortable, and for unusual strategies (such as Kang's for pronunciation; see Section 3.1.9) to be tolerated or even encouraged – after all, they might work!

4.10.4 Style and personality

Obviously, in any class, there is going to be a range of personality types. Some of the students may be extroverted and contribute willingly to speaking activities; others may be more introverted and more reluctant to get involved. Some may be intuitive and quick to pick up subtle inferences; others may need to think through information step by step in order to achieve understanding.

And personality may be related to learning style in the classroom. We might expect, for instance, that extroverted learners (such as Kira and Mikhail) would enjoy group work, while introverts (such as Kim and Kang) would probably prefer to work quietly on their own.

In turn, style and personality might be expected to influence students' choice of strategies. Extroverts will probably make use of social occasions to learn whereas introverts will probably prefer the self-study room or a library or their own rooms. Since there does not seem to be any strong evidence that one kind of style or personality is superior to another in terms of language learning (see Sections 3.2.6 and 3.2.7), the important thing from a pedagogical perspective would seem to be that classroom systems make allowances for individual differences.

4.10.5 Autonomy

There does seem to be some evidence that good language learners are autonomous, meaning that they are able to exercise control over their own learning (e.g. Cotterall, 2008). Certainly, in the study reported in Chapter 3, Kira, Kim and Kang all displayed autonomous behaviour, and all were successful. Furthermore, they were all active strategy users.

Learner autonomy can at times be threatening for teachers (e.g. Grundy, 1999). Truly autonomous students, however, are usually also aware that their teacher is a valuable resource, and they will develop strategies to maximise what they can obtain from their teacher (such as Kira's strategy of sitting beside the teacher in class whenever he could so that it was easy to get the teacher's attention).

4.10.6 Beliefs

Beliefs are a very personal matter and may manifest themselves in a classroom in a number of ways. These may include the way students dress, where they sit and with whom, the way they interact with classmates and/or the teacher, whether homework is done and how carefully, how regular they are in attendance or punctuality – all of these behaviours may indicate underlying belief systems.

These beliefs may, in turn, affect strategies. A student (like Yuki) who does not believe that the target language is worth learning, for instance, may not bother too much with homework. On the other hand, students who do believe that the target language is worthwhile will organise themselves in order to attend regularly and to be on time.

4.10.7 Aptitude

As discussed in Section 3.2.10, the aptitude concept has fallen rather out of favour for some time and the instruments with which to measure it are controversial. As a consequence, research regarding aptitude is scarce. Regarding the interviewees in Chapter 3, it is really not possible to say whether their success or otherwise might be attributable to natural aptitude or the lack thereof.

Perhaps in relation to strategies, the most sensible thing we can suggest is that all students should be given the benefit of the same instruction opportunities. From that point, what the student chooses to do is a matter of individual choice which may or may not be related to natural aptitude.

4.10.8 Affect, identity and investment

Although affect did not feature strongly among the strategies reported by the interviewees in Chapter 3, it would seem only sensible to assume that students who are anxious, who have negative attitudes, who attribute failure to deficiencies in their own ability, who do not empathise with speakers of the target language, who suffer from inhibitions or who have low self-concepts are less likely to be successful language learners than those who have more positive emotions. These feelings may be linked to a person's sense of identity, perhaps the extent to which he or she does or does not feel accepted by the target community (e.g. Norton & Toohey, 2001), and this may in turn relate to the amount of effort a learner is prepared to invest in learning the target language.

It is not easy to say how much influence a teacher may have over learners' affective states, sense of identity or willingness to invest in the language learning endeavour: this will vary according to both the individual learner and the individual teacher. It is obviously desirable for the teacher to maintain a positive and accepting classroom atmosphere and to ensure that all students are treated fairly and equally. Teachers should also try to remain sensitive to students' emotional states, since affective overload may well have an effect on students' work, as happened with Lily when her mother visited from Switzerland. In such cases it might be worth recommending affective strategies such as *positive self-talk, giving oneself a reward*, or *writing feelings in a diary*.

Learner variables

As discussed in Chapter 1, there are many individual learner variables and these may all affect the kinds of strategies students choose. From a pedagogical point of view, the important thing would seem to be that strategy instruction should be provided to all students and that the strategy choices that they make should be respected by teachers, even if (perhaps like Hiro's withdrawal strategy, see Section 3.1.7) they do not quite fit with the lesson plan, or (perhaps like Kang's pronunciation strategy, see Section 3.1.9) they are a little unusual.

4.11 Situational Variables

Although recognised as an important factor in language learning (e.g. Norton & Toohey, 2001), situational/contextual/environmental variables are often invisible when it comes to considering how students learn most effectively. White (1993) discovered the importance of metacognitive strategies for students studying in a distance learning situation. In a study-abroad situation, Griffiths (2008d) found that the strategies most strongly related to success were those related to lexical expansion and flexibility, the management of learning and the tolerance of ambiguity.

Although there is so little research in this area to go on, it would seem only sensible to suggest that teachers need to be sensitive to the learning situations in which they and their students operate. They also need to be aware that strategies that are appropriate and effective in one learning environment may or may not be suitable or useful in another, and students may need to adapt existing strategy patterns. The role of the teacher is to support this adaptation with patience, sensitivity and respect for the students' existing strategies, which may well have served them well in their previous learning environment. Teachers should remember that it is not always easy to change established behaviour, but with understanding and good will it is possible to co-construct a learning environment which will facilitate satisfactory outcomes for all concerned.

Situational variables

Clearly, the situation in which a learner is studying (for instance, in a classroom, in a distance education programme or abroad) will affect the strategies which are most likely to contribute to success in that environment. Students need, therefore, to be flexible with strategy choice, rather than rigidly keeping to familiar strategies. And teachers need to be tolerant and supportive during the period when students are adapting existing strategy repertoires to the new situation.

4.12 Target Variables

In spite of the fact that, intuitively, strategies must vary according to the learning purpose for which they are being employed, goal-appropriate strategies are another area where little research is available. Clearly, strategies which a student may find useful for studying grammar or developing skills, for instance, may or may not be useful for a student studying to pass a specific exam or working on a Business English course.

A number of pedagogical suggestions are made for a range of learning targets (vocabulary, grammar, function, pronunciation, reading, writing, listening, speaking) in Griffiths' (2008e) book *Lessons from Good Language Learners*, while reading strategies were discovered to be most significantly correlated with successful end-of-course outcomes for a Research Methods course (Griffiths, 2004: Section 2.7). However, further research needs to be done before it will be possible to know whether this finding applies to other learning targets.

Target variables

Goal-specific strategies are another area which is relatively under-researched. Although, intuitively, it would seem obvious that students will need different strategies for various learning targets and that teachers should make allowances for and facilitate the use of target-specific strategies, there is relatively little research to identify what these strategies may be.

4.13 Teacher Training

A number of writers have emphasised the importance of teacher training and cognition in recent years (e.g. Bailey *et al.*, 2001; Borg, 2009; Freeman & Richards, 1996; Harmer, 2012; Woods, 1996). Cohen (1998, 1999) suggests that teacher education is the key to progress on the strategy instruction front. If teacher education prospectuses and materials are examined, however, language learning strategy issues will rarely be dealt with prominently, if at all.

The studies presented in this book, however, indicate that language learning strategies are significantly related to achievement in language learning. Although the relationship is not uncomplicated (is any human behaviour uncomplicated?), there would appear to be enough of a relationship for strategies to be taken seriously as a means of promoting more effective learning. In fact, according to the results presented in Section 2.4, the *plus* group of strategies accounted for more than 10% of the variance in class level. When one considers how many variables there are in the equation (other kinds of strategies, motivation, nationality, sex, age, aptitude, beliefs, style, personality, autonomy, situation, goal, and so on), to find a group of strategies which accounts for a 10th of the variance in student achievement is surely worthy of pedagogical attention.

So, what do teachers need to know?

(1)   Teachers need to have an understanding of the terminology, definitions, classification and theory underlying the language learning strategy concept so that they are clear in their own minds about the issues and can therefore pass on to their students a clear vision of how strategies can be used to learn effectively. This conceptual perspective is dealt with in Chapter 1.

(2)   Teachers need to be informed of the current state of research in the area of language learning strategies. They should know, for instance, that research

has shown that higher level students do indeed use many more strategies more frequently than lower level students, and that some types of strategies (especially the *plus* strategies) do indeed seem to be significantly more related to successful learning (in terms of higher class levels) than others.

(3) Teachers should know that some learner variables (such as motivation and nationality) are significantly related to progress in English, and they should consider how to deal with this variability in their own classrooms.

(4) Teachers should consider how to manage aspects of the learning situation in which they and their students find themselves and strategies which may or may not be suitable for this particular environment.

(5) Teachers should consider the learning target at which their students are aiming and give careful thought to facilitating goal-appropriate strategies.

(6) Teachers should be aware that research has shown that strategies can and do change over time and that the students who appear to make the fastest progress in their language learning are those who most increase the frequency of their strategy use over a period (see Sections 2.8 and 2.9). Given this result, teachers should consider how best they can facilitate this development.

(7) Teachers should remain constantly aware that their students, although part of a class, are inevitably individuals who must be allowed, indeed encouraged, to apply their own unique approach to learning. From an individual perspective, quantitative statistics, although useful for providing generalised information, never quite describe any particular student exactly (see Chapter 3 for examples). Teachers must remain aware of, make allowances for, and even celebrate this basic variability of human nature.

(8) Teachers need to learn techniques for integrating language learning strategy instruction into the fabric of their lessons, making strategy instruction both explicit and embedded in order both to make students aware of their actions so that they may be able to transfer this knowledge to other situations, and to provide the practice required for new strategies to become automatic. By doing this, instead of strategy instruction being seen as a waste of time which holds up WHAT students want to learn, the HOW and the WHAT may be brought together in a mutually supportive partnership.

(9) Teachers should at all times be careful to promote student confidence so that they may be willing to risk their egos trying higher level strategies (such as reading without looking up every new word) and maybe learning from mistakes without fear of losing face. This learning then leads to more confidence, which encourages further risk-taking.

(10) Teachers should remember that strategy development is not linear but spiral, with one strategy (for instance, expanding vocabulary repertoires) facilitating the development of others (for instance, reading newspapers) which then supports the ability to read more advanced material, and so on. This spiral (Tornado?) effect potentially leads to accelerating language development. If we could only discover how to harness the power of this Tornado Effect, what a wonderful teaching/learning tool we would have!

Teacher training

If the potential of learning strategies to enhance learning is to be realised, teacher training needs to include an awareness of strategy theory and research as well as providing practical techniques for the promotion of strategy use in the classroom.

4.14 Conclusion

Much of the early pioneering strategy research (e.g. Rubin, 1975) was aimed at teaching good language learner strategies to less successful learners. Implications of this focus include:

(1) The cognitive theoretical paradigm within which language learning strategy theory essentially belongs suggests that language learning is a cognitive process involving conscious mental effort. Learners are capable of taking a conscious and active role in their own learning by the use of language learning strategies. Furthermore, language learning strategies are, themselves, able to be learnt, which allows for the possibility that individual students may be able to improve their language learning effectiveness by choosing appropriate strategies.

(2) It is possible that teachers might be able to facilitate the development of language learning strategies by raising awareness of strategy possibilities, by making strategy instruction both implicit and explicit, and by providing practice opportunities to develop automaticity and encouragement to develop confidence.

(3) An encouraging sign came from the study reported in Section 4.5. This indicated that teachers, contrary to the result of some other studies (e.g. Griffiths & Parr, 2001a; Nunan, 1988) rated their students' strategies as highly important. There was also a high degree of accord between the

teachers' importance ratings and the strategies the students reported using highly frequently.

(4) However, attempts at strategy instruction have not, on the whole, been hugely successful (e.g. Griffiths, 2003b; O'Malley, 1987; Wenden, 1987b). Nevertheless, there have been some success stories (for a summary, see Chamot, 2008).

(5) Perhaps the experience with the Study Skills class reported in Section 4.6 points generally to the need to include strategy instruction, whether explicit or embedded, in the general teaching programme since, in general, students seem to quickly lose interest in learning HOW to learn if it is not perceived as being directly relevant to WHAT they want to learn.

(6) This, in turn, would seem to point to the importance of teacher education, so that teachers are made aware of the need to integrate strategy instruction into the content of their lessons and are provided with training and practice in how to do this. Since higher level students report frequent use of a large number of language learning strategies, teachers should aim to raise students' awareness of strategy options and encourage students to practise and expand their language learning strategy repertoires. In order to do this effectively, teachers need to consider carefully the limitations and affordances existing in their particular learning situations given the learner and target variables with which they must deal.

4.15 Pedagogical Areas for Further Research

From a pedagogical perspective, many questions regarding language learning strategies remain to be answered. In particular:

(1) how to motivate students to become more strategically aware;
(2) how to allow for learner differences (such as age-related strategy choices) in a classroom;
(3) how strategies relate to particular learning targets;
(4) how strategies relate to particular learning situations;
(5) how to develop materials related to language learning strategies which can be built into the course as language learning exercises in their own right but with implicit strategy instruction underlying the language input;
(6) how to manage explicit strategy instruction in such a way as to help to circumvent student resistance;
(7) how to help students orchestrate strategies effectively;
(8) how the Tornado Effect can be used to maximise effective language learning.

5   Overview

5.1 The Strategy Concept

Although widely believed to be a significant factor in successful language learning, the language learning strategy concept, referring to behaviour employed by learners in order to promote language learning, has proven elusive, even at the basic level of terminology. However, even though a range of terms has been used to cover this kind of behaviour (including *learning behaviours, tactics, techniques,* and so on) the term *strategy* has probably been the most consistently used over the years, and for this reason it is probably the term best recognised and most widely accepted today.

Since it has been so difficult to achieve consensus even on a name, it is, perhaps, hardly surprising that defining this terminologically challenged concept has caused no less debate. An extensive review of the literature suggests that language learning strategies are actively and consciously selected by learners in order to achieve a particular learning goal. Language learning strategies might therefore be defined as *activities consciously chosen by learners for the purpose of regulating their own language learning.* It should be remembered, however, that this definition is value-neutral and does not relate to how effective a strategy may be. Strategy effectiveness can only be judged in relation to how useful it is for the user, the situation and the learning target.

Equally problematic has been the establishment of agreed theoretical underpinnings for the language learning strategy concept. However, the element of conscious choice evident in the definition suggested above would seem to indicate an essentially cognitive foundation. Nevertheless, some structuralist (for instance, learning grammar rules, looking for patterns, coming to terms with the systems of the new language), behaviourist (for instance drilling, repetition, practice) or sociocultural/communicative (for instance listening to or conversing with others, asking for help/advice/

correction) dimensions may also be present in some strategies. In addition, elements of Schemata Theory, Complexity/Chaos Theory, Activity Theory and perhaps others may well be present in the somewhat eclectic theoretical base which underlies the strategy concept.

Attempts to construct neat and tidy strategy taxonomies have failed to produce universal agreement, and learning strategies are often confused with other types of strategies (such as communication strategies) and other phenomena (such as styles and skills). Statistical procedures such as factor analyses have generally failed to produce coherent groupings, leading to the conclusion that a standardised classification system for language learning strategies may well not be viable. When undertaking language learning strategy research, researchers might be well advised either to write their own instruments or carefully to adapt existing instruments such as the *SILL* (*Strategy Inventory for Language Learning* – Oxford, 1990) or the *ELLSI* (*English Language Learning Strategy Inventory*, Griffiths, 2003b – see Appendix) to suit their own particular learners, situations and learning targets.

5.2 Quantitative Research

According to the research results presented in Chapter 2, language learning strategies are positively related to success in language learning. According to a study by Griffiths (2003a, 2003b), higher level students report using many more language learning strategies significantly more frequently than lower level students.

Furthermore, some strategy types appear to be more related to successful language learning than others. Memory strategies feature among those frequently used by lower level students, while metacognitive strategies used to manage the learning process feature frequently across all students. Higher level learners report the use of a wide range of various kinds of strategies: in other words, the more successful students frequently use a large number of different strategy types.

Can we assume that these findings will apply to all learners, contexts and learning goals? Although, according to Griffiths (2003b), some learner variables such as nationality and motivation do seem to be related to strategy choice and to class level, other factors such as sex and age do not appear to have a significant relationship. And there are indications that students are more likely to be successful if they are prepared to be flexible and adapt their strategies to suit situational and target variables.

Are strategies a fixed individual attribute, or are they variable? According to Griffiths (2003b, 2006), learners can adapt their strategy repertoires.

Furthermore, the most successful learners in this study were those who most increased their strategy frequency over the research period.

So does this suggest that frequent strategy use leads to more effective learning? We need to be careful here, since it is also possible that higher level students have access to more strategies merely because of their higher level of proficiency. It is rarely so easy to decide which is the chicken and which the egg. It might be reasonable, however, to suggest a spiral rather than a linear pattern of strategy development. This means, for instance, that a larger vocabulary facilitates wider reading, which increases exposure to previously unfamiliar vocabulary, and so on in an ever expanding spiral which might be termed a Tornado Effect.

5.3 Qualitative Research

These quantitative findings, however, although useful when looking at the situation overall, do not necessarily apply to every individual student, as is reported in Chapter 3. Although most of the interviewees who progressed to higher class levels or who passed the exams for which they were preparing reported a highly frequent overall average use of language learning strategies and gave ratings of 5 ('always or almost always') to a large number of language learning strategies of different types, there were individual exceptions to this general finding (for instance Kang and May).

Of the factors which emerged from the interview data as possible contributors to an explanation of varying levels of reported language learning strategy use and differing rates of progress, motivation may well be the strongest, although, as reported in Chapter 3, sex and age did not appear to be strongly related to strategy use or success on an individual level. Although not researched here directly, the interviews also provided some interesting insights into some other individual variables which are commonly researched in the literature (style, personality, autonomy, beliefs, affect, aptitude, identity, investment).

5.4 Pedagogical Research

If learners are capable of taking a conscious and active role in their own learning by the use of language learning strategies, it follows logically that language learning strategies are, themselves, able to be learnt. This allows for the possibility that individual students may be able to improve their language learning effectiveness by choosing appropriate strategies. Teachers, for their part, may be able to facilitate the process of strategy development by raising awareness, by making strategy instruction both implicit and explicit, and by providing practice opportunities to develop confidence and stimulate the Tornado Effect which has as its foundation the premise, based on research evidence, that the strategy factor is related to successful learning. Success then encourages strategy expansion, making learning even more effective, and creating an expanding and accelerating spiral resembling a tornado.

Although not all research has found a close accord between teacher and student perceptions regarding language learning strategies, and although not all attempts at strategy training have been particularly productive, there have been some successful strategy instruction initiatives. Key ingredients of successful strategy development programmes would seem to include awareness raising, explicit as well as implicit instruction, and opportunities for practice.

When training teachers to administer strategy instruction, it is important that they are made aware of the theoretical issues relating to the concept and of the research which has been conducted in the area. They also need to have a clear idea of strategy options available to students and of the learner variables that may help to determine which strategies are effective and for whom. Teachers also need to be trained to consider situational and target variables when considering strategy instruction for their students.

5.5 Conclusion

Although research into language learning strategies was begun in the 1970s, many unanswered questions and much controversy remains. By looking at the subject from conceptual, quantitative, qualitative and pedagogical perspectives, this book has attempted to provide answers for some of the questions and address some of the controversies. It is to be hoped that the search for solutions to some of the remaining issues will continue, since research to date has indicated that language learning strategies have the potential to be a powerful factor in successful language learning.

Appendix 1

LANGUAGE SKILLS DEVELOPMENT STRATEGY QUESTIONNAIRE

The following questionnaire contains some of the strategies which students report using in order to assist the development of skills in the language they are trying to learn. Please read the following strategy items and grade each one according to the frequency with which you use it:

BIODATA   M/F

BIRTHDATE: _____   NATIONALITY: _____

Why are you studying? _____

Are there any other strategies which you have found useful for developing the language skills you need for your study? _____

Strategies for Language Skills Development (LSD) Questionnaire, Griffiths, 2004

1. Very low   2. Low   3. Medium   4. High   5. Very high

READING SKILLS

_____1. I read extensively for information in the target language
_____2. I read for pleasure in the target language
_____3. I find reading material at my level
_____4. I use a library to obtain reading material
_____5. I first skim read a text then go back and read it more carefully
_____6. I look for how a text is organized
_____7. I make summaries of what I read
             8. I make predictions about what I will read next
_____9. I guess the approximate meaning by using clues from the context
_____10. I use a dictionary to get the exact meaning

WRITING SKILLS

_____1. I write letters or emails to friends in the target language
_____2. When my mistakes are corrected, I learn from the corrections
_____3. I write a variety of text types in the target language (e.g. notes, messages, lists)
_____4. I plan my writing before I start
_____5. If I cannot think of the correct expression I think of another way to express my meaning (e.g. synonyms)
_____6. I use reference materials (e.g. a dictionary, thesaurus or grammar book) to check that what I am writing is correct
_____7. If I am unsure about something I want to write I try to express my meaning and do not worry too much about correctness
_____8. I write a rough copy before writing a good copy
_____9. I write a diary in the target language
_____10. I get someone to proof read my writing

LISTENING SKILLS

_____1. I attend out-of-class events where I can listen to the new language being spoken

_____2. I use the media (e.g. radio, TV or movies) to practise my listening skills

_____3. I listen to native speakers in public places (e.g. shops, restaurants, buses) and try to understand what they are saying

_____4. I listen for key words which seem to carry most of the meaning

_____5. I predict what the other person will say next based on context, background knowledge or what has been said so far

_____6. I ask the speaker to slow down, repeat or clarify if I do not understand

_____7. I avoid translating what I hear word-for-word

_____8. I use the speaker's tone of voice, gestures, pauses or body language as a clue to meaning

_____9. If I am unsure about meaning I guess

_____10. I listen carefully to how native speakers pronounce the language I am trying to learn.

SPEAKING SKILLS

_____1. I repeat new language to myself in order to practise it

_____2. I seek out people with whom I can speak the target language

_____3. I plan in advance what I want to say

_____4. If I am corrected while speaking, I try to remember the correction and avoid making the same mistake again

_____5. I ask questions

_____6. I do not worry about correctness as long as I can communicate my meaning

_____7. If necessary, I use gestures to convey my meaning and keep a conversation going

_____8. I practise the target language with other students

_____9. If I do not know the vocabulary I want to use, I use similar words or phrases

_____10. I try to pronounce the target language like native speakers

Appendix 2

NAME: _____

**ENGLISH LANGUAGE LEARNING STRATEGY INVENTORY
(STUDENTS' VERSION)**

Dear student: *please read the following list of language learning strategies. Please mark each one according to the frequency with which you use it:*

1. Very low   2. Low   3. Medium   4. High   5. Very high

_____	1.	Doing homework
_____	2.	Learning from the teacher
_____	3.	Learning in an environment where the language is spoken
_____	4.	Reading books in English
_____	5.	Using a computer
_____	6.	Watching TV in English
_____	7.	Revising regularly
_____	8.	Listening to songs in English
_____	9.	Using language learning games
_____	10.	Writing letters in English
_____	11.	Listening to music while studying
_____	12.	Talking to other students in English
_____	13.	Using a dictionary
_____	14.	Reading newspapers in English
_____	15.	Studying English grammar
_____	16.	Consciously learning new vocabulary
_____	17.	Keeping a language learning notebook
_____	18.	Talking to native speakers of English
_____	19.	Taking note of language used in the environment
_____	20.	Controlling schedules so that English study is done
_____	21.	Pre-planning language-learning encounters
_____	22.	Not worrying about mistakes
_____	23.	Using a self-study centre
_____	24.	Trying to think in English
_____	25.	Listening to native speakers of English
_____	26.	Learning from mistakes
_____	27.	Spending a lot of time studying English
_____	28.	Making friends with native speakers
_____	29.	Watching movies in English
_____	30.	Learning about the culture of English speakers
_____	31.	Listening to the radio in English
_____	32.	Writing a diary in English

English Language Learning Strategy Inventory (ELLSI), Griffiths, 2003b

Appendix 3

INTERVIEW GUIDE

1. Which language learning strategies have you found most useful for learning English (key strategies)?

2. (a) What have you found most difficult about learning English?
   (b) Which strategies have you used to help overcome these difficulties?

3. Do you think the strategies you use have been affected by your
   (a) nationality?
   (b) gender?
   (c) age?
   (d) other factors?

If so, what effect have these factors had?

Appendix 4

NAME: _____

ENGLISH LANGUAGE LEARNING STRATEGY INVENTORY
(TEACHERS' VERSION)

Dear student: *please read the following list of language learning strategies. Please mark each one according to the frequency with which you use it:*

1. Very low   2. Low   3. Medium   4. High   5. Very high

_____	1.	Doing homework
_____	2.	Learning from the teacher
_____	3.	Learning in an environment where the language is spoken
_____	4.	Reading books in English
_____	5.	Using a computer
_____	6.	Watching TV in English
_____	7.	Revising regularly
_____	8.	Listening to songs in English
_____	9.	Using language learning games
_____	10.	Writing letters in English
_____	11.	Listening to music while studying
_____	12.	Talking to other students in English
_____	13.	Using a dictionary
_____	14.	Reading newspapers in English
_____	15.	Studying English grammar
_____	16.	Consciously learning new vocabulary
_____	17.	Keeping a language learning notebook
_____	18.	Talking to native speakers of English
_____	19.	Taking note of language used in the environment
_____	20.	Controlling schedules so that English study is done
_____	21.	Pre-planning language-learning encounters
_____	22.	Not worrying about mistakes
_____	23.	Using a self-study centre
_____	24.	Trying to think in English
_____	25.	Listening to native speakers of English
_____	26.	Learning from mistakes
_____	27.	Spending a lot of time studying English
_____	28.	Making friends with native speakers
_____	29.	Watching movies in English
_____	30.	Learning about the culture of English speakers
_____	31.	Listening to the radio in English
_____	32.	Writing a diary in English

English Language Learning Strategy Inventory (ELLSI), Griffiths, 2003b

Glossary

Note: The definitions given here are of the terms as they are used in relation to language learning.

Activity Theory – suggests that human activities are complex, socio-cultural phenomena aimed at achieving a desired outcome (Leont'ev, 1978).

Additional language – a language learnt in addition to the first language or mother tongue. Sometimes also known as the second language, L2 or target language.

Additive language – an alternative term to additional language (see above).

Affective (*adjective*) – relating to emotions or feelings. Noun = affect. Arnold's (1999) book deals with many aspects of the concept.

Affective overload – Originally used by Nahl (2005) in the context of information bahaviour, affective overload refers to the possibility that learning may be affected adversely if students experience strong emotional reactions which may distract attention from learning.

Anxiety – an affective condition which renders an individual nervous or worried and which may affect performance. Language learning anxiety is often classified according to whether it is a state (a temporary condition which will pass) or a trait (a permanent characteristic of the learner). The *Foreign Language Classroom Anxiety Scale* (*FLCAS*) was constructed by Horwitz *et al.* (1986) to measure the construct.

Aptitude – a natural ability to do anything, e.g. learn language. Perhaps the best-known test of aptitude is the *Modern Language Aptitude Test* (*MLAT*) by Carroll and Sapon (1959).

Attitude – a person's attitude relates to the manner in which he/she approaches and feels about the world, other people or tasks. Attitudes are typically seen as either positive or negative and are related to motivation.

Attribution – the process of ascribing responsibility for the perceived cause of success or failure, e.g. natural ability or lack of ability or good or bad luck (e.g. Weiner, 1974).

Audiolingualism – a system for learning language based on behaviourist beliefs (q.v.). In contrast to the grammar-translation method (q.v.) it emphasised the importance of aural/oral skills (e.g. Skinner, 1957).

Automatic – not dependent on deliberate decisions.

Autonomy – introduced to language learning by Holec (1981), autonomy refers to the ability to take charge of/manage/control/regulate one's own learning (e.g. Holec, 1981).

BALLI – the *Beliefs about Language Learning Inventory* developed by Horwitz (1987) to survey learners' beliefs.

Base **strategies** – these are the strategies which form the base level of students' strategy use and provide a foundation on which students can build as they become more expert. Memory strategies feature strongly at this level.

Behaviourism – a belief based on the idea that all human behaviour (including language) is developed as a habit by means of stimulus, response and reinforcement (e.g. Watson, 1930).

Belief – something which an individual holds to be true, e.g. 'I am/am not a good language learner', 'English is/is not a good language to learn'.

Big Five Model – a framework for conceptualising personality (McCrae & John, 1992). The Big Five factors are openness, conscientiousness, extraversion, agreeableness, and neuroticism (OCEAN).

CALLA – The *Cognitive Academic Language Learning Approach,* a strategy-based programme developed by Chamot and O'Malley (1987).

CANAL-F – an aptitude test (*Cognitive Ability for Novelty in Acquisition of Language – Foreign*) based on the premise that successful language learners are able to cope with new ideas (Grigorenko *et al.*, 2000).

Chaos/Complexity Theory – as applied to linguistics, this theory suggests that language is dynamic, complex and non-linear, and that learning language involves a process of imposing order on initial disorder (Larsen-Freeman, 1997).

Cognate – an element of one language which is recognisable to speakers of a different language because it is already known. For example, *makina* in Turkish is recognisable to English speakers because of its similarity to 'machine' in English.

Cognition – relating to thinking, knowledge or understanding. Adjective = cognitive.

Communication strategy – an activity (such as gesturing) whose basic purpose is to convey meaning (e.g. Tarone, 1980, 1981).

Communicative competence – a theoretical principle developed by Hymes (1972) which emphasised the ability to use language to convey and interpret meaning. The concept was later divided by Canale and Swain (1980) and Canale (1983) into:

> *grammatical competence* – relating to the learner's knowledge of the vocabulary, phonology and rules of the language;
>
> *discourse competence* – relating to the learner's ability to connect utterances into a meaningful whole;
>
> *sociolinguistic competence* – relating to a learner's ability to use language appropriately;
>
> *strategic competence* – relating to a learner's ability to employ strategies to compensate for imperfect knowledge.

Communicative language teaching (**CLT**) – an approach to language teaching based on the idea that the primary function of language is communication (e.g. Littlewood, 1981, 2001, 2012; Widdowson, 1978).

Comprehensible input – a hypothesis developed by Krashen (1985) which postulates that language is acquired when input is received which is slightly above the current level of competence, often represented by the formula I + 1.

Contrastive analysis (**CA**) – the hypothesis that target language difficulties could be predicted by contrasting the native language and the language the student is trying to learn (Lado, 1957).

Contrastive rhetoric – examines how a student's first language and culture influence target language acquisition (Connor, 1996; Kaplan, 1966). Studies of language learning strategy use according to nationality are not easy to find.

Core-plus **strategies** – these are the strategies used highly frequently by higher level students as well as those used highly frequently across all students.

Core **strategies** – consisting predominantly of metacognitive strategies, these activities are at the centre of a student's strategy repertoire and facilitate the management, control or regulation of a student's learning.

Correlation – this is a statistical concept which measures the relationship between two variables. Correlation values range from zero to 1 (a correlation of 1 means the variables are identical). Common correlation tests include Pearson (for parametric data) and Spearman (for nonparametric data).

Critical Period Hypothesis – the belief that there are maturational constraints on an individual's ability to develop language, and after this critical period has passed language development becomes difficult or impossible (Lenneberg, 1967).

Cultural capital – a metaphor introduced by Bourdieu (1977) to describe what learners hope to gain when they invest in the language learning enterprise.

Culture – culture is often understood to include the customs, language, family relationships, social organisation and artefacts of a people (e.g. Hofstede, 1980, 1997). It is frequently confused with other often closely related concepts such as ethnicity (q.v.) and nationality (q.v.).

Culture shock – refers to the negative feelings experienced by an individual who encounters an unfamiliar culture (e.g. Schumann, 1975).

Deliberate – requiring a decision of which the learner is aware.

Difference – a statistical concept which measures the degree to which variables are different from each other. Commonly used tests of difference include Student's *t*-tests (for parametric data) and Mann–Whitney U and Kruskal–Wallis (for non-parametric data).

Distance learning – a teaching method where students are not physically present in a classroom and do not have a face-to-face relationship with a teacher or with other students (e.g. White, 2003).

Eclecticism – a language teaching approach which chooses procedures from a wide variety of methods or techniques according to the needs of a particular set of learner characteristics, situations or goals.

Ego – a concept originally introduced by Freud (1910) to indicate an individual's sense of self.

Ego boundary – a concept introduced by Federn (1928) to indicate the mechanism used by individuals to distinguish the self from others and the world outside the self. Individuals with thin ego boundaries tend to be more open to the outside world, whereas those with thick ego boundaries tend to be more inhibited.

ELLSI – The *English Language Learning Strategy Inventory* (Griffiths, 2003b).

Empathy – the ability to identify with others and understand (though not necessarily agree with) their points of view (e.g. Guiora *et al.*, 1972).

Error – Something which is incorrect. According to Corder (1967) an error was something which a learner could not self-correct, which distinguishes it from a mistake (q.v.).

Ethnicity – often closely related to culture (q.v.) and nationality (q.v.), ethnicity refers to a person's racial origin.

Explicit strategy instruction – a teaching method whereby students are provided with overt information regarding strategy options and their use.

First language (L1) interference – this occurs when aspects of a student's first language interfere with target language acquisition, such as students who apply word order in their L1 inappropriately to English.

FLCAS – *Foreign Language Classroom Anxiety Scale* – a survey designed to investigate the anxiety phenomenon in foreign language classrooms (Horwitz *et al.*, 1986).

Foreign language (FL) – a language studied in an environment other than where it is spoken as a native language, for instance French as it is taught in England or Turkey, or English as it is taught in Korea.

Fossilisation – in language learning, fossilisation refers to the idea that if errors are not corrected they will become 'set in stone' – in other words, they will become a fixed habit and will not be able to be changed.

Gender – whereas the concept of 'sex' is biological, and therefore relatively fixed, the 'gender' concept relates more to the attributes accorded to 'male' or 'female' by society. However, 'gender' is quite often used as a softer way of expressing male/female differences even when it is essentially biological differences which are being referred to.

Grammar-Translation (GT) – a method of teaching language based (as the name suggests) on learning grammar and translating to and from the target language.

Heritage language – the language derived from a particular cultural heritage spoken in a dominant language environment, for instance Hebrew spoken by Jewish people in America.

Identity – the combination of the factors (such as nationality, culture, age, gender, etc.) which contribute to learner individuality (e.g. Norton, 1997, 2000, 2010).

Implicit strategy instruction – a teaching method which embeds strategy instruction in the regular classroom material.

Inhibition – something which causes an individual to retreat from open interaction with others.

Interaction Hypothesis – Long (1996) suggests that comprehensible input is more effective when learners must use the input to communicate.

Interlanguage – a term coined by Selinker (1972) to describe the language developed by learners which displays features of both the native and the target languages.

Investment – the resources in terms of time, effort, attention, money, etc. that a student is prepared to contribute to the learning endeavour (e.g. Bourdieu, 1977; Peirce, 1995).

Krashen's hypotheses – these were five proposals which have given rise to much controversy over the years and which have had a major effect on the way language teaching theory and practice has developed:

Acquisition/learning Hypothesis – language is acquired by means of natural communication and formal learning is of limited value;

Monitor Hypothesis – formal learning is only useful as a means of monitoring acquisition;

Input Hypothesis – language is learnt by means of being exposed to language one stage ahead of the learner's current level of competence;

Affective Filter Hypothesis – emotions can either facilitate or block language acquisition;

Natural Order Hypothesis – language is acquired in a set order.

Language Acquisition Device (LAD) – a concept originally promoted by Chomsky (1965) that humans are equipped with an area in the brain which predisposes them to be able to develop language.

Language function – an aspect of language which is concerned with what users do with the language, typically expressed in gerund form, e.g. *complaining, asking questions, giving directions,* etc. (e.g. Wilkins, 1976).

Language Skills Development (LSD) Questionnaire – a questionnaire designed to investigate the strategies students use to develop language skills (Griffiths, 2004).

Learned helplessness – a state in which learners believe they have no control over their learning (e.g. Kuhl, 1984).

Longitudinal – carried out over a period of time.

MBTI – based on Jung's (1921) theories of psychological types, the *Myers–Briggs Type Indicator* (Myers, 1962) is a widely used personality inventory which measures personality according to four dichotomous scales:

Extraversion–Introversion – focused towards an internal or an external reality;

Sensing–Intuitive – depending on the five senses versus non-sensory perceptions;

Thinking–Feeling – depending on logical versus affective judgments;

Judging–Perceiving – tending to depend on rational assessment versus instinctive impressions.

Mediation – the process of assisting with language learning (Vygotsky, 1978).

Mediator – someone or something who/which provides mediation.

Meta – a prefix meaning 'beyond', e.g. metacognition = beyond cognition.

Metacognition – refers to knowledge at the level of organising, managing, regulating or controlling.

Mistake – something which is incorrect. According to Corder (1967), a mistake is a slip which the learner can self-correct, whereas an error (q.v.) is beyond the learner's ability to self-correct.

MLAT – *Modern Language Aptitude Test* – a test of language aptitude published by Carroll and Sapon (1959).

Mother tongue – the language spoken in the home.

Motivation – refers to the drive to achieve a goal. Motivation is typically divided into four types:

Integrative – driven by the desire to be accepted by a particular group;
Instrumental – being used as a tool to achieve a particular purpose;
Intrinsic – aimed at one's own satisfaction;
Extrinsic – driven by the desire for external reward.

Of these pairs, the first two are generally attributed to Gardner and Lambert (1959), and the second two are generally attributed to Deci and Ryan (1980).

Nationality – refers to the geographical area (country) to which one belongs. Typically, nationality is what is on one's passport.

Native language/speaker – this is actually a complicated concept, but it refers essentially to the language spoken in the home and those who speak it. The native language is usually, but by no means always, the language spoken in the surrounding community.

Natural method – a method of language learning promoted by Krashen and Terrell (1983) based on the idea that non-native languages should be acquired in the same way as children develop their first languages.

Non-English-speaking background (**NESB**) – a background where English is not spoken as the native language.

Non-native language/speaker – this refers to a language other than the primary language spoken in the home and those who speak it.

Non-primary language – a language other than the one spoken in the home.

Notion – as applied to language, the term refers to particulate concepts, such as time, numerals, distance etc. (Wilkins, 1976).

Orchestration – when referring to strategies, this is a metaphorical use of the term and indicates the ability to use strategies in combination with each other.

Output Hypothesis – Swain (1985) suggests that language production can act as a complement to comprehensible input and help to facilitate language development.

Parametric – relating to numbers, as opposed to non-parametric. Age, income or test scores are examples of parametric (numerical) data, whereas data from Likert scales are non-parametric (ordinal), since the numbers represent attitudes rather than mathematical values. Nominal values given to variables such as sex (for example, male = 1, female = 2) are another example of non-parametric data.

Pedagogy – the study of teaching. Pedagogue is another word for teacher. Adjective = pedagogic; adverb = pedagogical.

Peer – one who is the same as oneself, e.g. a classmate, etc.

Personality – distinctive features of a person's behaviour such as attitudes, preferences or social relationships.

PLAB – *Pimsleur Language Aptitude Battery* – an aptitude test aimed at high school students (Pimsleur, 1966).

PLSPQ – the *Perceptual Learning Style Preference Questionnaire*, a learning style inventory developed by Reid (1987) involving five modalities:

visual (learning by seeing);
auditory (learning by hearing);
tactile (learning by touching);
kinaesthetic (learning by moving);
individual/ group (preferring to learn alone versus with others).

***Plus* strategies** – these strategies are the ones which tend to be used by higher level students in addition to the strategies used by all students. Plus strategies are very varied in their nature and seem to indicate that higher level learners are willing and able to employ a wide range of strategies in the pursuit of their goals.

Postmethod – refers to the idea that contemporary language teaching has moved beyond fixed methodologies (Kumaravadivelu, 2001).

Pragmatics – the area of linguistics which is concerned with how language is used for social interaction.

Primary language – the language spoken in the home, often also called the mother tongue or native language.

Proficiency – a difficult concept to measure, relating to one's level of competence in a language.

Qualitative – relating to non-numerical data obtained, for instance, from interviews, open-ended questions, think-aloud protocols, etc.

Quantitative – relating to numerical data obtained, for instance, from questionnaires, databases, etc.

Reliability – relating to the consistency of the data.

Repertoire – a musical metaphor used to refer to the range of strategies at a learner's disposal from which a selection can be made to suit a particular situation, goal or task.

Schema/schemata (plural) – an organized pattern of thought constructed in the brain which is used to interpret incoming information. (R. Anderson, 1977).

Second language (SL, L2) – studied in the environment where the language is spoken, for instance international students or immigrants studying English in New Zealand or the USA, or English speakers studying Japanese in Japan.

Self-concept – the way one conceives of oneself (e.g. Mercer, 2011).

Self-confidence – the degree to which one believes in oneself.

Self-efficacy – the belief in one's ability to achieve a particular goal (e.g. Bandura, 1997).

Self-esteem – a broader concept than self-efficacy, self-esteem refers more generally to one's confidence in oneself and is not necessarily related to a particular goal (e.g. Coppersmith, 1967).

Self-image – the way one visualises oneself.

Self-regulation – refers to learners' ability to manage their own learning (e.g. Dornyei, 2005; Winne, 1995).

Sensitive Period Hypothesis – a weaker version of the Critical Period Hypothesis which suggests that language development becomes steadily more difficult as a learner matures, but not necessarily impossible.

Sex – the biological difference between males and females.

Significance – a statistical concept indicating that a result is more than would be expected merely by chance.

Silent way – a method which relies for its effectiveness on the teacher being silent as much as possible (Gattegno, 1963).

SILL – the *Strategy Inventory for Language Learning* (Oxford, 1990), used to assess frequency of reported strategy use.

Skill – refers to the ability to use language to communicate, typically divided into reading, writing, listening and speaking, each of which may have sub-skills, such as skim reading, letter writing, listening for gist, conversation management, etc.

Social distance – a concept which describes the differences between/among various cultures (Schumann, 1976).

Socio-cultural – an adjective used to describe characteristics which are dependent on social and/or cultural influences (e.g. Lantolf, 2000; Vygotsky, 1978).

Speakers of other languages (SOL) – a general term used to include those who are in an environment or learning situation where they do not speak the dominant or target language, for instance English speakers in China or in a Chinese class elsewhere. In other words, the term covers what is generally understood by both *second language* and *foreign language*.

SPSS – *Statistical Package for Social Sciences* – a commonly used statistical programme in linguistic research.

SSBI – *Styles and Strategies-based Instruction* – an approach to language learning based on students' learning styles and strategies, developed by Cohen (1998).

Style – a person's preferred ways of learning, e.g. aural, visual, kinaesthetic, etc.

Strategy – an activity consciously chosen by learners for the purpose of regulating their own learning (Griffiths, 2008a).

Suggestopaedia – a teaching method which relies on positive suggestion such as a pleasant environment, music, colour, art, etc. (Lozanov, 1978).

Target language – the language the learner is aiming to learn.

Task based language teaching (**TBL**) – TBL is based on the idea that language is learnt most effectively by engaging students in communicative activities which approximate those they might be required to perform in real life, such as going to the supermarket, renting a flat or planning a holiday (e.g. Ellis, 2003; Nunan, 2004).

Teachability Hypothesis – developed by Pienemann (1985, 1989), the Teachability Hypothesis postulates that language can be taught and learnt when the learner is ready.

Tornado Effect – a hypothesised effect which suggests that strategy development is spiral rather than linear, and that as students develop their strategies and increase their proficiency, more and more strategies become available to them (for instance, higher level students can improve their listening skills by watching TV, which lower level students would be unable to understand). This means that the learner has a constantly widening spiral (resembling a tornado) of strategies which s/he can utilise (Griffiths, 2003b).

Total Physical Response (**TPR**) – a teaching method which relies on physical movement for its effect (Asher, 1969).

Universal Grammar (**UG**) – the idea that all human languages have elements in common (Chomsky, 1965).

Validity – the degree to which an instrument measures what it is supposed to be measuring. A number of different types of validity have been identified, including:

Construct/concept validity – how well the target concept is measured (e.g. does a learning strategy questionnaire really measure learning strategies?);

Content validity – the degree to which the content is appropriate for the context (e.g. an instrument designed for adults might not be suitable for younger learners);

Convergent validity – the degree to which an instrument correlates with the results of other instruments;

Concurrent validity – the degree to which an instrument correlates with others done at the same time;

Criterion validity – the relationship between the results of the instrument and a given standard;

External validity – the degree to which the results are generalisable to a wider population;

Face validity – the degree to which an instrument appears to be measuring what it is supposed to be measuring;

Internal validity – the degree to which results can be used to infer cause and effect;

Predictive validity – the degree to which the results of an instrument are able to predict outcomes.

VARK – a questionnaire produced by Fleming and Mills (1992) based on Visual, Aural, Read/write and Kinaesthetic learning styles.

Volition – the will to persevere with a chosen course of action (e.g. Corno, 2001).

Zone of Proximal Development (ZPD) – the difference between what a learner can do with and without help (Vygotsky, 1978).

References

Abraham, R. and Vann, R. (1987) Strategies of two language learners: A case study. In A. Wenden and J. Rubin (eds) *Learner Strategies in Language Learning* (pp. 85–102). New York: Prentice Hall.

Aldridge, A. and Levine, K. (2001) *Surveying the Social World: Principles and Practice in Survey Research.* Buckingham: Open University Press.

Allan, D. (1995) *Oxford Placement Test.* Oxford: Oxford University Press.

Allen, P. and Harley, B. (eds) (1992) *Issues and Options in Language Teaching.* Oxford: Oxford University Press.

Anderson, J. (1980) *Cognitive Psychology and its Implications.* San Francisco, CA: W.H. Freeman.

Anderson, N. (2008) Metacognition and good language learners. In C. Griffiths (ed.) *Lessons from Good Language Learners* (pp. 99–109). Cambridge, UK: Cambridge University Press.

Anderson, R. (1977) The notion of schemata and the educational enterprise. In R. Anderson, J. Spiro and W. Montague (eds) *Schooling and the Acquisition of Knowledge* (pp. 415–431). Hillsdale, NJ: Erlbaum.

Aoki, N. and Smith, R. (1999) Learner autonomy in cultural context: The case of Japan. In S. Cotterall and D. Crabbe (eds) *Learner Autonomy in Language Learning: Defining the Field and Effecting Change* (pp. 19–27). Frankfurt am Main: Lang.

Arnold, J. (ed.) (1999) *Affect in Language Learning.* Cambridge: Cambridge University Press.

Arnold, J. and Brown, H.D. (1999) A map of the terrain. In J. Arnold (ed.) *Affect in Language Learning* (pp. 1–24). Cambridge: Cambridge University Press.

Asher, J. (1969) The total physical response approach to second language learning. *Modern Language Journal* 53 (1), 3–17.

Atkinson, R. (1975) Mnemotecnics in second-language learning. *American Psychologist* 30, 821–828.

Ausubel, D. (1964) Adults vs. children in second language learning: Psychological considerations. *Modern Language Journal* 48, 420–424.

Ausubel, D. (1968) *Educational Psychology: A Cognitive View.* New York: Holt, Rinehart & Winston.

Bacon, S. (1992) The relationship between sex, comprehension, processing strategies and cognitive and affective response in second-language listening. *Modern Language Journal* 76, 160–178.

Baddeley, A. and Hitch, G. (1974) Working memory. In G. Bower (ed.) *The Psychology of Learning and Motivation: Advances in Research and Theory* (Vol. 8) (pp. 47–89). New York: Academic Press.

Bade, M. (2008) Grammar and good language learners. In C. Griffiths (ed.) *Lessons from Good Language Learners* (pp. 174–184). Cambridge: Cambridge University Press.

Bailey, K., Curtis, A. and Nunan, D. (2001) *Pursuing Professional Development.* Boston, MA: Heinle & Heinle.

Baker, C. (1988) *Key Issues in Bilingualism and Bilingual Education.* Clevedon: Multilingual Matters.

Bandura, A. (1997) *Self-efficacy: The Exercise of Control.* New York: W.H. Freeman.

Barcelos, A. (2003) Researching beliefs about SLA: A critical review. In P. Kalaja and A. Barcelos (eds) *Beliefs About SLA: New Research Approaches* (pp. 7–33). Dordrecht: Kluwer.

Bedell, D. and Oxford, R. (1996) Cross-cultural comparisons of language learning strategies in the Peoples' Republic of China and other countries. In R. Oxford (ed.) *Language Learning Strategies Around the World: Cross-Cultural Perspectives* (pp. 47–60). Honolulu, HI: Second Language Teaching and Curriculum Centre, University of Hawai'i at Manoa.

Bellingham, L. (2000) Language acquisition after 40? *Babel* 35 (1), 24–38.

Benson, P. (2001) *Teaching and Researching Autonomy in Language Learning.* Harlow: Pearson.

Benson, P. (2007) Autonomy in language teaching and learning. *Language Teaching* 40 (1), 21–40.

Benson, P. and Voller, P. (eds) (1997) *Autonomy and Independence in Language Learning.* London: Longman.

Bialystok, E. (1978) A theoretical model of second language learning. *Language Learning* 28 (1), 69–83.

Bialystok, E. (1981) The role of conscious strategies in second language proficiency. *Modern Language Journal* 65, 24–35.

Bialystok, E. (1991) Achieving proficiency in a second language: A processing description. In R. Phillipson, E. Kellerman, L. Selinker, M. Sharwood-Smith and M. Swain (eds) *Foreign/Second Language Pedagogy Research* (pp. 63–77). Clevedon: Multilingual Matters.

Bialystok, E. (1999) Confounded age: Linguistic and cognitive factors in age differences for second language acquisition. In D. Birdsong (ed.) *Second Language Acquisition and the Critical Period Hypothesis* (pp. 161–181). Mahwah, NJ: Lawrence Erlbaum.

Birdsong, D. (1999a) Whys and why nots of the Critical Period Hypothesis for second language acquisition. In D. Birdsong (ed.) *Second Language Acquisition and the Critical Period Hypothesis* (pp. 1–22). Mahwah, NJ: Lawrence Erlbaum.

Birdsong, D. (ed.) (1999b) *Second Language Acquisition and the Critical Period Hypothesis.* Mahwah, NJ: Lawrence Erlbaum.

Borg, S. (2009) *Teacher Cognition and Language Education: Research and Practice.* London: Continuum.

Bourdieu, P. (1977) The economics of linguistic exchanges. *Social Science Information* 16, 645–668.

Bowler, B. and Parminter, S. (1992) *Literature.* Oxford: Oxford University Press.

Boyle, J. (1987) Sex differences in listening vocabulary. *Language Learning* 37, 273–284.

Breen, M. (ed.) (2001) *Learner Contributions to Language Learning.* London: Longman.

Brown, H.D. (1980) *Principles and Practices of Language Learning and Teaching.* Englewood Cliffs, NJ: Prentice Hall.

Brown, H.D. (1994) *Principles of Language Learning and Teaching.* Englewood Cliffs, NJ: Prentice Hall.

Brown, H.D. (2001) In the minds of the methodologists. *EL Teaching Matters* April, v.

Brown, H.D., Yorio, C. and Crymes, R. (eds) (1977) *On TESOL '77.* Washington DC: TESOL.

Brumfit, C. (1984) *Communicative Methodology in Language Teaching.* Cambridge: Cambridge University Press.

Bruner, J. (1960) *The Process of Education.* Cambridge, MA: Harvard University Press.

Burling, R. (1981) Social constraints on adult language learning. In H. Winitz (ed.) *Native Language and Foreign Language Acquisition* (pp. 279–290). New York: New York Academy of Sciences.

Burstall, C. (1975) Factors affecting foreign-language learning: A consideration of some relevant research findings. *Language Teaching and Linguistics: Abstracts* 8, 5–25.

Burstall, C., Jamieson, M., Cohen, S. and Hargreaves, M. (1974) *Primary French in the Balance.* Windsor: NFER Publishing.

Bysgate, M., Tonkyn, A. and Williams, E. (eds) (1994) *Grammar and the Language Teacher.* London: Prentice Hall.

Canale, M. (1983) On some dimensions of language proficiency. In J. Oller (ed.) *Issues in Language Testing Research* (pp. 333–342). Rowley, MA: Newbury House.

Canale, M. and Swain, M. (1980) Theoretical bases of communicative approaches to second language teaching and testing. *Applied Linguistics* 1, 1–47.

CARLA (Centre for Research in Language Acquisition) website. www.carla.umn.edu. Accessed 19 Feb, 2013.

Carrell, P., Pharis, B. and Liberto, J. (1989) Metacognitive strategy training for ESL reading. *TESOL Quarterly* 23 (4), 647–673.

Carroll, J. (1965) The prediction of success in intensive foreign language training. In R. Glaser (ed.) *Training Research and Education* (pp. 87–136). Pittsburgh, PA: University of Pittsburgh Press.

Carroll, J. and Sapon, S. (1959) *Modern Language Aptitude Test.* New York: Psychological Corporation.

Chamot, A. (1987) The learning strategies of ESL students. In A. Wenden and J. Rubin (eds) *Learner Strategies in Language Learning* (pp. 71–83). London: Prentice Hall.

Chamot, A. (2001) The role of learning strategies in second language acquisition. In M. Breen (ed.) *Learner Contributions to Language Learning* (pp. 25–43). Harlow: Longman.

Chamot, A. (2005) The Cognitive Academic Language Learning Approach (CALLA): An update. In P. Richard-Amato and M. Snow (eds) *Academic Success for English Language Learners: Strategies for K-12 Mainstream Teachers* (pp. 87–101). White Plains, NY: Longman.

Chamot, A. (2008) Strategy instruction and good language learners. In C. Griffiths (ed.) *Lessons from Good Language Learners* (pp. 266–281). Cambridge, UK: Cambridge University Press.

Chamot, A. and O'Malley, M. (1986) *A Cognitive Academic Language Learning Approach: An ESL Content-based Curriculum.* Wheaton, MD: National Clearing house for Bilingual Education.

Chamot, A. and O'Malley, M. (1987) The Cognitive Academic Language Learning Approach: A bridge to the mainstream. *TESOL Quarterly* 21 (2), 227–250.

Chamot, A. and Rubin, J. (1994) Comments on Janie Rees-Miller's 'A critical appraisal of learner training: Theoretical bases and teaching implications'. *TESOL Quarterly* 28 (4), 771–781.

Chamot, A., Barnhardt, S., El-Dinary, P. and Robbins, J. (1999) *The Learning Strategies Handbook.* White Plains, NY: Addison Wesley Longman.

Chapelle, C. (1988) Field independence: A source of language variance? *Language Testing* 5, 62–82.

Chaudron, C. (1986) The interaction of quantitative and qualitative approaches to research: A view of the second language classroom. *TESOL Quarterly* 20 (4), 709–717.

Chaudron, C. (1995) *Second Language Classrooms.* Cambridge: Cambridge University Press.

Chihara, T. and Oller, J. (1978) Attitudes and attained proficiency in EFL: A sociolinguistic study of adult Japanese speakers. *Language Learning* 28, 55–68.

Ching, T. (1992) Chinese learning styles: A personal view. *Many Voices* 3, 9–10.

Chomsky, N. (1959) Review of *Verbal Behaviour* by B.F. Skinner. *Language* 35, 26–58.

Chomsky, N. (1965) *Aspects of the Theory of Syntax.* Cambridge, MA: MIT Press.

Chomsky, N. (1968) *Language and Mind.* New York: Harcourt, Brace & World.

Clarke, J. (1996) Face-directed behaviour in the language classroom. *TESOLANZ Journal* 4, 13–20.

Clarke, M. and Handscombe, J. (eds) (1982) *On TESOL.* Washington, DC: TESOL.

Cohen, A. (1991) Strategies in second language learning: Insights from research. In R. Phillipson, E. Kellerman, L. Selinker, M. Sharwood-Smith and M. Swain (eds) *Foreign/Second Language Pedagogy Research* (pp. 107–119). Clevedon: Multilingual Matters.

Cohen, A. (1998) *Strategies in Learning and Using a Second Language.* New York: Longman.

Cohen, A. (1999) Language learning strategies instruction and research. In S. Cotterall and D. Crabbe (eds) *Learner Autonomy in Language Learning: Defining the Field and Effecting Change* (pp. 61–68). Frankfurt am Main: Lang.

Cohen, A. (2003) The learner's side of foreign language learning: Where do styles, strategies and tasks meet? *IRAL* 41, 279–291.

Cohen, A. (2011) *Strategies in Learning and Using a Second Language* (2nd edn). Harlow: Longman.

Cohen, A. (2012) Strategies: The interface of styles, strategies and motivation on tasks. In S. Mercer, S. Ryan and M. Williams (eds) *Language Learning Psychology: Research, Theory and Pedagogy* (pp. 136–150). Basingstoke: Palgrave Macmillan.

Cohen, A. and Chi, J. (2002) *Language Strategy Use Survey.* http://carla.acad.umn.edu/profiles/cohenpapers/lg_strat_srvy.html.

Cohen, A. and Dornyei, Z. (2002) Focus on the language learner: Motivation, styles and strategies. In N. Schmitt (ed.) *An Introduction to Applied Linguistics* (pp. 170–190). London: Edward Arnold.

Cohen, A. and Macaro, E. (2007) *Learner Strategies.* Oxford: Oxford University Press.

Cohen, A., Weaver, S. and Li, T. (1998) The impact of strategies-based instruction on speaking a foreign language. In A. Cohen (ed.) *Strategies in Learning and Using a Second Language* (pp. 107–156). New York: Longman.

Cohen, A., Oxford, R. and Chi, J. (2002) *Learning Styles Survey.* Minneapolis, MN: Center for Advanced Research on Language Acquisition. See www.carla.umn.edu.

Connor, U. (1996) *Contrastive Rhetoric: Cross-cultural Aspects of Second-language Writing.* Cambridge, UK: Cambridge University Press.

Cook, V. (1991) *Second Language Learning and Language Teaching.* London: Edward Arnold.

Coppersmith, S. (1967) *Antecedents of Self-Esteem.* San Francisco, CA: Freeman.

Corbett, J. (1999) 'Chewing the fat' is a cultural issue. *IATEFL Issues* 48, 2–3.

Corder, S.P. (1967) The significance of learners' errors. *International Review of Applied Linguistics* 5, 160–170.

Corno, L. (2001) Volitional aspects of self-regulated learning. In B. Zimmerman and D. Schunk (eds) *Self-regulated Learning and Academic Achievement: Theoretical Perspectives* (pp. 191–225). Mahwah, NJ: Erlbaum.

Cotterall, S. (2008) Autonomy and good language learners. In C. Griffiths (ed.) *Lessons from Good Language Learners* (pp. 110–120). Cambridge: Cambridge University Press.

Cotterall, S. and Crabbe, D. (eds) (1999) *Learner Autonomy in Language Learning: Defining the Field and Effecting Change*. Frankfurt am Main: Lang.

Cotterall, S. and Reinders, H. (2000) Learner's perceptions and practice in self access language learning. *TESOLANZ Journal* 8, 23–47.

Crabbe, D. (1993) Fostering autonomy from within the classroom: The teacher's responsibility. *System* 21 (4), 443–452.

Cummins, J. (1996) *Negotiating Identities: Education for Empowerment in a Diverse Society*. Ontario: California Association for Bilingual Education.

Cummins, J. (2001) *Negotiating Identities: Education for Empowerment in a Diverse Society* (2nd edn). Los Angeles, CA: California Association for Bilingual Education.

Curry, L. (1983) *Learning Style in Continuing Medical Education*. Ottawa: Canadian Medical Association.

Dam, L. (1995) *Autonomy: From Theory to Classroom Practice*. Dublin: Authentik.

Dansereau, D. (1978) The development of a learning strategies curriculum. In H.F. O'Neil, Jr (ed.) *Learning Strategies* (pp. 1–29). New York: Academic Press.

Day, E. (2002) *Identity and the Young English Language Learner*. Clevedon: Multilingual Matters.

de Andres, V. (1999) Self-esteem in the classroom or the metamorphosis of butterflies. In J. Arnold (ed.) *Affect in Language Learning* (pp. 87–102). Cambridge: Cambridge University Press.

Deci, E. and Ryan, R. (1980) The empirical exploration of intrinsic motivational processes. In L. Berkowitz (ed.) *Advances in Experimental Social Psychology* (Vol. 13) (pp. 39–80). New York: Academic Press.

DeKeyser, R. (2009) Cognitive-psychological processes in second language learning. In M. Long and C. Doughty (eds) *Handbook of Second Language Teaching* (pp. 119–138). Oxford: Blackwell.

DeKeyser, R. and Koeth, J. (2011) Cognitive aptitudes for second language learning. In E. Hinkel (ed.) *Handbook of Research in Second Language Teaching and Learning* (Vol. 2) (pp. 395–406). New York: Routledge.

de Vaus, D. (1995) *Surveys in Social Research* (4th edn). London: Allen & Unwin.

Diller, K. (ed.) (1981) *Differences and Universals in Language Learning Aptitude*. Rowley, MA: Newbury House.

Donato, R. (2000) Sociocultural contributions to understanding the foreign and second language classroom. In J. Lantolf (ed.) *Sociocultural Theory in Second Language Learning* (pp. 27–50). Oxford: Oxford University Press.

Dornyei, Z. (1995) On the teachability of communication strategies. *TESOL Quarterly* 29 (1), 55–85.

Dornyei, Z. (2001) *Motivational Strategies in the Language Classroom*. Cambridge: Cambridge University Press.

Dornyei, Z. (2003) *Questionnaires in Second Language Research*. Mahwah, NJ: Lawrence Erlbaum.

Dornyei, Z. (2005) *The Psychology of Language Teaching*. Mahwah, NJ: Lawrence Erlbaum.

Dornyei, Z. (2007) *Research Methods in Applied Linguistics*. Oxford: Oxford University Press.

Dornyei, Z. and Skehan, P. (2003) Individual differences in second language learning. In C. Doughty and M. Long (eds) *Handbook of Second Language Acquisition* (pp. 589–630). Oxford: Blackwell.

Dornyei, Z. and Ushioda, E. (2010) *Teaching and Researching Motivation* (2nd edn). Harlow: Pearson Longman.

Doughty, C. and Long, M. (eds) (2003) *Handbook of Second Language Acquisition*. Oxford: Blackwell.

Dowsett, G. (1986) Interaction in the semi-structured interview. In M. Emery (ed.) *Qualitative Research* (pp. 51–59). Canberra: Australian Association of Adult Education.

Dreyer, C. and Oxford, R. (1996) Learning strategies and other predictors of ESL proficiency among Afrikaans speakers in South Africa. In R. Oxford (ed.) *Language Learning Strategies Around the World: Cross-Cultural Perspectives* (pp. 61–74). Honolulu, HI: Second Language Teaching and Curriculum Centre, University of Hawai'i at Manoa.

Dulay, H., Burt, M. and Krashen, S. (1982) *Language Two*. New York: Oxford University Press.

Dunn, R., Dunn, K. and Price, G. (1975) *The Learning Style Inventory*. Lawrence, KS: Price Systems.

Eckman, F., Bell, L. and Nelson, D. (eds) (1984) *Universals of Second Language Acquisition*. Rowley, MA: Newbury House.

Ehrman, M. (1999) Ego boundaries and tolerance of ambiguity in second language learning. In J. Arnold (ed.) *Affect in Language Learning* (pp. 68–86). Cambridge: Cambridge University Press.

Ehrman, M. (2008) Personality and good language learners. In C. Griffiths (ed.) *Lessons from Good Language Learners* (pp. 61–72). Cambridge, UK: Cambridge University Press.

Ehrman, M. and Leaver, B. (2003) Cognitive styles in the service of language learning. *System* 31, 393–415.

Ehrman, M. and Oxford, R. (1989) Effects of sex differences, career choice, and psychological type on adult language learning strategies. *Modern Language Journal* 73 (1), 1–13.

Ehrman, M. and Oxford, R. (1990) Adult language learning styles and strategies in an intensive training setting. *Modern Language Journal* 74 (3), 311–327.

Ehrman, M. and Oxford, R. (1995) Cognition plus: Correlates of language learning success. *Modern Language Journal* 79 (1), 67–89.

Eisenstein, M. (1982) A study of social variation in adult second language acquisition. *Language Learning* 32, 367–391.

Ellis, G. and Sinclair, B. (1994) *Learning to Learn English*. Cambridge: Cambridge University Press.

Ellis, R. (1986) *Understanding Second Language Acquisition*. Oxford: Oxford University Press.

Ellis, R. (1994) *The Study of Second Language Acquisition*. Oxford: Oxford University Press.

Ellis, R. (2003) *Task-based Language Teaching and Learning*. Oxford: Oxford University Press.

Ellis, R. (2006) Current issues in the teaching of grammar: An SLA perspective. *TESOL Quarterly* 40 (1), 83–107.

Ellis, R. (2008) *Understanding Second Language Acquisition*. Oxford: Oxford University Press.

Ellis, R. (2008) *The Study of Second Language Acquisition* (2nd edn). Oxford: Oxford University Press.

Ely, C. (1995) Tolerance of ambiguity and the teaching of ESL. In J. Reid (ed.) *Learning Styles in the ESL/EFL Classroom* (pp. 87–95). Boston, MA: Heinle & Heinle.

Emery, M. (ed.) (1986) *Qualitative Research*. Canberra: Australian Association of Adult Education.

Eslami Rasekh, Z. and Ranjbary, R. (2003) Metacognitive strategy training for vocabulary learning. *TESL-EJ* 7 (2). http://tesl-ej.org/ej26/rasekh.html.

Faerch, C. and Kasper, G. (eds) (1983) *Strategies in Interlanguage Communication*. London & New York: Longman.

Farhady, H. (1982) Measures of language proficiency from the learner's perspective. *TESOL Quarterly* 16, 43–59.

Fathman, A. (1975) The relationship between age and second language productive ability. *Language Learning* 25, 245–253.

Federn, P. (1928) Narcissism in the structure of the ego. *International Journal of Psychoanalysis* 9, 401–419.

Finkbeiner, C. (2008) Culture and good language learners. In C. Griffiths (ed.) *Lessons from Good Language Learners* (pp. 131–141). Cambridge: Cambridge University Press.

Fleming, N. and Mills, C. (1992) Not another inventory, rather a catalyst for reflection. *To Improve the Academy* 11, 137–149.

Freed, B. (1998) An overview of issues and research in language learning in a study abroad setting. *Frontiers* 4, 31–60.

Freeman, D. and Richards, J. (eds) (1996) *Teacher Learning in Language Teaching*. Cambridge: Cambridge University Press.

Freud, S. (1910) The origin and development of psychoanalysis. *American Journal of Psychology* 21 (2), 196–218.

Gage, N. and Berliner, D. (1992) *Educational Psychology*. Boston, MA: Houghton Mifflin.

Gardner, R. (1985) *Social Psychology and Second Language Learning: The Role of Attitude and Motivation*. London: Edward Arnold.

Gardner, R. and Lambert, W. (1959) Motivational variables in second language acquisition. *Canadian Journal of Psychology* 13, 266–272.

Gardner, R. and Lambert, W. (1972) *Attitudes and Motivation in Second Language Learning*. Rowley, MA: Newbury House.

Gardner, R. and MacIntyre, P. (1991) An instrumental motivation in language study: Who says it isn't effective? *Studies in Second Language Acquisition* 13, 57–72.

Gardner, R. and MacIntyre, P. (1993) A student's contribution to second language learning. Part II: affective factors. *Language Teaching* 26, 1–11.

Gass, S. (1991) Grammar instruction, selective attention, and learning processes. In R. Phillipson, E. Kellerman, L. Selinker, M. Sharwood-Smith and M. Swain (eds) *Foreign/Second Language Pedagogy Research* (pp. 134–141). Clevedon: Multilingual Matters.

Gattegno, C. (1963) *Teaching Foreign Languages in Schools: The Silent Way*. Reading: Educational Explorers.

Gillam, B. (2000) *Case Study Research Methods*. London & New York: Continuum.

Grabe, W. and Stoller, F. (2011) *Teaching and Researching Reading* (2nd edn). Harlow: Pearson Longman.

Graham, S. (1997) *Effective Language Learning: Positive Strategies for Advanced Level Language Learning*. Clevedon: Multilingual Matters.

Green, J. and Oxford, R. (1995) A closer look at learning strategies, L2 proficiency and sex. *TESOL Quarterly* 29 (2), 261–297.

Gregg, K. (1984) Krashen's monitor and Occam's razor. *Applied Linguistics* 5, 78–100.

Gregorc, A. (1979) Learning/teaching styles: Potent forces behind them. *Educational Leadership* 36, 236–238.

Grenfell, M. and Harris, V. (1999) *Modern Languages and Learning Strategies: In Theory and Practice*. London: Routledge.

Grenfell, M. and Macaro, E. (2007) Claims and critiques. In A. Cohen and E. Macaro (eds) *Language Learner Strategies* (pp. 9–28). Oxford: Oxford University Press.

Griffiths, C. (2002) Using reading as a strategy for teaching and learning language. *ERIC Database of Educational Documents*. http://www.ericfacility.org.

Griffiths, C. (2003a) Patterns of language learning strategy use. *System* 31, 367–383.

Griffiths, C. (2003b) Language learning strategy use and proficiency: The relationship between patterns of reported language learning strategy (LLS) use by speakers of other languages (SOL) and proficiency with implications for the teaching/learning situation. PhD thesis, University of Aukland. http://hdl.handle.net/2292/9.

Griffiths, C. (2004) Studying in English: Language skills development. Occasional Paper No. 5. Auckland: Centre for Research in International Education. http://www.crie.org.nz.

Griffiths, C. (2006) Strategy development and progress in language learning. *Prospect* 21 (3), 58–76.

Griffiths, C. (2008a) Strategies and good language learners. In C. Griffiths (ed.) *Lessons from Good Language Learners* (pp. 83–98). Cambridge: Cambridge University Press.

Griffiths, C. (2008b) Age and good language learners. In C. Griffiths (ed.) *Lessons from Good Language Learners* (pp. 35–48). Cambridge: Cambridge University Press.

Griffiths, C. (2008c) Teaching/learning method and good language learners. In C. Griffiths (ed.) *Lessons from Good Language Learners* (pp. 255–265). Cambridge: Cambridge University Press.

Griffiths, C. (2008d) Learning successfully in a target language environment. *TESOLANZ Journal* 16, 34–43.

Griffiths, C. (ed.) (2008e) *Lessons from Good Language Learners*. Cambridge: Cambridge University Press.

Griffiths, C. (2011) The traditional–communicative dichotomy: Defining the terms and re-examining the constraints. *ELT Journal* 65, 300–308.

Griffiths, C. (2012) Learning styles: traversing the quagmire. In S. Mercer, S. Ryan and M. Williams (eds) *Psychology for Language Learning: Insights from Research, Theory and Practice* (pp. 151–168). Houndmills: Palgrave MacMillan.

Griffiths, C. and Parr, J. (2000) Language learning strategies, nationality, independence and proficiency. *Independence* 28, 7–10.

Griffiths, C. and Parr, J. (2001a) Language-learning strategies: Theory and perception. *ELT Journal* 55 (3), 247–254.

Griffiths, C. and Parr, J. (2001b) Strategies for success: How language learning strategies relate to proficiency in language learning. *Many Voices* 17, 27–31.

Grigorenko, E., Sternberg, R. and Ehrman, M. (2000) A theory-based approach to the measurement of foreign language learning ability: The CANAL_F theory and test. *Modern Language Journal* 84, 390–405.

Grundy, P. (1999) From model to muddle. *ELT Journal* 53 (1), 54–55.

Gruneburg, M. (1987) *Linkword French, German, Spanish, Italian*. London: Corgi.

Gu, P.Y. (1996) Robin Hood in SLA: What has the learning strategy researcher taught us? *Asian Journal of English Language Teaching* 6, 1–29.

Gu, Y. (2002) Gender, academic major and vocabulary learning strategies of Chinese EFL learners. *RELC Journal* 33 (1), 35–54.

Gu, Y., Wen, Q. and Wu, D. (1995) How often is *Often*? Reference ambiguities of the Likert-scale in language learning strategy research. Occasional Paper in English Language Teaching No. 5 (pp. 19–35). ELT Unit, Chinese University of Hong Kong.

Guiora, A., Brannon, R. and Dull, C. (1972) Empathy and second language learning. *Language Learning* 22 (1), 111–130.

Harley, B. (1986) *Age in Second Language Acquisition*. Clevedon: Multilingual Matters.

Harley, B., Allen, P., Cummins, J. and Swain, M. (eds) (1990) *The Development of Second Language Proficiency*. Cambridge: Cambridge University Press.

Harmer, J. (1995) Taming the big 'I': Teacher performance and student satisfaction. *ELT Journal* 49 (4), 337–345.

Harmer, J. (2012) *Essential Teacher Knowledge: Core Concepts in English Language Teaching*. Harlow: Pearson.

Harris, V. (2001) *Helping Learners Learn: Exploring Strategy Instruction in Language Classrooms Across Europe*. Strasbourg: Council of Europe Publishing.

Hartmann, E. (1991) *Boundaries in the Mind: A New Psychology of Personality*. New York: Basic Books.

Henning, C. (ed.) (1977) *Proceedings of the Los Angeles Second Language Research Forum*. Los Angeles, CA: English Department, University of California.

Hofstede, G. (1980) *Culture's Consequences*. Newbury Park: Sage.

Hofstede, G. (1997) *Cultures and Organizations: Software of the Mind. Intercultural Cooperation and its Importance for Survival*. New York: McGraw-Hill.

Hogan, R. (1969) Development of an empathy scale. *Journal of Consulting and Clinical Psychology* 33, 307–316.

Holec, H. (1981) *Autonomy and Foreign Language Learning*. Oxford: Pergamon.

Honey, P. and Mumford, A. (1982) *The Manual of Learning Styles*. Maidenhead: Peter Honey Publications.

Horwitz, E. (1987) Surveying student beliefs about language learning. In A. Wenden and J. Rubin (eds) *Learner Strategies in Language Learning* (pp. 119–132). London: Prentice Hall.

Horwitz, E. (1988) The beliefs about language learning of beginning university foreign language students. *Modern Language Journal* 72 (3), 283–294.

Horwitz, E. (1999) Cultural and situational influences on foreign language learners' beliefs about language learning: A review of BALLI studies. *System* 27, 557–576.

Horwitz, E., Horwitz, M. and Cope, J. (1986) Foreign language classroom anxiety. *Modern Language Journal* 70 (2), 125–132.

Hosenfeld, C. (1976) Learning about learning: Discovering our students' strategies. *Foreign Language Annals* 9, 117–129.

Huang, X. and van Naerssen, M. (1987) Learning strategies for oral communication. *Applied Linguistics* 8 (3), 287–307.

Hutchinson, T. and Waters, A. (1990) *English for Specific Purposes: A Learning-Centred Approach*. Cambridge: Cambridge University Press.

Hyltenstam, K. and Abrahamsson, N. (2003) Maturational constraints in SLA. In C. Doughty and M. Long (eds) *The Handbook of Second Language Acquisition* (pp. 539–588). Malden, MA: Blackwell.

Hyltenstam, K. and Pienemann, M. (eds) (1985) *Modelling and Assessing Second Language Acquisition*. Clevedon: Multilingual Matters.

Hymes, D. (1972) On communicative competence. In J. Pride and J. Holmes (eds) *Sociolinguistics* (pp. 269–293). Harmondsworth: Penguin.

Ikeda, M. and Takeuchi, O. (2003) Can strategy instruction help ESL learners to improve their reading ability? An empirical study. *JACET Bulletin* 37, 49–60.

Ioup, G., Boustagui, E., El Tigi, M. and Moselle, M. (1994) Reexamining the critical period hypothesis. *Studies in Second Language Acquisition* 16, 73–98.

Isabelli-Garcia, C. (2003) Development of oral communication skills abroad. *Frontiers* 9, 149–173.

Jones, J. (1995) Self-access and culture: Retreating from autonomy. *ELT Journal* 49 (3), 228–234.

Juffs, A. and Harrington, M. (2011) Aspects of working memory in L2 learning. *Language Teaching* 44 (2), 137–166.

Jung, C. (1921) *Psychological Types*. Princeton, NJ: Princeton University.

Kaplan, R. (1966) Cultural thought patterns in intercultural education. *Language Learning* 16 (1), 1–20.

Kline, R. (1998) Literacy and language learning in a study abroad context. *Frontiers* 4, 139–163.

Kolb, D. (1976) *The Learning Style Inventory: Self-scoring Test and Interpretation*. Boston, MA: McBer & Company.

Krashen, S. (1976) Formal and informal linguistic environments in language acquisition and language learning. *TESOL Quarterly* 10, 157–168.

Krashen, S. (1977) Some issues relating to the Monitor Model. In H. Brown, C. Yorio and R. Crymes (eds) *On TESOL '77* (pp. 144–158). Washington, DC: TESOL.

Krashen, S. (1981) *Second Language Acquisition and Second Language Learning*. Oxford: Pergamon Press.

Krashen, S. (1982) *Principles and Practices in Second Language Acquisition*. Oxford: Pergamon Press.

Krashen, S. (1985) *The Input Hypothesis*. London: Longman.

Krashen, S. and Terrell, T. (1983) *The Natural Approach*. Hayward, CA: Hayward Press.

Kuhl, J. (1984) Volitional aspects of achievement motivation and learned helplessness: Toward a comprehensive theory of action control. In B. Maher and W. Maher (eds) *Progress in Experimental Personality Research* (pp. 101–171). Orlando, FL: Academic Press.

Kumaravadivelu, B. (2001) Towards a postmethod methodology. *TESOL Quarterly* 35, 537–560.

Lado, R. (1957) *Linguistics Across Cultures: Applied Linguistics for Language Teachers*. Ann Arbor, MI: University of Michigan Press.

Lam, W. and Wong, J. (2000) The effects of strategy training on developing discussion skills in an ESL classroom. *ELT Journal* 54 (3), 245–255.

Lantolf, J. (ed.) (2000) *Sociocultural Theory in Second Language Learning*. Oxford: Oxford University Press.

Larsen-Freeman, D. (1991) Second language acquisition research: Staking out the territory. *TESOL Quarterly* 25 (2), 315–350.

Larsen-Freeman, D. (1997) Chaos/complexity science and second language acquisition. *Applied Linguistics* 18 (2), 141–165.

Larsen-Freeman, D. (2001) Individual cognitive/affective learner contributions and differential success in second language acquisition. In M. Breen (ed.) *Learner Contributions to Language Learning* (pp. 12–23). Harlow: Longman.

Larsen-Freeman, D. and Long, M. (1991) *An Introduction to Second Language Acquisition Research*. London & New York: Longman.

Lavine, R. (2001) *Beyond the Boundaries: Changing Contexts in Language Learning*. New York: McGraw-Hill.

Lazar, G. (1993) *Literature and Language Teaching*. Cambridge: Cambridge University Press.

Legato, M. (2005) *Why Men Never Remember and Women Never Forget*. New York: Rodale.

Lenneberg, E. (1967) *Biological Foundations of Language*. New York: Wiley.

Leont'ev, A. (1978) *Activity, Consciousness and Personality*. Englewood Cliffs, NJ: Prentice Hall.

Lewis, M. (1993) *Lexical Approach: The State of ELT and the Way Forward*. Hove: Language Teaching Publications.

Lewis, M. (1997) *Implementing the Lexical Approach*. Hove: Language Teaching Publications.

Little, D. (1999) Learner autonomy is more than a western cultural concept. In S. Cotterall and D. Crabbe (eds) *Learner Autonomy in Language Learning: Defining the Field and Effecting Change* (pp. 11–18). Frankfurt am Main: Lang.

Littlewood, W. (1981) *Communicative Language Teaching.* Cambridge: Cambridge University Press.

Littlewood, W. (1984) *Foreign and Second Language Learning.* Cambridge: Cambridge University Press.

Littlewood, W. (2001) Students' attitudes towards classroom English learning: A cross-cultural study. *Language Teaching Research* 5 (1), 3–28.

Littlewood, W. (2012) Communication-oriented language teaching: Where are we now? Where do we go from here? *Language Teaching* 45, 1–14.

Lo Bianco, J., Orton, J. and Yihong, G. (eds) (2009) *China and English: Globalisation and the Dilemmas of Identity.* Bristol: Multilingual Matters.

LoCastro, V. (1994) Learning strategies and learning environments. *TESOL Quarterly* 28 (2), 409–414.

Loewen, S. and Ellis, R. (2001) The relationship of receptive vocabulary knowledge to academic success and learner beliefs. Occasional Paper No. 15, Auckland: Department of Applied Language Studies and Linguistics.

Long, M. (1990) Maturational constraints on language development. *Studies in Second Language Acquisition* 12, 251–285.

Long, M. (1996) The role of the linguistic environment in second language acquisition. In W.C. Ritchie and T.K. Bhatia (eds) *Handbook of Second Language Acquisition* (pp. 413–468). San Diego, CA: Academic Press.

Lozanov, G. (1978) *Suggestology and Outlines of Suggestopedy.* New York: Gordon & Breach.

Lunt, H. (2000) The learning strategies of adult immigrant learners of English. Unpublished doctoral thesis, University of Melbourne.

Macaro, E. (2001) *Learning Strategies in Foreign and Second Language Classrooms.* London & New York: Continuum.

Macaro, E. (2006) Strategies for language learning and for language use: Revising the theoretical framework. *Modern Language Journal* 90 (3), 320–337.

Manchon, R., Roca de Larios, J. and Murphy, L. (2007) A review of writing strategies: Focus on conceptualizations and impact of first language. In A. Cohen and E. Macaro (eds) *Language Learner Strategies* (pp. 229–250). Oxford: Oxford University Press.

McCrae, R. and John, O. (1992) An introduction to the five-factor model and its applications. *Journal of Personality* 60 (2), 175–215.

McLaughlin, B. (1978) The Monitor model: Some methodological considerations. *Language Learning* 28, 309–332.

McLaughlin, B. (1990) 'Conscious' versus 'unconscious' learning. *TESOL Quarterly* 24 (4), 617–634.

McLaughlin, B., Rossman, T. and McLeod, B. (1983) Second language learning: An information-processing perspective. *Language Learning* 33 (2), 135–158.

Mehrabian, A. and Epstein, N. (1972) A measure of emotional empathy. *Journal of Personality* 40, 525–543.

Mercer, S. (2011) *Towards an Understanding of Language Learner Self-Concept.* Berlin: Springer.

Moir, J. and Nation, P. (2002) Learners' use of strategies for effective vocabulary learning. *Prospect* 17 (1), 15–35.

Moir, J. and Nation, P. (2008) Vocabulary and good language learners. In C. Griffiths (ed.) *Lessons from Good Language Learners* (pp. 159–173). Cambridge: Cambridge University Press.

Munoz, C. and Singleton, D. (2011) A critical review of age-related research on L2 ultimate attainment. *Language Teaching* 44 (1), 1–35.

Myers, E. (1962) *The Myers–Briggs Type Indicator.* Palo Alto, CA: Consulting Psychologists Press.

Nahl, D. (2005) Affective load. In K. Fisher, S. Erdelez and L. Mckechnie (eds) *Theories of Information Behavior* (pp. 39–44). Old Marlton Pike Medford, NJ, USA: Information Today Inc.

Naiman, N., Frohlich, M., Stern, H. and Todesco, A. (1978) *The Good Language Learner.* Research in Education Series No. 7. Toronto: Ontario Institute for Studies in Education.

Nakatani, Y. (2005) The effects of awareness-raising training on oral communication strategy use. *Modern Language Journal* 89 (1), 76–91.

Nation, I.S.P. (1990) *Teaching and Learning Vocabulary.* Boston, MA: Heinle & Heinle.

Nation, I.S.P. (2008) *Teaching Vocabulary: Strategies and Techniques.* Boston, MA: Heinle & Heinle.

Nel, C. (2008) Learning style and good language learners. In C. Griffiths (ed.) *Lessons from Good Language Learners* (pp. 49–60). Cambridge: Cambridge University Press.

Neufeld, G. (1978) On the acquisition of prosodic and articulatory features in adult language learning. *Canadian Modern Language Review* 32 (2), 163–174.

Nisbet, J. and Shucksmith, J. (1984) *The Seventh Sense: Reflections on Learning to Learn.* Edinburgh: Scottish Council for Research in Education.

Noels, K., Pelletier, L., Clement, R. and Vallerand, R. (2000) Why are you learning a second language? Motivational orientations and self-determination theory. *Language Learning* 50, 57–85.

Norton, B. (1997) Language, identity and the ownership of English. *TESOL Quarterly* 31 (3), 409–427.

Norton, B. (2000) *Identity and Language Learning: Gender, Ethnicity and Educational Change.* Harlow: Longman.

Norton, B. (2010) *Identity and Language Learning: Gender, Ethnicity and Educational Change* (2nd edn). London: Longman/Pearson.

Norton, B. and Toohey, K. (2001) Changing perspectives on good language learners. *TESOL Quarterly* 35 (2), 307–322.

Nunan, D. (1988) *The Learner-Centred Curriculum.* Cambridge: Cambridge University Press.

Nunan, D. (1992) *Research Methods in Language Learning.* Cambridge: Cambridge University Press.

Nunan, D. (1995) Learner strategy training in the classroom: A case study. Unpublished paper.

Nunan, D. (2004) *Task-based Language Teaching.* Cambridge: Cambridge University Press.

Nyikos, M. (1987) The effects of color and imagery as mnemonic strategies on learning and retention of lexical items in German. Unpublished doctoral dissertation, Purdue University, West Lafayette, IN.

Nyikos, M. (1990) Sex related differences in adult language learning: Socialisation and memory factors. *Modern Language Journal* 3, 273–287.

Nyikos, M. (2008) Gender and good language learners. In C. Griffiths (ed.) *Lessons from Good Language Learners* (pp. 73–82). Cambridge: Cambridge University Press.

O'Malley, J.M. (1987) The effects of training in the use of learning strategies on learning English as a second language. In A. Wenden and J. Rubin (eds) *Learner Strategies in Language Learning* (pp. 133–143). Englewood Cliffs, NJ: Prentice Hall.

O'Malley, J.M. and Chamot, A. (1990) *Learning Strategies in Second Language Acquisition.* Cambridge: Cambridge University Press.

O'Malley, J.M., Chamot, A., Stewner-Manzanares, G., Kupper, L. and Russo, R. (1985) Learning strategies used by beginning and intermediate ESL students. *Language Learning* 35 (1), 21–46.

O'Neil, H. (ed.) (1978) *Learning Strategies.* New York: Academic Press.

Oxford, R. (1989a) Use of language learning strategies: A synthesis of studies with implications for strategy training. *System* 17 (2), 235–247.

Oxford, R. (1989b) 'The best and the worst': An exercise to tap perceptions of language-learning experiences and strategies. *Foreign Language Annals* 22 (5), 447–454.

Oxford, R. (1990) *Language Learning Strategies: What Every Teacher Should Know.* New York: Newbury House.

Oxford, R. (1993) *Style Analysis Survey (SAS).* Tuscaloosa, AL: University of Alabama.

Oxford, R. (ed.) (1996a) *Language Learning Strategies around the World: Cross-Cultural Perspectives.* Honolulu, HI: Second Language Teaching and Curriculum Centre, University of Hawai'i at Manoa.

Oxford, R. (1996b) Employing a questionnaire to assess the use of language learning strategies. *Applied Language Learning* 7 (1& 2), 25–45.

Oxford, R. (1999) Anxiety and the language learner: New insights. In J. Arnold (ed.) *Affect in Language Learning* (pp. 58–67). Cambridge: Cambridge University Press.

Oxford, R. (2001) The bleached bones of a story: Learners' constructions of language teachers. In M. Breen (ed.) *Learner Contributions to Language Learning* (pp. 86–111). Harlow: Longman.

Oxford, R. (2011a) Research timeline: Strategies for learning a second or foreign language. *Language Teaching* 44 (2), 167–180.

Oxford, R. (2011b) *Teaching and Researching Language Learning Strategies.* Harlow: Pearson Longman.

Oxford, R. and Burry-Stock, J. (1995) Assessing the use of language learning strategies worldwide with the ESL/EFL version of the Strategy Inventory for Language Learning (SILL). *System* 25 (1), 1–23.

Oxford, R. and Cohen, A. (1992) Language learning strategies: Crucial issues of concept and classification. *Applied Language Learning* 3 (1 & 2), 1–35.

Oxford, R. and Lee, K. (2007) L2 grammar strategies: The second Cinderella and beyond. In A. Cohen and E. Macaro (eds) *Language Learner Strategies* (pp. 117–140). Oxford: Oxford University Press.

Oxford, R. and Lee, K. (2008) The learners' landscape and journey: A summary. In C. Griffiths (ed.) *Lessons from Good Language Learners* (pp. 306–317). Cambridge: Cambridge University Press.

Oxford, R. and Nyikos, M. (1989) Variables affecting choice of language learning strategies by university students. *Modern Language Journal* 73 (iii), 291–300.

Oxford, R., Nyikos, M. and Ehrman, M. (1988) Vive la difference? Reflections on sex differences in use of language learning strategies. *Foreign Language Annals* 21, 321–329.

Oxford, R., Lavine, R. and Crookall, D. (1989) Language learning strategies, the communicative approach and their classroom implications. *Foreign Language Annals* 22 (1), 29–39.

Oyama, S. (1976) A sensitive period in the acquisition of a non-native phonological system. *Journal of Psycholinguistic Research* 5, 261–285.

Pavlenko, A. and Blackledge, A. (eds) (2003) *Negotiation of Identities in Multilingual Contexts.* Clevedon: Multilingual Matters.

Pavlenko, A. and Lantolf, J. (2000) Second language learning as participation and the (re) construction of selves. In J. Lantolf (ed.) *Sociocultural Theory in Second Language Learning* (pp. 1–26). Oxford: Oxford University Press.

Pearsall, J. (1998) *The New Oxford Dictionary of English*. Oxford: Clarendon Press.

Pearson, E. (1988) Learner strategies and learner interviews. *ELT Journal* 42 (3), 173–178.

Peirce, B.N. (1995) Social identity, investment and language learning. *TESOL Quarterly* 29, 9–31.

Pellegrino, V. (1998) Student perspectives on language learning in a study abroad context. *Frontiers* 4, 91–120.

Pemberton, R. (1996) The learner and the learning process. In R. Pemberton, E. Li, W. Or and H. Pierson (eds) *Taking Control: Autonomy in Language Learning* (pp. 59–60). Hong Kong: Hong Kong University Press.

Pemberton, R., Li, E., Or, W. and Pierson, H. (eds) (1996) *Taking Control: Autonomy in Language Learning*. Hong Kong: Hong Kong University Press.

Pennycook, A. (1997) Cultural alternatives and autonomy. In P. Benson and P. Voller (eds) *Autonomy and Independence in Language Learning* (pp. 35–53). London & New York: Longman.

Phillipson, R., Kellerman, E., Selinker, L., Sharwood-Smith, M. and Swain, M. (eds) (1991) *Foreign/Second Language Pedagogy Research*. Clevedon: Multilingual Matters.

Pienemann, M. (1984) Psychological constraints on the teachability of languages. *Studies in Second Language Acquisition* 6, 186–214.

Pienemann, M. (1985) Learnability and syllabus construction. In K. Hyltenstam and M. Pienemann (eds) *Modelling and Assessing Second Language Acquisition* (pp. 23–75). Clevedon: Multilingual Matters.

Pienemann, M. (1989) Is language teachable? Psycholinguistic experiments and hypotheses. *Applied Linguistics* 10, 52–79.

Pierson, H. (1996) Learner culture and learner autonomy in the Hong Kong Chinese context. In R. Pemberton, E. Li, W. Or and H. Pierson (eds) *Taking Control: Autonomy in Language Learning* (pp. 49–58). Hong Kong: Hong Kong University Press.

Pimsleur, P. (1966) *Pimsleur Language Aptitude Battery*. New York: Harcourt, Brace, Jovanovic.

Politzer, R. (1983) An exploratory study of self-reported language learning behaviours and their relation to achievement. *Studies in Second Language Acquisition* 6, 54–65.

Politzer, R. and McGroarty, M. (1985) An exploratory study of learning behaviours and their relationship to gains in linguistic and communicative competence. *TESOL Quarterly* 19, 103–123.

Porte, G. (1988) Poor language learners and their strategies for dealing with new vocabulary. *ELT Journal* 42 (3), 167–171.

Pride, J. and Holmes, J. (eds) (1972) *Sociolinguistics*. Harmondsworth: Penguin.

Purpura, J. (1999) *Learner Strategy Use and Performance on Language Tests: A Structural Equation Modelling Approach*. Cambridge: Cambridge University Press.

Ranta, L. (2008) Aptitude and good language learners. In C. Griffiths (ed.) *Lessons from Good Language Learners* (pp. 142–154). Cambridge: Cambridge University Press.

Rees-Miller, J. (1993) A critical appraisal of learner training: Theoretical bases and teaching implications. *TESOL Quarterly* 27 (4), 679–687.

Regan, V. (1998) Sociolinguistics and language learning in a study abroad context. *Frontiers* 4, 61–89.

Reid, J. (1987) The learning style preferences of ESL students. *TESOL Quarterly* 21 (1), 87–111.

Reid, J. (1990) The dirty laundry of ESL survey research. *TESOL Quarterly* 21 (2), 323–338.

Reid, J. (ed.) (1995) *Learning Styles in the ESL/EFL Classroom*. Boston, MA: Heinle & Heinle.

Reid, J. (1998a) Preface. In J. Reid (ed.) *Understanding Learning Styles in the Second Language Classroom* (pp. ix–xiv). Upper Saddle River, NJ: Prentice Hall.

Reid, J. (ed.) (1998b) *Understanding Learning Styles in the Second Language Classroom.* Upper Saddle River, NJ: Prentice Hall.

Richards, J. (1996) Teachers' maxims in language learning. *TESOL Quarterly* 30 (2), 281–296.

Richards, J. (2006) *Communicative Language Teaching Today.* Cambridge: Cambridge University Press.

Richards, J. and Rodgers, T. (1986) *Approaches and Methods in Language Teaching.* Cambridge: Cambridge University Press.

Richards, J., Platt, J. and Platt, H. (1992) *Longman Dictionary of Language Teaching and Applied Linguistics.* Harlow: Longman.

Rigney, J. (1978) Learning strategies: A theoretical perspective. In H. O'Neil, Jr (ed.) *Learning Strategies* (pp. 165–205). New York: Academic Press.

Robinson, P. (2012) Individual differences, aptitude complexes, SLA processes and aptitude test development. In M. Pawlak (ed.) *New Perspectives on Individual Differences in Language Learning and Teaching* (pp. 57–76). Berlin: Springer.

Roebuck, R. (2000) Subjects speak out: How learners position themselves in a psycholinguistic task. In J. Lantolf (ed.) *Sociocultural Theory in Second Language Learning* (pp. 79–96). Oxford: Oxford University Press.

Rubin, J. (1975) What the 'good language learner' can teach us. *TESOL Quarterly* 9 (1), 41–51.

Rubin, J. (1981) Study of cognitive processes in second language learning. *Applied Linguistics* 11, 117–131.

Rubin, J. (1987) Learner strategies: Theoretical assumptions, research history and typology. In A. Wenden and J. Rubin (eds) *Learner Strategies in Language Learning* (pp. 15–19). Englewood Cliffs, NJ: Prentice Hall.

Ryan, R. and Deci, E. (2000) Intrinsic and extrinsic motivations: Classic definitions and new directions. *Contemporary Educational Psychology* 25, 54–67.

Schmidt, R. (1983) Interaction, acculturation, and the acquisition of communicative competence: A case study of an adult. In N. Wolfson and E. Judd (eds) *Sociolinguistics and Second Language Acquisition* (pp. 137–174). New York: Newbury House.

Schmidt, R. (1990) The role of consciousness in second language learning. *Applied Linguistics* 11 (2), 129–158.

Schumann, J. (1975) Affective factors and the problem of age in second language acquisition. *Language Learning* 25, 209–235.

Schumann, J. (1976) Second language acquisition: The pidginisation hypothesis. *Language Learning* 26 (2), 391–408.

Schumann, J. (1978) *The Pidginisation Process: A Model for Second Language Acquisition.* Rowley, MA: Newbury House.

Scollon, R. and Scollon, S. (2000) *Intercultural Communication: A Discourse Approach.* Beijing: Foreign Language Teaching and Research Press.

Scovel, T. (1978) The effect of affect on foreign language learning: A review of the anxiety research. *Language Learning* 28, 129–142.

Seliger, H. (1984) Processing universals in second language acquisition. In F. Eckman, L. Bell and D. Nelson (eds) *Universals of Second Language Acquisition* (pp. 36–47). Rowley, MA: Newbury House.

Seligman, M. (1975) *Helplessness: On Depression, Development, and Death.* San Francisco, CA: W.H. Freeman.

Selinker, L. (1972) Interlanguage. *International Review of Applied Linguistics* 10, 209–230.

Sharwood Smith, M. (1994) *Second Language Learning: Theoretical Foundations*. London & New York: Longman.

Short, E. and Ryan, E. (1984) Metacognitive differences between skilled and less skilled readers: Remediating deficits through story grammar and attribution training. *Journal of Educational Psychology* 76, 225–235.

Simmons, D. (1996) A study of strategy use in independent learners. In R. Pemberton, E. Li, W. Or and H. Pierson (eds) *Taking Control: Autonomy in Language Learning* (pp. 61–76). Hong Kong: Hong Kong University Press.

Singleton, D. (1989) *Language Acquisition: The Age Factor.* Clevedon: Multilingual Matters.

Singleton, D. and Lesniewska, J. (2012) Age and SLA: Research highways and bye-ways. In M. Pawlak (ed.) *New Perspectives on Individual Differences in Language Learning and Teaching* (pp. 97–117). Berlin: Springer.

Singleton, D. and Munoz, C. (2011) Around and beyond the Critical Period Hypothesis. In E. Hinkel (ed.) *Handbook of Research in Second Language Teaching and Learning* (Vol. 2) (pp. 407–425). New York: Routledge.

Skehan, P. (1989) *Individual Differences in Second-Language Learning*. London: Edward Arnold.

Skehan, P. (1998) *A Cognitive Approach to Language Learning*. Oxford: Oxford University Press.

Skinner, B. (1957) *Verbal Behaviour.* New York: Appleton-Century-Crofts.

Skyrme, G. (2005) English as cultural capital in the decision to study abroad: 'I want to show my English is very good'. Paper presented at the Conference on Value of English for Asian Students and 'Added Value' of Studying in New Zealand, University of Auckland, October.

Snow, C. and Hoefnagel-Hohle, M. (1978) The critical period for language acquisition: Evidence from language learning. *Child Development* 49, 1119–1128.

Snow, R. (1987) Aptitude complex. In R. Snow and M. Farr (eds) *Aptitude, Learning and Instruction* (pp. 11–34). Hillsdale, NJ: Lawrence Erlbaum.

Spada, N. (2007) Communicative language teaching: Current status and future prospects. In J. Cummins and C. Davison (eds) *International Handbook of English Language Teaching*, 15 (pp. 271–288). Berlin: Springer.

Spada, N. and Lightbown, P. (2002) Second language acquisition. In N. Schmitt (ed.) *An Introduction to Applied Linguistics* (pp. 115–133). London: Edward Arnold.

Spolsky, B. (1989) *Conditions for Second Language Learning.* Oxford: Oxford University Press.

Stern, H. (1975) What can we learn from the good language learner? *Canadian Modern Language Review* 34, 304–318.

Stern, H. (1992) *Issues and Options in Language Teaching* (edited posthumously by P. Allen and B. Harley). Oxford: Oxford University Press.

Sturtridge, G. (1997) Teaching and language learning in self-access centres: Changing roles? In P. Benson and P. Voller (eds) *Autonomy and Independence in Language Learning* (pp. 66–78). London & New York: Longman.

Sunderland, J. (1998) Girls being quiet: A problem for foreign language classrooms. *Language Teaching Research* 2 (1), 48–82.

Sunderland, J. (2000) New understandings of gender and language classroom research: Texts, teacher talk and student talk. *Language Teaching Research* 4 (2), 149–173.

Swain, M. (1981) Time and timing in bilingual education. *Language Learning* 31, 1–6.

Swain, M. (1985) Communicative competence: Some roles of comprehensible input and comprehensible output in its development. In S. Gass and C. Madden (eds) *Input in Second Language Acquisition*. Rowley, MA: Newbury House.

Takeuchi, O., Griffiths, C. and Coyle, D. (2007) Applying strategies to contexts: The role of individual, situational and group differences. In A. Cohen and E. Macaro (eds) *Language Learner Strategies* (pp. 69–92). Oxford: Oxford University Press.

Tanaka, K. and Ellis, R. (2003) Study-abroad, language proficiency, and learner beliefs about language learning. *JALT Journal* 25 (1), 63–85.

Tang, H. and Moore, D. (1992) Effects of cognitive and metacognitive pre-reading activities on the reading comprehension of ESL learners. *Educational Psychology* 12 (3 & 4), 315–331.

Tarone, E. (1980) Communication strategies, foreigner talk, and repair in interlanguage. *Language Learning* 30 (2), 417–429.

Tarone, E. (1981) Some thoughts on the notion of communication strategy. *TESOL Quarterly* 15 (3), 285–295.

Tarone, E. and Yule, G. (1989) *Focus on the Language Learner.* Oxford: Oxford University Press.

Tonkyn, A. (1994) Introduction: Grammar and the language teacher. In M. Bysgate, A. Tonkyn and E. Williams (eds) *Grammar and the Language Teacher* (pp. 1–14). London: Prentice Hall.

Toohey, K. (2000) *Learning English at School: Identity, Social Relations and Classroom Practice.* Clevedon: Multilingual Matters.

Tran, T. (1988) Sex differences in English language acculturation and learning strategies among Vietnamese adults aged 40 and over in the United States. *Sex Roles* 19, 747–758.

Turner, J. (1993) Using Likert scales in L2 research. *TESOL Quarterly* 27 (4), 736–739.

Ushioda, E. (2008) Motivation and good language learners. In C. Griffiths (ed.) *Lessons from Good Language Learners* (pp. 19–34). Cambridge, UK: Cambridge University Press.

Usuki, M. (2000) A new understanding of Japanese students' views on classroom learning. *Independence* 27, 2–6.

Vandergrift, L. and Tafaghodatari, M. (2010) Teaching L2 learners how to listen does make a difference: An empirical study. *Language Learning* 60 (2), 470–497.

Van Houtte, M. (2004) Why boys achieve less at school than girls: The difference between boys' and girls' academic culture. *Educational Studies* 30 (2), 159–173.

Vann, R. and Abraham, R. (1990) Strategies of unsuccessful language learners. *TESOL Quarterly* 24 (2), 177–198.

Voller, P. (1997) Does the teacher have a role in autonomous language learning? In P. Benson and P. Voller (eds) *Autonomy and Independence in Language Learning* (pp. 98–113). London & New York: Longman.

Vygotsky, L. (1978) *Mind in Society.* Cambridge, MA: Harvard University Press.

Vygotsky, L. (1987) *Thought and Language.* Cambridge, MA: MIT Press.

Watson, J. (1930) *Behaviourism.* New York: Norton.

Weiner, B. (1974) *Achievement Motivation and Attribution Theory.* Morristown, NJ: General Learning Press.

Weiner, B. (1985) An attributional theory of achievement, motivation and emotion. *Psychological Review* 92, 548–573.

Weinstein, C. (1978) Elaboration skills as a learning strategy. In H. O'Neil, Jr (ed.) *Learning Strategies* (pp. 30–62). New York: Academic Press.

Wenden, A. (1985) Learner strategies. *TESOL Newsletter* 19 (5), 1–7.

Wenden, A. (1987a) How to be a successful language learner: Insights and prescriptions from L2 learners. In A. Wenden and J. Rubin (eds) *Learner Strategies in Language Learning* (pp. 103–117). Englewood Cliffs, NJ: Prentice Hall.

Wenden, A. (1987b) Incorporating learner training in the classroom. In A. Wenden and J. Rubin (eds) *Learner Strategies in Language Learning* (pp. 159–167). Englewood Cliffs, NJ: Prentice Hall.

Wenden, A. (1991) *Learner Strategies for Learner Autonomy.* Englewood Cliffs, NJ: Prentice Hall.

Wenden, A. and Rubin, J. (eds) (1987) *Learner Strategies in Language Learning.* Englewood Cliffs, NJ: Prentice Hall.

Wesche, M. (1977) Learning behaviours of successful adult students on intensive language training. In C. Henning (ed.) *Proceedings of the Los Angeles Second Language Research Forum* (pp. 355–370). Los Angeles, CA: English Department, University of California at Los Angeles.

Wesche, M. (1981) Language aptitude measures in streaming, matching students with methods, and diagnosis of learning problems. In K. Diller (ed.) *Differences and Universals in Language Learning Aptitude* (pp. 119–154). Rowley, MA: Newbury House.

White, C. (1989) Negotiating communicative language learning in a traditional setting. *ELT Journal* 43 (3), 213–220.

White, C. (1993) Strategy use in foreign language learning: A comparative study. Unpublished doctoral thesis, Massey University, Palmerston, New Zealand.

White, C. (1999) Expectations and emergent beliefs of self-instructed language learners. *System* 27, 443–457.

White, C. (2003) *Language Learning in Distance Education.* Cambridge, UK: Cambridge University Press.

White, C. (2008) Beliefs and good language learners. In C. Griffiths (ed.) *Lessons from Good Language Learners* (pp. 121–130). Cambridge: Cambridge University Press.

Widdowson, H. (1978) *Teaching Language as Communication.* Oxford: Oxford University Press.

Wilkins, D. (1972) *Linguistics and Language Teaching.* London: Edward Arnold.

Wilkins, D. (1976) *Notional Syllabuses.* Oxford: Oxford University Press.

Wilkinson, S. (1998) On the nature of immersion during study abroad: Some participant perspectives. *Frontiers* 4 (5), 121–138.

Williams, M. and Burden, R. (1997) *Psychology for Language Teachers: A Social Constructivist Approach.* Cambridge: Cambridge University Press.

Willing, K. (1987) *Learning Styles in Adult Migrant Education.* Sydney: National Centre for English Language Teaching and Research.

Willing, K. (1989) *Teaching How to Learn: Learning Strategies in ESL.* Sydney: National Centre for English Language Teaching and Research.

Winitz, H. (ed.) (1981) *Native Language and Foreign Language Acquisition.* New York: New York Academy of Sciences.

Winne, P. (1995) Inherent details in self-regulated learning. *Educational Psychologist* 30, 173–187.

Witkin, H. (1962) *Psychological Differentiation.* New York: Wiley.

Witkin, H. (1971) *Embedded Figures Test.* Menlo Park, CA: Mind Garden.

Wolfson, N. and Judd, E. (eds) (1983) *Sociolinguistics and Second Language Acquisition.* New York: Newbury House.

Wong Fillmore, L. (1982) The language learner as an individual: Implications of research in individual differences for the ESL teacher. In M. Clarke and J. Handscombe (eds) *On TESOL* (pp. 157–171). Washington, DC: TESOL.

Woods, D. (1996) *Teacher Cognition in Language Teaching: Beliefs, Decision-Making and Classroom Practice.* Cambridge, UK: Cambridge University Press.

Yang, N. (1998) An interviewing study of college students' English learning strategy use. *Studies in English Language and Literature* 4, 1–11.

Yang, N. (1999) The relationship between EFL learners' beliefs and learning strategy use. *System* 27, 515–535.

Young, D. and Oxford, R. (1997) A gender-related analysis of strategies used to process written input in the native language and a foreign language. *Applied Language Learning* 8 (1), 26–43.

Index